BRINGING OUR LANGUAGES HOME

Language Revitalization for Families

BRINGING OUR LANGUAGES HOME

LANGUAGE REVITALIZATION FOR FAMILIES

Edited with a How-to Guide for Parents
by Leanne Hinton

Heyday, Berkeley, California

The publisher wishes to thank Lawrence Crooks and other donors to Heyday's California Indian Publishing Program.

Library of Congress Cataloging-in-Publication Data
Bringing Our Languages Home : Language Revitalization for Families / Edited with a How-to Guide for Parents by Leanne Hinton.
    pages cm
Includes bibliographical references.
ISBN 978-1-59714-200-7 (pbk. : alk. paper)
1. Language revival. 2. Families—Language. 3. Native language. 4. Bilingualism in children. I. Hinton, Leanne, editor of compilation.
P40.5.L356B75 2013
418—dc23
                              2012039484

5153 8493 3/13

Cover Art and Design: Lorraine Rath
Interior Design/Typesetting: Rebecca LeGates
Printing and Binding: Worzalla, Stevens Point, MI
Orders, inquiries, and correspondence should be addressed to:
        Heyday
        P.O. Box 9145, Berkeley, CA 94709
        (510) 549-3564, Fax (510) 549-1889
        www.heydaybooks.com

10 9 8 7 6 5 4 3 2 1

*To my fellow Advocates for Indigenous California Language Survival,
past and present, for all I have learned from them and through them
over the past twenty years*

CONTENTS

ACKNOWLEDGMENTS

I am deeply indebted to the Lannan Foundation, who have been supportive of the work of my colleagues and myself in language revitalization for many years and, most relevant to this book, provided me with a fellowship for a six-week stay in Marfa, Texas, where they have homes set up specifically for writers to get away from the multitasking responsibilities of daily life and simply write. Before that trip, I had long been wanting to write a book about language revitalization for families. Originally I had thought that I would write it myself, but the prospect of doing this seemed overwhelming. I figured that I would have to go all over the world interviewing families and then turn the interviews into a book. "And who am I," I thought, "who never braved raising a child to speak an endangered language, to write for people who might want to do this?" It was not until I settled down in Marfa and thought about nothing else for the first week that the simple answer suddenly dawned on me: why should I write this book at all? It was the families who had done it themselves who should write it. And thus it was that my wonderful weeks in Marfa were spent calling and emailing the people who have become the main authors of this book.

I thank too these authors themselves, who wrote such moving, honest, and powerful chapters about their lives and their families and communities, throwing such great insight on the issues involved in bringing endangered languages into use in their families. Additional thanks go to Cedric Sunray, whose conversations and letters to me added several quotes and much wisdom to the book, and to many other families not personally represented here, but whose efforts to use their heritage languages at home have been inspirational in the development of this book.

The Advocates for Indigenous California Language Survival (AICLS) have been a very important part of my life for the last twenty years. I thank the board members, staff members, and funders, past and present, for support, companionship, and shared wisdom in our mutual journey to learn how best to be of use to communities and individuals who are trying to learn their endangered languages and bring them back into use. Thanks also to all the people in California and elsewhere who have taken part in our programs, especially the Master-Apprentice Language Learning Program, the Breath of Life Language Workshops, and the Language is Life conferences. The participants, mentors, and volunteers have all provided their own wisdom and lessons learned, a "mutual help society" that has led us all to become better at what we do.

The University of California at Berkeley was my professional home for thirty-five years, and remains so now, at least in my heart, even though I am physically elsewhere most of the time. Many academics feel that they are the lonesome stewards of their fields of interest and worry that their specializations will be neglected by their departments when they retire. But I retired in 2006 knowing that the enterprises I held dear would thrive. My colleague Andrew Garrett took over the directorship of the Survey of California and Other Indian Languages and has turned it into something much greater than it was before. He and Lev Michael, the linguist hired into the position I vacated, continue to make the collaboration with indigenous communities in language documentation and revitalization an ever stronger part of the department's enterprise. I am grateful to have them as colleagues. I am also grateful to our department staff, especially Paula Floro and Belen Flores, for their many years of making my professional life (along with everyone else's) run smoothly, both as an active professor and as emerita.

Finally, I thank my husband, Dr. Gary Scott, for his constant loving support and encouragement of my work, and for the family he brought into my life: Stephanie, Lauren, Robert, and Jessy—and now their own children—have been and continue to be the most valuable project of our lives.

INTRODUCTION

Leanne Hinton

Deep in a misty mountain range in Northern California, a young family is visiting with elderly relatives who are members of the last generation to grow up speaking the Karuk language as their first and primary language. The elders are chuckling over the children of the family, who understand and speak Karuk as much as their parents are able to teach them. "*teexúriha hum?*" (are you hungry?), Violet asks. "*hãa!*" (yes!), answers Machnátach, three years old. Violet then asks, "*fâat ivishtáanti?*" (what do you want to eat?). He answers "*moosh!*" (meaning "mush," spoken with a true Karuk accent) and all the elders laugh in delight. These are the first Karuk children in three generations to grow up having their language spoken to them at home from infancy—indeed, since before their births, when their mother laid a tape recorder over her womb every night to play tapes of Karuk stories to them.

On the other coast, in Massachusetts, a mother and her five-year-old daughter are walking through the aisles of a grocery store, picking out items for the week's meals. "*Tyâqas wah nutahtôm?*" (What can I have?), the child asks, and her mother answers, "*Wah kutahtôm wutâhumuneash*" (You can have some strawberries). Other shoppers walking by, strangers to the family, may hear this snippet of conversation and have no idea what language they are listening to. Depending on their ideologies or their moods of the moment, they may think, "How sweet to hear a five-year-old talking a foreign language" or perhaps, "Darned immigrants! Why don't they learn English?" What they probably do not know is that this mother, a native speaker of English, has devoted many years of her life to learning this profoundly American language, Wampanoag—and that this child is the first one to be raised as a native speaker of Wampanoag in close to two hundred years.

These small scenes between parent and child can be viewed against the backdrop of deep time. In our first hundred thousand years of human history, our species has spread across the planet in multiple waves. People have adapted in ingenious ways to the tremendous variety of environments they have come to, and we have created a vast array of cultures, each with its own customs, rituals, belief systems, and forms of artistic expression—and each with its own language. Language is one of the great adaptations of the human species. It allows members of a group to communicate with each other in great detail and to express and create great verbal art; and it is also a self-identifying mechanism that allows groups to differentiate from each other and take their thinking in different directions. The wonderful plasticity of the human brain allows people to become multilingual, able to communicate across groups. And so languages and cultures also interact with each other, influence each other, and form new synergies and even new languages.

But it is of course not always the case that contact between cultures is benign and mutually beneficial. The pattern we see all around us in today's world is the massive development of a global economy and technology backed by centuries of military might steamrolling over ecosystems and the human cultures that had been part of them. Over and over again we have seen the marginalization, enslavement, or even genocide of groups of people who were the stewards of their land before the arrival of political, economic, or military imperial forces. This vast military-industrial complex has threatened the very diversity of adaptation that is the hallmark of the human species.

Language is one of the casualties of this process. Groups of indigenous people and long-term minorities are dispossessed of their land and livelihood, and may be scattered into diaspora or forced into missions or reservations or cities belonging to the new order and characterized by other languages. Governments and the majority groups they represent want to impose their own language on the developing nations; they see other languages as a threat to their hegemony. School systems (such as the early twentieth-century boarding schools for indigenous peoples of the US and Canada) are sometimes founded with specific aims to teach the dominant language and eradicate the other endemic languages within the nation's borders. In another tragic twentieth-century case of forced cultural and linguistic assimilation, that of the "stolen generation" of Australian aborigines, mixed-blood children were taken away from their parents. All these oppressive policies have led to worldwide erosion of the languages spoken by indigenous and minority populations. Of close to 7,000 languages that are still spoken in the world, most are spoken by fewer and fewer people each decade, and hundreds have lost their last speakers in our own lifetimes. At least 250 languages have gone extinct since 1950, and UNESCO estimates that almost half of the languages of the world for which there is sufficient data to know their status are in danger of extinction.[1]

But there is also another pattern emerging in the current era, of individuals and communities striving to strengthen or regain aspects of their heritage cultures even within the context of the larger, newer society. Such efforts are often part of a backlash against the encroaching society, a movement by people to strengthen autonomy and have a voice about their own future. It is a movement away from the cultural annihilation that comes from complete assimilation.

Inside the big picture I have just painted are individuals and families from both sides of this human collision, just trying to survive, to thrive, and to live ethically. People can and often have voluntarily given up language, along with other aspects of their heritage culture and way of life, for the sake of their own welfare and that of their children. And language is often one of the core components of the movement for cultural survival. This book is about families who so love their endangered languages of heritage that they have made them a part of their homes and their daily lives, despite all the pressures against doing so. And it is for families who might wish to do this brave act themselves.

The revitalization of endangered languages has been an active and growing movement for several decades now. It takes place in many venues—through community classes, summer camps, master-apprentice programs, the development of pedagogical books and multimedia materials, and most visibly schools, where, depending on community capability, there have been classes, or bilingual programs, or full immersion programs in the local language. In immersion schools such as those for Māori and Hawaiian, Scottish and Irish Gaelic, Welsh, Secwepemc (Shuswap) in Canada, and Mohawk, Seneca, and Blackfeet on the US mainland (and more), we see a new generation of fluent speakers of

endangered languages growing up. Newer and more tolerant government policies in the Americas, Europe, and Australia have led to funding (though never sufficient, and never safe from the "axe") for indigenous and minority language programs in schools and the wider
communities.

On a more informal level, communities around the world have regular language classes taught by elder native speakers; or they run language camps; or individuals who did not learn their languages at home
attach themselves to elders to learn as adults. It has been a great under-
taking, with language activists overcoming many obstacles. The lack of
support by policy makers and school officials, lack of steady funding,
lack of school subject material in the languages and the paucity of language-learning programs and opportunities all still create roadblocks to
the goal of language revitalization, yet the communities persevere and
make progress, often astounding progress. These efforts have been documented over the last couple of decades in an increasing amount of literature by linguists, anthropologists, and educators.[2]

And yet, many of us would say that the most important locus of language revitalization is not in the schools, but rather the home, the last
bastion from which the language was lost, and the primary place where
first language acquisition occurs. Those who dream of language revitalization ultimately desire the natural transmission of the language from
parent to child and its use in daily life. Most communities have not paid
much attention to language in the home; or to be fair, they are only
beginning to do so. Even teachers of heritage languages might not use
them with their children. True "reversal of language shift" cannot be
successful in the long run unless families make it their own process.[3] It
may be the lead generation of parent activists, who in many cases have
had to learn their heritage languages as second languages, who initi-
ate the return to using them at home. Or it may be the children of the
activists, who have learned the language at school, and as adults bring
the language to their home so that their own children will learn it as a
first language. Either way, it is that step—of actually using the language
in daily life at home—that is essential for true language revitalization.
Margaret Noori put it like this in her profound essay "Wenesh Waa
Oshkii-Bmaadizijig Noondamowaad? What Will the Children Hear"[4]:

Many have rightly reviled [Carlisle boarding school founder Capt. Richard H.] Pratt's 1892 call for "killing the Indian and saving the man."[5] But few have given him credit for understanding something we would do well not to forget. Taking aim at the language was indeed an effective form of cultural genocide.[6] Tearing children away from their homes is how it was accomplished. History has proven it is incredibly difficult to maintain ethnic identity without the language running like lifeblood through every daily act. If we are to learn from this lesson, the language must certainly be restored. And more importantly, the educational system that took it away cannot be depended upon to bring it back. We should not look for an answer in politics, policy or pedagogy alone. We must find the answer in practice and action. To reverse the damage, the language must be returned to the children and the home.

About the Chapters

The heart of this book is a set of autobiographical chapters by people who have done this very act of bringing their endangered (or even "extinct") languages into their homes and speaking them with their children. We begin with the most extreme situation: languages that have had no speakers at all for generations. Shying away from the hopelessness of the word "extinct," we call these languages "dormant," or "sleeping."[7] One such case is the Myaamia (Miami) language, whose speakers originally lived throughout what is now known as Indiana and much of Michigan, Illinois, and Ohio, and now, after two removals, live in areas of Kansas, Oklahoma, and elsewhere (Chapter 1). The last fluent native speaker of the language died sometime before Myaamia language activist Daryl Baldwin was born. Yet Daryl learned Myaamia, purely from documentation, going back to school for a degree in linguistics to assist him in the effort. He started using the language at home with his children as he learned, and now has four children who speak it proficiently. Two of them are old enough to write their own language life stories, and they do so in that chapter. This family's accomplishment demonstrates how a committed group can bring their language from being "extinct" to having native speakers with just two generations working together. Daryl is also the only linguist I know personally who has had dissertations written *about* him.[8]

Jessie Little Doe Baird (Chapter 2) has a similar history. Like Daryl, she learned her language—Wampanoag—purely from documentation, getting herself a degree in linguistics from MIT along the way. She brought the language to her community in the form of language classes, and into the home for her youngest child, age five at the time of this writing. In 2010 Jessie received the prestigious MacArthur "genius award" for her great accomplishments and inspiration. An award-winning film about her work and the language revitalization efforts of Wampanoag has since been produced.[9]

Part II has two chapters by families who began their quest for their ancestral language when the last generation of native speakers was still alive, of grandparent and great-grandparent age. With the languages no longer being spoken aloud around the community, in each case the parents had to search out elders to learn their heritage tongue. Ellie Supahan-Albers (Chapter 3) and her twin sister, Nisha, had a great-aunt and great-uncle living at their home in Orleans, California, and were able to hear some Karuk as young children, though never enough to acquire it as a language of communication. Later they began a more focused effort at learning the language through the help of the Master-Apprentice Language Learning Program run by the Advocates for Indigenous California Language Survival.[10] Phil Albers did not begin learning Karuk until he was college age—he was initially taught by Ellie, and soon thereafter by her great-aunt and other elders. Ellie and Phil began talking to their children in Karuk in utero. Theirs is a deeply honest account that says much about the emotional basis of decisions to use an endangered language in one's family, and how heart-wrenching it is to go on when the elders who know the language pass away.

In the Yuchi case (Chapter 4), Richard Grounds and his daughter Renée did a great deal of their language learning together. Richard took his daughter to elders on a regular basis to learn, and then they both made a habit of using whatever they learned in place of English from then on. Now a young adult, Renée can tell her own language story, and she writes probingly about the joys of knowing her heritage tongue as well as the burden of responsibility that comes with it.

Part III is about families who use their languages at home and also have strong community support in the way of immersion schools and other community-based programs. The Peters family (Chapter 5) were fluent native speakers of Mohawk but began using it at home with their own children only after acquiring inspiration from their immersion school program and the Longhouse ceremonial tradition.

Hana O'Regan (Chapter 6), a second-language learner of Māori, is also a leader in the great and multifaceted Māori revitalization movement. She writes movingly about her own childhood and the meaning of the Māori language in her life, and also forthrightly discusses the fears and difficulties attached to bringing up her children in an endangered language.

Husband and wife William Wilson and Kauanoe Kamanā (Chapter 7) learned most of their Hawaiian as college students and have been leaders in the development of Punana Leo and the Hawaiian immersion schools, as well as in the important university support programs for the Hawaiian language. They were also the first family in the Hawaiian revitalization movement to use only Hawaiian at home with their children.

Margaret Noori (Chapter 8), writing from her long experience with language revitalization in the Anishinaabe schools and with her family, shares her wisdom about how Anishinaabemowin at home fits into both the community culture, where immersion is possible, and more restrictive academic environments, where literacy and assessment are required.

Finally, Aodán Mac Póilin writes about the Shaw's Road Gaeltacht, a neighborhood founded by Irish-speaking families in order to give their children a fully Irish-speaking community to live in.

Part IV is about two unusual cases, to show the scope of variation within the language revitalization movement. Chapter 10 is about efforts to maintain an endangered dialect of Greek, and it makes some strong points about the difficulty of bringing up children to full fluency in isolation from a speech community. Brian Bielenberg and Aigli Pittaka's commitment to raising their son to be a balanced bilingual— or actually trilingual, in this case—led to the difficult choice of giving up promising careers in the United States in order to move to Cyprus, Aigli's country of origin, so that their child would be able to grow up fluent in Aigli's heritage dialect, Kypriaka. Nonetheless, the family still finds obstacles in the path to language learning. Even though Kypriaka is the Greek dialect of Cyprus, it is still threatened; the schools all teach in Standard Greek, and Kypriaka is in danger of giving way to the Standard.

In Chapter 11, Ezra Hale, son of the famous multilingual linguist Kenneth Hale, writes about the singular case of being brought up in the Warlpiri language half a world away from where it is spoken, showing the possibilities and limitations of achieving bilingualism away from the speech community a language comes from. Doing fieldwork in Australia, Ken fell deeply in love with the language, and, saddened by the thought that the younger generations no longer knew it, he decided to make it the language of his own home. He and his two sons conversed all their lives together in Warlpiri, up to the time of Ken's death. Ezra gave a speech about his father at a memorial ceremony at MIT, all in Warlpiri.

Part V is about two programs designed specifically to help families learn language together. Chapter 12 is about the California language Kawaiisu, where an extended family is learning their language together under the mentorship of language educators. Their learning is specifically geared to language they can use every day at home with each other. This chapter illustrates in detail how a highly structured mentored language-learning program can function to help a family learn together.

Chapter 13 is about a multifaceted program designed by Finlay Macleoid for learning home-style Scottish Gaelic. Concerned that the Gaelic taught in the schools in Scotland does not transfer to everyday conversation at home, Macleoid developed a program that helps parents learn how to interact with their children in Gaelic, from diaper-changing to teen talk.

We end this volume with a final chapter on how a family who wishes to use their own heritage language at home can get started in that process. Summarizing the wisdom from the first thirteen chapters, we provide ideas on parent language learning, how to get started using the language with one's children, and how to deal with the various obstacles that get in the way.

Each of these chapters is written from the heart, and each writer has his or her own personal style. I have done very little editing on most chapters, for they are so personal, so expressive of the feelings of the families, that they should stand as they were first expressed. The writers' voices are fresh and clear and very much their own.

Yet the authors also have much in common. You will note, to begin with, that all the authors are committed to raising bilingual children. None have any desire to keep their children from learning the majority language of their country—they strive for balanced bilingualism, not for monolingualism in the heritage tongue. Yet because the majority language is everywhere, and the endangered language almost nowhere, the parents' focus is always necessarily on how to bring more of the endangered language into their children's lives. It will also be seen in these chapters that almost all the authors go beyond their immediate families to help lead their languages into the community. Furthermore, each author keeps in mind an audience of readers who would like to know how one goes about starting the journey of bringing an ancestral language back into the home, and so these writings impart a great deal of good advice and wisdom.

Finally, each author speaks eloquently to the efforts, heartaches, and joys of language revitalization in the home, and the wonder of hearing one's children speak in what Joshua Fishman has so aptly called "the beloved language."[11]

Notes

1. UNESCO, *UNESCO Interactive Atlas of the World's Languages in Danger*, at http://www.unesco.org/culture/languages-atlas/, 2010.
2. For example: Joshua A. Fishman, *Can Threatened Languages Be Saved?* (Clevedon, UK.: Multilingual Matters, 2000). Lenore A. Grenoble and Lindsay J. Whaley, *Saving Languages: An Introduction to Language Revitalization* (Cambridge: Cambridge Univ. Press, 2006). Leanne Hinton and Ken Hale (eds.), *The Green Book of Language Revitalization in Practice* (Bingley, UK: Emerald Group, 2001). John Hobson, Kevin Lowe, Susan Poetsch, and Michael Walsh, *Re-awakening languages; Theory and Practice in the Revitalisation of Australia's Indigenous Languages* (Sydney: Sydney Univ. Press, 2010). Another important set of publications is the Stabilizing Indigenous Languages Series, published from the annual conference of the same name and available at http://jan.ucc.nau.edu/~jar/books.html.
3. Joshua Fishman coined the term "Reversing language shift" in his book by that title: Joshua A. Fishman, *Reversing Language Shift* (Clevedon, UK: Multilingual Matters, 1991).
4. Margaret Noori, "Wenesh Waa Oshkii-Bmaadizijig Noondamowaad? What Will the Young Children Hear?" in *Indigenous Language Revitalization: Encouragement, Guidance & Lessons Learned*, ed. Jon Reyhner and Louise Lockard (Flagstaff: Northern Arizona Univ. College of Education, 2009).
5. R. H. Pratt, "The Advantages of Mingling Indians with Whites" (an extract of the Official Report of the Nineteenth Annual Conference of Charities and Correction), in *Americanizing the American Indians: Writings by the "Friends of the Indian," 1880–1900*, ed. F. P. Prucha (Cambridge, MA: Harvard Univ. Press, 1973).

6. Tove Skutnabb-Kangas, *Linguistic Genocide in Education—Or Worldwide Diversity and Human Rights?* (Mahwah, NJ: Lawrence Erlbaum, 2000).
7. Wesley Leonard, "When Is an 'Extinct Language' Not Extinct? Miami, a Formerly Sleeping Language," in *Sustaining Linguistic Diversity: Endangered and Minority Languages and Language Varieties,* ed. Kendall King et al. (Georgetown: Georgetown Univ. Press, 2008).
8. Melissa A. Rinehart, "Miami Indian Language Shift and Recovery" (Ph.D. diss., Michigan State University, 2006); Wesley Leonard, "Miami Language Reclamation in the Home: A Case Study" (Ph.D. diss., UC Berkeley, 2007).
9. Anne Makepeace, *We Still Live Here* (Lakeville, CT: Makepeace, 2010). DVD available from www.MakepeaceProductions.com.
10. Leanne Hinton, Matt Vera, and Nancy Steele, *How to Keep Your Language Alive: A Commonsense Approach to One-on-One Language Learning* (Berkeley: Heyday, 2002).
11. Joshua Fishman, "Maintaining Languages: What Works and What Doesn't," in *Stabilizing Indigenous Languages,* ed. Gina Cantoni (Flagstaff: Northern Arizona Univ., 1996).

Part I

STARTING FROM ZERO

1: Miami

myaamiaataweenki oowaaha: MIAMI SPOKEN HERE

Daryl, Karen, Jessie, and Jarrid Baldwin

ceeleelintamaani niišwi iilaataweenkia. myaamia neehi english
(I like having two languages, Miami and English)
—awansaapia, nine years old

Daryl

Aya. kinwalaniihsia weenswiaani. karen weekimaki neehi niiwi piloohsaki eehsakiki. keemaacimwihkwa, ciinkwia, amehkoonsa, neehi awansaapia weenswiciki. myaamiaataweentiaanki wiihsa pipoonwa. ileeši kati neepwaanki ayoolhka.

Greetings! My name is Daryl. I am married to Karen and have four children. Their names are Jessie, Jarrid, Emma, and Elliot. We have been speaking to each other in the Myaamia language for many years, but there is more to learn.

For me personally, language is something that came to me later in life. I was always aware of my Myaamia (Miami) heritage through my father and grandfather, and fortunate to have had a great deal of historical knowledge about previous generations passed on to me. Culture for me was primarily shaped early in life through the intertribal experience, especially powwows. The only language I heard growing up was ancestral names, many of which I did not know the meanings of.

weecikiintiaanki 'our family'. Photo by Karen Baldwin, courtesy of Myaamia Project Archive

Previous generations of my family were divided by our forced relocation in 1846 from homelands in north central Indiana to a reservation in the unorganized territory, which later became Kansas. In the 1870s our Kansas relatives underwent a second removal to Indian Territory (Oklahoma). Some of my ancestors stayed in Kansas and still others remained behind in Indiana and northwest Ohio. As a result of these removals, we as Myaamia people today find ourselves scattered from Indiana, Kansas, and Oklahoma, with families living in almost every state. We are a fragmented community with tribal lands currently consisting of a checkerboard of approximately 1,319 acres primarily located in our jurisdictional area in Ottawa County, in northeastern Oklahoma. The Miami Tribe of Oklahoma is a federally recognized tribe with thirty-seven hundred on its citizenship rolls, but there are easily twice that number of individuals throughout the Midwest with Myaamia ancestry.

Linguists refer to our language as "Miami-Illinois." The Illinois people were a loose confederation of villages located throughout what is now the state of Illinois. Their descendants are today recognized as members of the Peoria Tribe of Oklahoma. The Miami and Illinois groups all spoke slightly different dialects of the same language. All things considered, there are likely ten thousand individuals who can claim ancestry to the Miami-Illinois people.

A desire to pursue my heritage on a deeper level through the language coincided with a key moment in my life. My wife and I had just had our first child and I was entertaining the idea of pursuing higher education, which would bring to an end a successful ten-year career as a carpenter. As a first-generation college student who was married with young children, I knew that college would be very challenging. Determined not to wait any longer to pursue a new path, I quit my career in carpentry, my wife quit her job as a schoolteacher, we sold most of what we owned, and I went back to school. I had no way of knowing the hardships that would come over the next ten years and how deeply my commitment to learning my heritage language would be tested.

During these years of transition, I distinctly remember finding a word list of the Myaamia language buried in my grandfather's personal papers, which I had recently received. The language was not his, as he was not a speaker, but it was the first time I had seen what I considered my heritage language and I was curious to know if it was still spoken. I asked my father if he knew any speakers and he suggested I travel to both Indiana and Oklahoma to find if any speakers existed in the two Myaamia communities. I followed through with his recommendation and soon learned that the last speakers had passed nearly at the same time I was born, in the early 1960s. There would be no speakers to learn from, and at the time, it wasn't fully known what documentation was available or if there were any audio recordings.

I remember feeling a sense of loss but also a sense of responsibility when I learned of the status of our language. I became determined to try and learn what I could. At the time I was not familiar with the use of the term "extinct" in referring to our ancestral language. I would soon become familiar with the terms "dead," "dying," and "extinct" in reference to languages and would eventually come to challenge these notions as inappropriately applied to well-documented languages that have communities interested in reclamation.

We really didn't start actively learning the language until my second child came along in 1991. In the beginning, the language consisted of word lists and the desire to name things: household items, birds, animals, and other familiar items common to everyday activities served as our starting point. Word lists taped to walls, counters, and cabinets

served as the learning mechanism, along with folded notes in my pockets as I went about my day. My first two children were still very young
and so they naturally became part of the learning process, as rudimentary as our effort was. We approached the effort collectively as a family.
We were young and uninformed but we were very committed.

During our home efforts of the early 1990s, I remember struggling
with pronunciation and understanding the verb system. At that time, a
graduate student named David Costa was studying linguistics at Berkeley and was reconstructing the Miami-Illinois language as part of his
dissertation research. I remember getting a draft of his dissertation
in the mail and, upon opening it, becoming overwhelmed by the linguistic description and jargon. I was just finishing up my undergradu-
ate degree in biology at the University of Montana and decided at that
moment that I would pursue graduate studies in linguistics at the same
school. My desire to pursue a linguistics degree was not motivated by
an interest in being a linguist. Instead, I was interested in obtaining
enough training to interpret Costa's dissertation and use these skills for
language reclamation. I was very fortunate to have the guidance of Dr.
Anthony Mattina and his wife, Dr. Nancy Mattina, for graduate studies
as both understood the complex nature of language revitalization, what
I was up against, and what my personal needs were. My best educational experience was my graduate studies in linguistics.

In the early years, my approach to home learning was much more formal than it is now, both in terms of our homeschooling efforts and from
my own personal "study" of the language. I learned about the phonol-
ogy, morphology, and grammar of my language and did tend to teach it
based on what I was learning in college. Even on the community level I
used to lean heavily towards teaching language from the perspective of
grammar, but I have since learned that teaching grammar and teaching
to speak are not the same thing. It wouldn't be until my second two children came along, years later, that we would move towards an immersive
approach to teaching. Immersion is much more efficient and effective in
passing on the language to young children. However, in the fragmented
speaking environment that we have created in our home, due to an
evolving fluency, I do think that a certain amount of structured learning
has had its benefits. I would say that structured learning is much harder
for me to do, primarily because of my own developing fluency level
after nineteen years of learning. Sometimes I find myself just wanting to

speak and not worry about developing learning aids for the home, but I know learning aids would be useful to my youngest children, who are now ten and thirteen years old.

I would like to turn my attention to some other aspects of home language learning. Learning to think differently is an issue that comes up repeatedly in our home. Just as I was writing this section, my youngest daughter, *amehkoonsa,* approached me to ask for some of what I was snacking on. I gave her only a very small portion with a smile, knowing that the amount I gave her would not be satisfactory to her. In English she replied, "You know I want more than that," and my response to her was *"taaniši ilweenki"* 'how is that said' (our typical way to ask for Myaamia to be spoken). She struggled to respond, but not because the vocabulary wasn't there. She knows from previous instances that the construct of the Myaamia sentence, hence the thought process, is situational and would not exactly match the English. After giving her adequate time to think about it, I supplied, *"kiihkeelintamani ayoolhka meeciaani"* 'you know I will eat more', which I did not translate into English, and she repeated without any trouble, knowing exactly what I said. This is a common struggle for our youngest children, less so for the older ones because the translation skills are better. One of the cautions in second-language learning is to understand "how the language thinks," and we consciously teach that as a skill, always pointing out how Myaamia thinks differently from English. As a side note, I could have translated my daughter's original English sentence to match the English exactly: *kiihkeelintamani neetaweelintamaani ayoolhka iiniini* 'you know I want more than that', but this would have been anglicizing the language and destroying its own unique thought process.

Staying in the language also has its challenges from a reclamation perspective. As indicated previously, complete fluency is not for this generation. There is no complete and total immersive environment that one can experience in our language. Fluency is an evolving process for us that will come from being immersed in documentation. This is the generation of reintroduction to the language and its unique way of thinking, and rebuilding cultural context for a future fluent environment. From my personal vantage point I see work towards immersion and eventual fluency as a process that will easily take us two to three generations. This is our reality without fluent conversational speakers. With that said, I do believe that communal fluency is achievable in the future, but I likely will not live to see it. Our work in understanding our language, developing cultural fluency, building culturally appropriate teaching models and technologies, building communal educational infrastructure, and developing proven educational pedagogy builds the kind of foundational understanding needed for a future community-wide immersion effort.

Since our language fell dormant in the early to mid-twentieth century, speakers stopped building new vocabulary as they shifted to English. This is why we don't have words for "refrigerator," "microwave," or "airplane," or not yet at least. Those terms will come with time, but in the interim, I feel strongly that staying with "whole language" utilizing already established vocabulary is important when working with children. In cases where the Myaamia term is clearly known as a non-English word, for instance kinship terms, then it will appear in an English sentence. But depending on the situation, we will either try to speak entirely in Myaamia or entirely in English and not mix the languages to compensate for lack of Myaamia vocabulary. If the Myaamia terms are not available or known, then we simply use English, knowing that with time we will eventually be able to say them in Myaamia.

It's important to understand that we are not under heavy pressure to "save a language" like so many communities who are witnessing the loss of first-generation speakers. Instead, we are under heavy critique and pressure from our own community to "do this well." I remember vividly many years ago a well-respected community elder shaking her finger at me and saying, "Don't screw this up!" I have not forgotten that moment and know that our language is not something to "mess with," but to handle cautiously with patience and respect. Without speakers there are lots of places for us to "screw up," but if we allow ourselves adequate time to learn and reflect, I feel confident we can revive our language in a way that honors our past and serves our present needs. We will continue to witness a degree of loss when working with our documentation, and we will continue to see major shifts over time, but I also acknowledge the creative human spirit that has the potential to bring new meaning and purpose to the language we speak today. I am not afraid of that reality.

As for making new terms, we have taken on that challenge when we feel comfortable with the situation at hand. For instance, we now have words such as *kiinteelintaakani* 'computer', *aacimwaapiikwi* 'Internet', and *hohowa* 'Santa Claus'. But in cases where language was historically absent, such as for concepts like religion, nature, race, and democracy, we have chosen not to translate those terms for the moment, out of fear that forced translations could affect the way in which the culture handles those ideas. Sometimes there is more to learn from the lack of certain vocabulary than there is from forced translations. Realistically, we know that people in the future will do whatever they want with the language, but for now we want the opportunity to reflect on why our ancestors would not have conceived of these ideas as defined institutional thoughts, and what the implications might be if we "name" and thus "define" them as nominal concepts. I feel this dialogue is essential for language and cultural preservation. If we want to preserve certain aspects of our culture, we must know how our culture differs from others, and our language gives some insight into this important issue. This type of discussion can provide a framework for developing language in culturally appropriate ways for any concept we may want to talk about in the future.

Another important aspect that has emerged with time is the knowledge that our ancestors have always lived directly connected to their food source. Food is at the heart of our culture as ecologically based people. In precontact times all of their sustenance came from the local environment, and food was a product of their ecological knowledge and their skills at growing, harvesting, and intimately knowing what was around them. During the early to mid-nineteenth century our landscape was dramatically altered due to settlement, and our ancestors took up domestic farming, with hogs, cattle, chickens, and a variety of crops, but remained involved in the production of their food.

As a family committed to cultural revitalization as much as we are to language reclamation, we felt this was an important cultural context worth preserving within the home, and we have worked to reconnect to natural processes and participate in the production of our own foods and medicines to some extent. This was a wonderful opportunity for language growth because our linguistic documentation was rich in farm-related vocabulary. Terms for raising animals, butchering, and food preparation are well established, even for animals and plants that were not indigenous to this region. We found that butchering chickens could be done entirely in the language and could even serve as a great opportunity to learn and teach about the internal and external anatomy of the bird.

A farm activity that we became involved in that was absent from our linguistic record was producing milk from dairy goats. The term *paapiciihsia* 'goat' was already established, but there were no milking terms available in the documentation. So we had to create them. We first considered the existing terms *noonaakanaapowi* 'milk', *noonaakani* 'female breast (of human or animal)', and *noon-* 'to nurse'. Using the stem *noon-* we added *-en* 'by hand' to create *noonin-* 'nurse by hand', and this created a verb stem that could be used to produce terms such as *nooninaki* 'I milk her (by hand)'. So now it's common to hear ringing out in the home around milking time, *"šaaye aawiki nooninenc"* 'its time to milk' or *"aašite kiila nooninaci"* 'it's your turn to milk'. The older children were involved in creating this new vocabulary, which serves as an important lesson in the ability of our language to create new terms when needed.

Our longtime friend and colleague Dr. David Costa continues to work with Miami language documentation, and he has been extracting from these valuable resources since the late 1980s. After more than twenty years of working from this documentation to reclaim our language, we estimated that we had used only about 10 percent of the available materials. Without this documentation, along with our work in the fields of linguistics, second-language learning, cultural preservation, and issues around Indigenous language revitalization, none of this progress would have been possible. But the work yet to come reaches far beyond our natural lives, and we hope someone will be there to pick up where we leave off.

Karen

aya karen weenswiaani. kinwalaniihsia eenaapeemimaki neehi keemaacimwihkwa, ciinkwia, amehkoonsa, awansaapia eeniicaanhsemakiki. "iinka" iiši-wiinšiciki niniicaanhsaki. mayaawi kweeteeliaani kaakinšimi myaamiaatawiaani.

Hello, my name is Karen. Daryl is my husband and Jessie, Jarrid, Emma, and Elliot are my children. My children call me *"iinka"* 'mother'. I really try to speak the Myaamia language often.

In the Miami Tribe community I am known as a "tribal spouse." This designation simply means that I am not an enrolled tribal member but am married to one, and in our case I am the mother of tribal youth (my four children). It's been my experience that the Myaamia community respects their tribal spouses and in many ways I feel as much a part of

meehkintaminki eeyoonsaaweekiša peehkateekia meeloohkamike 'gathering redbud flowers in spring'. Photo by Karen Baldwin, courtesy of Myaamia Project Archive

the community as any tribal member. The only difference is that I cannot vote or personally access benefits or resources afforded to enrolled tribal members. However, I would say that as a tribal spouse who has been intimately involved over the years in community language and cultural development, this experience has enriched my life in ways that go far beyond voting power and benefits.

As a participant in Myaamia language and culture revitalization efforts, I have experienced a way of life and knowing that differs from my American upbringing. I have come to value this experience and the many relationships I have built over the years with community members. If there is one thing my community and cultural experience have taught me, it is that life is about respectful relationships, and the use of the Myaamia language reinforces this concept in a deep way.

I recall the excitement of being exposed to the language in the beginning. I was driven by the desire for my children to not only know their heritage, but to experience it, and as their mother I wanted to share that experience with them. We started when the children were quite young, before any formal schooling began. At that time, language learning consisted of simple words and word games. The kids couldn't read, so we were limited in what we could present, and Daryl and I were just starting to learn the language ourselves.

As the children approached school age, I began homeschooling with great enthusiasm. I absolutely loved being with the kids and having the responsibility and opportunity of teaching them. This included the language. I made lots of games, activities, and several storybooks. It was a lot of work, as there were no language learning materials at the time, but I was very committed. I just wanted the kids to learn their language.

As the years went on, our efforts continued to evolve and change. The kids picked up the language quickly, almost too quickly for me to keep up with them. It was very challenging for me to learn as fast as they did. Exposing their young minds to the language challenged me as an adult second-language learner. I remember becoming frustrated with the intensity that comes with "staying in the language," which I knew they were more able to do. The newness and excitement had worn off. This was real work and our challenges were just beginning.

The test of any lifelong commitment is the ability to continue adapting and growing with it. This includes remaining motivated for years and years in a larger English-dominant social environment. We found ourselves having to limit the TV and focus more on family activities as a way to keep talking to each other. I continually try new approaches, techniques, methods, and anything that will help us maintain a need to use the language. It was and is difficult for me.

Currently, as I homeschool our two younger children, *amehkoonsa* (age 13) and *awansaapia* (age 10), my approach to language mainte-nance and teaching is vastly different than it was in the beginning, with our older children. Today, I use very few activities specific to language learning. I encourage the use of the language all the time, during school and otherwise. It feels more like an immersion environment, at least as immersive as it can be at this stage. I consciously incorporate cultural knowledge into their daily lessons and naturally apply the specific lan-guage for those activities. We have moved away from language being the target to language just being part of life in the home. This feels more natural.

My commitment to language learning has remained constant over the years, but our approach to teaching and maintaining has changed with time. I feel everyone has to find what works for his or her situation. Family dynamics, lifestyles, personal commitments, available resources, and personal skills and knowledge all factor into how much a family can actually do. Keep trying new things until you find what works.

I know more fully as a result of my experience that language and culture are directly tied to one's identity. The confidence I see in my grown children is amazing. They know who they are, they know their people's history, they just simply know. They aren't afraid to say who they are or be who they are, and that is the power of knowing. Pro-viding a helping hand in promoting my children's sense of identity is incredibly rewarding as a parent. I am very proud of them and feel their confidence as *myaamiinsaki* 'young Miami adults'.

Jarrid

aya, ciinkwia weenswiaani. eeweemakiki iiši-wiinšiciki. myaamia mihši-neepwaantikaaninkiši neepwaamikwaani niišwi pipoonwe aawiki. neepwaaminki myaamiaataweenki ceeki meehtohseeniwiaani.

Greetings! My name is Jarrid. I am a sophomore at Miami Univer-sity. I have been learning *myaamiaataweenki* (the Myaamia language) all my life.

At a very young age *nimihsa* (my older sister) and I started learning the language through our parents. My earliest memories are of when we lived in Missoula, Montana, and I had a very limited grasp of the language. I recall having a few good friends of native descent and teaching them simple words in my language, such as greeting terms: "hello," "good-bye," etc. The extent of my knowledge of the language at that age included greeting terms, kinship terms, earth and sky terms, and more dominantly, animal terms. Animal terms were the easiest to learn and are a good starting point for beginners.

Growing up, my parents always told me that being bilingual was a very important skill. They told me it would help me when I'm older to be able to understand situations from a different point of view, so this is the outlook I've always had on learning the language.

As for my thoughts on how I feel about the language, I am really glad I grew up learning to speak it at home. It is something different and very unique about me that I can put on resumés, scholarship applications, etc., and I feel good knowing a language and culture other than English. I have grown up learning the language and culture of an oppressed people, so that has really helped me relate to other groups of people who are going through things similar to what my ancestors went through.

Since I went away to college, the language has lessened itself in my life. As a sophomore in college, living in the dorms and surrounded by almost 100 percent English-speaking students, it is difficult to use the language as I once did at home. I still use it in texting with my family and some friends, and we have a tribe class here at Miami University that we attend once a week where I use it. Otherwise, I do not get to use it a lot unless I go home or go to a tribal event. I can feel myself forgetting words that I used to know when I lived at home, when I was around it all the time. I use it with my friends in the dorm, and many of them think it's really cool to be able to speak another language, and they ask me questions about how to say certain things and what their Miami name would be if they had one, which is a common question from people who have never known anyone from a Native American tribe.

In the future, I will continue to be a student of the language and learn as much as I can. However, in many places on campus it is very difficult to practice and continue learning when there is no one else around to speak it to. It is yet to be seen if I will work with the tribe and the language when I am out of college and go out to work in the world. I have made no plans but will not be surprised if I do end up

ciinkwia nooninaaci akowali 'Jarrid milking a dairy goat'. Photo by Karen Baldwin, courtesy of Myaamia Project Archive

continuing to work with the community and help teach the language. It is something I want to continue learning and pass on to other tribal members so they can have the experience I have had growing up bilingual. The language is very important to have and I think it shows a lot of dedication and commitment to something if you are learning the language of your heritage.

Jessie

aya keemaacimwihkwa weenswiaani. niila myaamiihkwia. myaamia mihši-neepwaantiikaaninki neepwaaminki. neepwaamikwaani nihswi pipoonwe aawiki. aancimaaci kati niila neepwaankia meehciweele neepwaaminki.

Hi, my name is Jessie and I am Myaamia. I am a student at Miami University in Oxford, Ohio. I am in my junior year. My major is Early Childhood Education and I hope to be a teacher after I graduate.

I have very strong memories of growing up and learning a language spoken by few. I had friends that spoke Spanish or just English, and they would always be curious about the language and want me to say something in my language. When I was young those moments seemed awkward and I would be hesitant to say something, but now I am much more comfortable talking about my heritage. It has become very much a part of who I am. I am thankful that I had the opportunity to be so immersed with the language as a young child.

When we were very young, there were many ways that we came to learn the language, but repetition and frequent use were important. For practice, my family and I would make name cards and tape them to objects around the house and say the word every time we used that object. We also made games as incentives to learning the language with our parents. The penny game was one of my favorites. Every time we would use the language we would get a penny, and when we forgot to use it, whoever caught us would take a penny from our jar. Once our jars were filled with pennies we would walk down the street to the gas station and buy a piece of candy. I think this was very beneficial to getting us to learn the language, because we did not realize how valuable it was as young children.

We were homeschooled, so that was also helpful in learning our language, since we were around it all the time. During math we would practice counting in the language and for science we learned the phases of the moon and the Myaamia names of all the months. We also wrote

amehkoonsa peempaalita

keemaacimwihkwa eewikiita aacimooni 'Jessie writes a story'. Courtesy of the Baldwin family

stories in the language. All of these ways of integrating the language into our daily activities were very beneficial to our homeschooling.

There are many benefits I have realized to knowing my own language. Most important is just being able to pass it on and teach my younger siblings and other tribal members. In order to keep our language alive we have to spread it around and share it with others. If we just kept the language to ourselves where would it be today? I help pass it on to my younger siblings and will pass it on to our future children.

There have been a lot of changes in our use of the language throughout the years as we keep learning more about it. So I end up learning new things while teaching my younger two siblings to learn to use it; having younger siblings to teach the language to encouraged me to learn more of it and improve my speaking skills. When my sister was born, our goal was to talk to her solely in the language, so she would learn to use it as her first language.

Today, I use the language as much as I can, which can be challenging because I am not living at home anymore. I use it with *nihšiima* (my younger brother), whom I go to school with, and other tribal students on campus. Many of them are still learning it and have not been exposed to the language as much as my brother and I have, so it is fun teaching them funny sayings that we have come up with over the years! If my brother and I are talking in the language amongst other people, we get some strange looks, but most of our friends have gotten used to it and love to hear it. They are always asking what we said and how do we say this or that. It is comforting to use our language where people do not criticize us.

Conclusion—Darryl

We have not only had the unique opportunity to see the immeasurable impact of language reclamation in our own home, but we have all been involved in developing programs in our community since 1995. This work continues through a unique relationship the Myaamia People have with an institution that bears their name, Miami University, located in Oxford, Ohio. Over forty tribal students have attended Miami University since 1991, and today we have eighteen currently on campus. All of our tribal students today are engaged in language and cultural education on campus. The Myaamia Project was developed at Miami University in 2001 to advance the language and cultural educational needs of the Myaamia People. What an opportunity for us, to take what started in the home nineteen years ago to a college campus and to be present during the education of our youth.

I remember well the day a young *myaamiihkwia* 'Myaamia woman' arrived on campus ready to take the next steps in her educational journey. I remember it well because thirteen years before, she was a seven-year-old coming to language camp for the first time. A year later my own daughter entered college at MU, joining her fellow language learners, and by this time they had become close friends. I am reinforced by the simple fact that this younger generation knows more about being Myaamia than I knew at that age. Our language, in the context of our culture, provided that growth and experience. This kind of personal development doesn't come from something dead or extinct. Our language is giving new life to a generation because our language is life-giving, and I believe it has no bounds for a way of life it can provide for the future.

2: Wampanoag

HOW DID THIS HAPPEN TO MY LANGUAGE?

jessie little doe baird

Wôpanâôt8âôk, also termed Wampanoag, Massachusett, Massachusee, and Natick, is the language of the Wampanoag Nation. It is one of the languages in the Algonquian family. It was spoken across a geographic area of southern New England from Cape Ann, Massachusetts, southwest to Dudley, Massachusetts, then south to Narragansett Bay. In the period from 1616 to 1619, an estimated two-thirds of the nation (some forty thousand Wampanoag) was wiped out by yellow fever brought by a trading ship. Hardest hit were children and Elders, the most critical speaker populations for any language. However, with the landing of the Europeans in 1620 came further devastating social and cultural losses to the Wampanoag Nation. Through the settlers' processes of religious conversion, laws against the use of the language, mainstream education, and commerce, the Wampanoag People had their land, their spirituality, and their language taken away. By the 1860s, the Wampanoag language had ceased to be spoken, and by 1900, the Wampanoag Nation, once sixty-nine tribes strong, was reduced to three remaining Wampanoag governments: the Mashpee Wampanoag Tribe, the Wampanoag Tribe of Gay Head Aquinnah, and the Herring Pond Wampanoag Tribe.

If there was a small glimmer of hope in the earliest parts of this story, it lay, ironically, in the fact that John Eliot, a Congregationalist missionary from England, supervised the translation of many religious documents into the language. This includes the King James Version of the Holy Bible. This was the first bible put to press on this continent. We also held the hope of our language prophecy. The prophecy proclaims that the Wampanoag language—which the Wampanoag People consider a living and animate thing—was destined to go away but also promised that the language would return when it could be welcomed back. It further tells us that the descendants of those who broke the

jessie (left) with student Berta Welch. Courtesy of jessie little doe baird

circle—the common language linking the Wampanoag to their Ancestors—would have a hand in closing it again.

What Can We Do about This Situation?

From the period of the 1850s or so until the late 1990s, there were no speakers of the language at any level. In 1994, the Mashpee and Aquinnah Wampanoag tribes formed the Wampanoag Language Reclamation Project (WLRP). The Assonet Band of Wampanoag, descendants from several historic Wampanoag tribes, joined us in 1996. In 2007, the Herring Pond Wampanoag Tribe joined the effort and in 2008, the Chappaquiddick Wampanoag, descendants of the historic Chappaquiddick People, who are trying to revive their tribe, joined the project. Today we have speakers from the levels of complete novice to proficient speakers able to have conversation. We have one first-language speaker, who is five years old. It is very important to note here that any reclamation effort would have been impossible without the written documents from the 1600s forward. i have heard various points of view from Indian folks on the subject of whether to employ a writing system for their languages. Only each community can decide what is best for their language and their own People. i am truly thankful that the Elders of my tribe decided, nearly four hundred years ago, that they would use an alphabetic writing system to codify our language. In this way, each generation has had the opportunity to decide whether the appointed time for language to come home has arrived.

How Can i Learn When There Are No Speakers?

Step one of my language journey was accepting that i was responsible for, and capable of, making a place for my language to be welcomed back into my community, and that creation of such a place had to begin in my own home. Step two involved having to do some work outside of my community. Since we had no speakers and could not afford to hire a linguist to teach us about the documents written in our language, i went back to school. i learned about Algonquian linguistics and began to work with the documents that my Ancestors wrote.

i am still in the process of becoming an eloquent speaker. i will be learning to speak for the rest of my life. i began learning my language by teaching myself. Let me explain how i did it. As i discussed earlier, Wampanoag has a very large body of native written documents. This collection includes documents of various types. Once i had decided upon a new standardized spelling system, some of the documents were transcribed using that system. Professor Kenneth Hale was invaluable on my journey and suggested that i keep the orthography (writing system) as close to the original texts as possible. Next, i would read those documents, looking for examples of certain parts of speech. For example, i might have had an assignment that involved finding one hundred phrases that had English glosses, listing them in a row, and then identifying the following:

- The part of the phrase that means "my," or "i am"
- The part of the phrase that means "your," or "you are"
- The plural of a noun
- Any question words

After documenting the words, i recorded myself reading them. i translated into English as well. Then, i added questions to the phrases and did other things, like pretending i was two different speakers and recording little conversations. Another method was to write out exercises and then record them and try to complete them audibly. i recorded sentences that said something like *nutahtôm mutâhs* 'i have a sock'. i then learned that the plural of *mutâhs* was *mutâhsash,* and so i could record myself saying, "*nutahtôm mutâhsash* 'i have some socks'.

It was then pretty simple to modify the phrase by adding a question word at the front, the prefix on the verb to mean "you," and pretending to be a different person. i could then say things like "*sun kutahtôm mutâhsash*" 'Do you have socks?' and "*nukees, nutahtôm mutâhsash*" 'Yes, i have socks'.

my professor guided me through a slow progression of more complex forms of the verb. i slowly learned about the complicated and very productive system of prefixes and suffixes that turned small parts of words (stems) into complete phrases.

i think that some of the most effective learning aids i had, and still have, are my student speakers. Teaching something to others helps me to understand the "whys" and "hows" of my language. i have been teaching for fifteen years now, and i have new questions from new speakers every single year. i also learn by talking with my husband around the house each day. i have discovered that i have made forms of words that i have never read anywhere. The human need to be understood really goes a long way where production and motivation are concerned. i keep a copy of the dictionary handy. The fact that it is not finished does not matter. It helps to find a word when i need to be understood. If i cannot find the word that i need, it is still helpful practice, since i have to find another way to describe my thoughts.

Maybe We Should Try Speaking Just Our Language

By the time my youngest was born, my husband, Jason, and i were both good speakers. i met my husband in language class. He is a very smart man and he worked very hard at learning his language. Naturally, this caused me to fall head-over-heels in love with him! i think that we agreed that we would use our language at home as soon as we decided to have a baby. We now felt that if we used the language continually, Mae Alice might be a native speaker. Jason said she might even be able to eventually teach us a thing or two.

We discussed the fact that our daughter would not be exposed to the language on a daily basis anywhere else and we acknowledged and accepted our responsibility to the language. Sometimes i think Indian folks recognize our responsibilities to provide cultural instruction to our children but we do not always see our heritage languages as part of that responsibility. We want to ensure that our daughters and sons know about ceremony, story, and dance. We think it is important for our children to know how to catch and prepare traditional foods. We find it almost as important as teaching them how to make a particular recipe taste better than anyone else's dish. Maybe we do not realize that our children have a birthright to their language. Maybe when we think of our language as a vital part of our children's cultural education, we become a little afraid. Maybe we do not want to talk about it because we feel that we may not be good enough speakers to try to pass on what we do know. i have thought about all of these things and felt the emotion from these thoughts too. i also know that if i put out the language i do have, then i have given my child everything i have. i have given her a chance and can feel satisfied with my efforts to pass on my culture. On my way into the room where Mae would come into the world, i asked my obstetrician to support us in our endeavor. i told the doctor that i understood that she had never heard our language and that she was not expected to understand or use the language. We just wanted her to allow ours to be the first voices our new daughter heard. She agreed. In this way, the first language our new little one heard was her language of heritage.

my husband's words were prophetic. Mae Alice did eventually correct his language usage. We were getting into the car one hot summer day. Jason opened the car door and exclaimed, *"whooo, kusaputeâw!"*

And Mae responded, *"mata, n8hsh...kusutâw."*

What happened here was that Jason had said, "Whooo, it is hot (to the touch)!" and Mae corrected him by saying, "No, father...it is hot (weather/air)." The two verbs sound similar, but Mae knew the difference. We were actually very happy about this and wrote down the date and what had been said. She was three years old at the time.

What's the Language Scoop around the House?

Mae Alice is the last child at home on a full-time basis. The next youngest, Rachael, is away at college. The other three have their own families and homes. We also have three grandchildren, and we use Wampanoag with them whenever they visit or we visit them. We use our language in the home on a daily basis. We do not use the language exclusively. The fact that we do not use it exclusively is most probably driven by my desire rather than any other reason. i find that most decisions made in the home are made by me. The woman of the house typically makes the decisions about the household atmosphere, activities, and schedule in Wampanoag society. If i demanded that the family use Wampanoag exclusively, we probably would. All three of us use both Wampanoag and English. There has been much less time spent using Wampanoag since Mae began attending public school. If she hears us using the language exclusively, that is what she will speak some of the time. Prior to her attendance in public school, it took less effort to elicit Wampanoag speech from her. If we have company and she hears English, she will use that exclusively.

Outside of the Wampanoag ceremonies and Wampanoag language games that we play, there are no activities that are exclusively conducted in Wampanoag or English. Everything in the home, from cleaning the house to dinner conversation, involves the use of both Wampanoag and English. This seems to be the place where we have found comfort without extra effort. This is not necessarily a good thing and this may be changing soon.

Jason and Mae Alice getting ready for hunting. Courtesy of jessie little doe baird

So What's the Language Scoop outside the House?

It is important for our families to hear language outside of the home, and the Wampanoag language was not heard anywhere in the community for over 150 years prior to the work of the Wampanoag Language Reclamation Project. There are some pretty easy and practical activities that can be conducted in any community in order to create opportunities for language to be heard outside of the home. The WLRP created a prayer of thanksgiving for the opening of every type of language class or language gathering. The prayer was in the same format and tradition as the ones that were Wampanoag in nature but being said in English. The prayer was printed in the language with the English gloss next to it on the page. Student speakers began to use this prayer at other meetings and gatherings outside of the language project. Student speakers of the language also began to be asked quite often to open all different sorts of gatherings in the language. It is now very common to hear the language at every type of gathering in our communities.

Another strategy that worked well was sending an invitation to the singing groups in our communities. The invitation allowed the singers to sit with speakers of the language and to create new songs using our language. There are now songs in our language for 49s, socials, pow-wow, traveling, honor, veteran's honor, marriage ceremony, and burial ceremony. People that attend these events now sing these songs along with the singers, and the sounds of the language signal familiarity, comfort, and enjoyment.

In each community, greetings and good-byes are daily items heard in the language. This was not by design or plan but rather organic in occurrence.

Certain ceremonies are now conducted in the language. Due to the protocols surrounding ceremony, that specific information will not be discussed here. However, it is important to realize that this is a place where opportunity may be created if it is appropriate in your community.

Work on What You Can Change and Accept What You Cannot!

There are several problems involving language use in our home. One problem is that everything we get in the mail, see on the television, hear on the radio, and read in the paper is written in English. i have written children's books for Mae Alice but beyond that, i am not sure that there is a whole lot i can do about the medium of the rest of the information coming into our home. Another problem is that Mae now feels awkward using her language. i think the reason for this is the fact that she goes to a public school where no one speaks the language. The language project is currently working on ways to solve this problem. One other solution to her using English too much came in an unplanned way. Mae's "Auntie Alice" (Alice Lopez) gave her two Indian puppets for Christmas. i picked one up and said, "*nutus8ees mukayuhs kah weepee nuwôpanâôt8âm*" 'my name is Baby and i only speak Wampanoag'. Mae absolutely loved it. She did try to respond to my puppet in English. i simply said nothing until she spoke to me in Wampanoag.

Another problem i have encountered is the resistance of individuals within our own tribes. Sometimes, when i was speaking only Wampanoag, people became visibly disturbed by my refusal to use English. i think this has to be expected and ignored. If we are using our languages around nonspeakers, it can cause our People to feel a wide range of emotions, not least of which are shame, inadequacy, fear of the unknown, and frustration. Eventually, these folks will learn to accept it and move on. As an advocate for your language, you can help folks that are nonspeakers by taking responsibility for effective communication. This may mean being *really* patient and even miming when necessary.

What's Going On These Days?

Today, i have just completed a research fellowship and written a grammar of the language that can be used by the layperson. This is good news for our language speakers, as the current materials available in regard to grammar are almost entirely written for the linguist. Naturally, this is a significant increase in opportunity to use the language, since the speakers can work with the grammar as well the dictionary to create novel speech. The Wôpanâak Language Reclamation Project was awarded a grant this year by the Administration for Native Americans. This master-apprentice fluency project, modeled on the work of Leanne Hinton and speaker communities employing master-apprentice methods, aims to increase the fluent speaker population by the addition of three more fluent speakers by the end of 2012. These speakers will then begin to work on curriculum for our Wampanoag medium charter elementary school (scheduled to open in 2015) as well as take on four new apprentices in order to replicate our speaker pool growth. We have seen the fluency of two speakers move from the Novice Mid level on the American Council for the Teaching of Foreign Language scale to Advanced Low for one speaker and Advanced Mid for another. One of the apprentices came to the master-apprentice project as a Novice Low speaker and has moved all the way up to Intermediate Low, a stunning amount of progress for nine months.

jessie little doe baird, enjoying Mashpee Wampanoag Women's Fishing Day. Courtesy of jessie little doe baird

This is a very busy time for my family. After i received a MacArthur "Genius" fellowship, the attention given to the cause of language reclamation and our project specifically was helpful, but the recognition has caused a demand for my time and i have had to be very selective about the time away. We certainly would not profit at all by my turning my attention in every direction except my own language. There are times, however, when other communities need assistance and the time away cannot be avoided. One of the fantastic products of the master-apprentice grant has been the opportunity to have so many hours of daily life be conducted in our language and with a group of my contemporaries. This has also increased opportunities for my family to use the language in our home. i find that teaching another to speak exponentially increases my own ability to speak.

So, What's on Deck?

There are exciting projects in the works for the WLRP. We are currently in discussion with an expert in the production of children's television programming to produce a series of children's DVDs. The series is called *Wôpanây May* (Wampanoag Street). The DVDs will feature characters and puppets that teach basic concepts. The series will be in Wampanoag and distributed to families in the community. The goal is to produce five of these half-hour DVDs in a period of six to nine months. The hope is that the parents will also watch and learn from them and be encouraged to take their language learning further. Student speakers will be producing story lines, props, and puppets. The local cable television station will provide free lessons in using Final Cut, an editing program for media projects.

Another idea that i have been developing is an after-school program that focuses on theatre and the language. The idea is to have two after-school theatre clubs: one for first through sixth graders, and another for seventh through twelfth graders. Both clubs will meet one day per week for three hours. The structure of the program will allow the kids to produce plays in the language. This project will require considerable cooperation from the tribes in the way of parental input, transportation, supervision, and a budget for materials. No English language will be used in the theatre clubs.

Our Board of Directors for WLRP commenced meetings in the fall of 2011 with consultants that are expert in the area of charter school development and implementation.

Immersion school is in the works as part of WLRP's five-to-ten-year goal. The apprentices from the master-apprentice work will be the individuals who become state certified as teachers. These speakers will be our first teachers. The immersion school will open with pre kindergarten through grade 5. Our target date for opening is 2015. We will then add one grade every two years thereafter.

The prospects for the Wôpanâak Language Reclamation Project and our family's language use are bright. Stay tuned for an update in the next volume! One last word of advice is to keep your language in your mind as a living member of your household and community. Try to do any and everything that you can for your language and work in a respectful way. Treat your language with patience and love and do the same for yourself and your family.

Part II

LEARNING FROM THE ELDERS

3: Karuk

KARUK LANGUAGE AND THE ALBERS BASKET

Phil Albers and Elaina (Supahan) Albers

The Karuk language is one of many in California. The Karuk culture was naturally preserved through location, as contact was limited and delayed until much later than most of Northwest America. Although contact was late, much of the language, culture, and lifestyle have assimilated and lost connection with the tribal roots and understandings.

Today the federally recognized tribe has over thirty-five hundred tribal members, and fewer than ten fluent first-language speakers. Many have gone on, leaving their legacy to our people through a variety of documentation, recordings, and relationships that may live forever. The tribe has a published dictionary with over seven thousand entries (and growing). The Karuk Language Restoration Committee has existed since nearly the time of federal recognition and works with a passionate dedication to revitalize cultural understandings and the identity of Karuk people through language. The Karuk Language Program has language materials, recordings, and videos.

Our family, Phil Albers, Elaina (Supahan) Albers, Machnátach, Íhaan, and Sasipuraan Albers, have been studying and teaching language for more than ten years now. As a family, we practice speaking at home with each other.

Phil Albers and Elaina Supahan Albers with their children (left to right): Gavyn Machnátach, Irysa Sasipuraan, and Íhaan Cayden. Courtesy of the Albers family

The Karuk language has always been a part of me, Elaina (Supahan) Albers, a part of who I am, and I have always wanted it to be a part of the future for many generations. My twin sister, Nisha Supahan, and I began "working on language" near the age of ten, joining the Master-Apprentice Language Learning Program (MALLP) with Advocates for Indigenous California Language Survival (AICLS) with our "master" speaker, our great-great-aunt Violet Super, whom everyone called "Auntie." Before we officially went to work ourselves, every week we joined our parents, Terry and Sarah Supahan, who were teaching Karuk community language classes in the Orleans/Somes Bar area, along with teaching weekly classes in our classroom at Orleans Elementary School. The Karuk language was a part of my life since childhood. Again, in high school, my sister and I and our best friend, Emilio Tripp, began the MALLP as a team effort. We worked with Auntie on a weekly basis while attending our high school Karuk language class taught by Susan Gehr, which also qualified for our required two years of a "foreign" language.

Even with hours and hours of language classes, and listening to hours of language, my language learning became lax in the later part of high school and the motivation began to slip. I didn't feel like I was advancing beyond basic vocabulary and simple phrases. This was upsetting, to feel like I had hit a wall, a wall constructed with only basic nouns and common sentences. Once that wall is hit it is hard to rebuild confidence. After years and years of learning I felt like I should be so much further along than just the toddler stage of speaking. I felt that the community was praising me for the years of work, not really understanding that I had only gotten a few steps down the road.

I met my husband the first day of school, my freshman year in college. We are both Karuk from the Klamath River and had never met until we were both in school in Ashland, Oregon. His desire for the language was translucent, it shone through him at first sight. He was intrigued that I grew up with a fluent speaker and he couldn't wait to know everything I knew. It didn't take him long to absorb what I had to offer. I started by giving him a phrase a week to use instead of English. He grew beyond that almost immediately and began speaking all the Karuk he knew first, and then translating it into English with every sentence. He continued to crave the language and began to work with my auntie Violet at every opportunity.

I found out I was pregnant with our first son in the spring of 2003, when I was twenty years old. Phil was twenty-three and preparing to graduate from college. It was a stressful time in our lives. I hung up the phone with the midwife and looked at Phil's wide eyes. All he had to say was…"We have nine months to become fluent!" The language was all we could think about in the preparations for our first child. I filled a cassette tape with recordings of Phil and my aunt telling stories and speaking only in Karuk to the baby inside of me. I played the cassette softly every night as I propped it against my growing belly, only to wake up in the middle of the night to turn the tape over and push "play" again. I knew that this was probably going to contribute to my son's being a night owl, but it was the only time I could guarantee I would be still for a length of time and expose the baby to effortless Karuk conversations. We worked endlessly on learning, translating, and creating language material for our child.

Gavyn Machnátach Albers was born December 9, 2003, into the arms of his father with the Karuk language in his ears. We worked hard to stay in the language while at home in the presence of our son. We were learning as we went, writing down phrases for translation and hanging cards with common phrases around the house in appropriate locations. His doctor, in Ashland, was concerned that he was not developing well since he was not making typical sounds as defined by the standard for English-speaking babies. "He isn't making any 'dadada' or 'lalala' sounds, which he should be at this point," said Dr. Olsen. Once we explained to her that we only spoke Karuk in the home, which doesn't have a "d" or "l," and demonstrated the sounds and speech, she marveled to see the effects on the child's development of speech and to hear that the sounds that flowed from his little voice were Karuk sounds. Later as he began to speak English he would pronounce English words with a noticeable Karuk accent. As he grew, he would identify the different languages and he learned to speak accordingly. While at Ke'Pel Head Start he said to me, *"yáxa, yuraschíshii îikam,"* then he looked at the teacher and said to her, "Look, horse outside." Then while playing with a dear friend, L. Frank, he would speak to her in English, yet maintain Karuk to us. Sometimes he would translate our statements into English for her, so she could still play with him. I would say to him, *"yáxa, yuraschíshih tu'áhoo,"* and he would look to L. Frank and say, "Look, horsey walking" while doing the action with a toy horse.

For most of my "adult" life, during that time a person begins to worry about life and death and all the things in between, I began to worry that someday I would be without my aunt. This went on for many, many years, worry that I would wake up one morning and get the devastating news. My auntie Violet, who had lived next door to my family my entire life, was my confidence in Karuk language survival. I knew that if I didn't know how to say a phrase in Karuk, I could walk up the hill to her house and ask, which I did almost every day.

Machnátach's brother, Íhaan (Dancer), was born almost two years later, on January 30, 2006. He was exposed to Karuk as much as we could, but Auntie passed away in a tragic house fire on November 29, 2006, when Íhaan was only ten months old. Still tied into his baby basket, he sat at the site of the fire, next to the ashes that were our language in my mind. He didn't even have a chance to learn from his aunt during the critical speaking years. I stopped talking at home. After the fire I lost all motivation to speak Karuk. I was afraid that when I needed a translation and it wasn't right there from the lips of my aunt it would hurt too much. I began to not even try to find the words, in order to prevent the hurt from inside. Both boys quickly followed my example in my devastation; they began to speak English on a regular basis...

As for me, Phil Albers, I did not have the foundation that my wife had. I had language terms and phrases that I had no recollection of learning, only that I knew them, and used them minimally. Very limited. My parents, Philip and Rhonda Albers, and the rest of my family supported my language learning and speaking, yet had minimal experience or skills to be of much help beyond where I was already. Arch Super shared and understood my craving for language and was supportive and helpful in learning and speaking language. My grandmother Lucille Albers was quite apprehensive. As a fluent first-language speaker, she chose not to teach her children, out of concern for their best interest and safety, based on her own experiences growing up. It wasn't until I met my wife, Elaina, that I had an environment and partner that could offer liquid to a parched thirst. She fed me anything I asked for, and introduced me to a new world of language learning through her great-aunt. I quickly became an apprentice with that truly unique and incredible woman, first-language speaker "Auntie" Violet Super.

Auntie was my teacher, mentor, and best friend. We spoke language together as if we had known each other all our lives. She had a strong cultural tie and traditional way of speaking. She held that and spoke in that way, in Karuk, and in English. Learning language from her, especially in conversational and contemporary speech, forced that concept. She wouldn't say things how they "should" be said in English. She would say them the way she spoke, with a traditional and cultural framework. Learning this accelerated my learning faster than all other techniques combined. We had conversations from smoking fish to smoking cigarettes, from bathtime to bedtime, from fighting to loving, and from being born to growing old. We included our entire family, many friends, and even an occasional stranger in our language-speaking opportunities.

In November of 2006 she went on to another stage of her existence. It was abrupt, unexpected, and painful. The loss struck our family, our community, and our entire tribe. It stunned my outlook on life, my

Violet Super with great-nephew Andre Cramblit.
Photograph courtesy of Andre Cramblit

perspective on Karuk language revitalization and our actual language survival. At first I felt only two emotions when anyone or anything triggered memories of her, pain and fear. It hurt to lose such a close and special person, and it scared me to learn that my strongest language tool was gone.

In living through this ordeal I learned about process. I discovered how to appreciate what I have, remember what I have lost, earn what I wish to gain, and respect life. Without my dear family member, friend, and language teacher I was left confused and scared. It impacted our entire family's daily living. We were no longer able to walk the seventy-five feet or so up to speak with Auntie. We were no longer able to write down our questions and phrases that we needed to learn in order to stay that half-step ahead of our children. We could not simply check on our language use, grammar, structure, and choice of words with our living key to the precious past. Losing her meant losing a portion of our past and our future, and we were not prepared.

I had to learn how to continue. Even though my greatest language asset was gone, my hunger and desire for language were not. I had to identify the hard, painful truth of her death, and let her go. I had to learn to remain consistent with speaking at home, using what I had as much as possible. There were times that even speaking the language hurt because of the connection and associations. I was dependent on her, on that safety of knowing someone could tell me, show me, and be my language teacher.

My boys, Machnátach and Íhaan, were quickly beyond what I could fluently speak. They flew past me while I struggled to look up the new words, find the proper translation, and then speak the language accurately. I lost patience, I lost motivation, and I lost the discipline to practice until it felt right. Auntie would say, "Just say it, Karuks would just say things..." After Machnátach started school at Ke'Pel Head Start and began using English more than Karuk, I felt pressure in my chest. Like someone was squeezing my heart from the inside. I couldn't compete with English, not at school, and now not at home. I missed Auntie more than ever. As I looked at my two boys, I realized how much I needed the language to teach them about who our people are and how we think. At that point I finally accepted the responsibility of being my own teacher.

While I, Elaina, was a nostalgic speaker, Phil continued to learn and grow, teaching his Karuk language class at Hoopa Valley High School and occasionally visiting with fluent speakers Vina Smith, Charlie Thom, Sonny Davis, Alvis Johnson, Jeanerette Jacups-Johnny, and his grandmother Lucille Albers. He amazes me on a daily basis with his ability to grasp, understand, and retain the Karuk language. It is now a little intimidating for me at home. I feel like I cannot keep up with Phil and his advanced understanding of the Karuk language.

I, Phil, use Violet's knowledge, her life, and her love to rise up and grow. I speak of her to my children, and teach them of her contribution to our family. I share stories of the way she spoke, the words she chose, and the gift she contributed. Today we still hold true to our language efforts. Our children, our families, and our friends know us as Karuk language speakers. Auntie, *hitíhaan kúma súpaah nupikrôok. yôotva yôotva.*

After all these years the most inspiration for us is our children. Seeing them respond and understand their Native language, and hearing them comfortably speak in their Native language, is the most rewarding feeling we could ever imagine. It is bigger than the first day of school or the first lost tooth. It is an experience that can happen every day of our lives as long as we continue to encourage it. Even after reaching the last step into complete surrender and then starting all over, it is worth every minute.

When our third child was born, our first daughter, I was lying with her in the evening gazing into her eyes, as mothers sometimes do, with our foreheads pressed together. She was only a month old. As I was looking at her, a scenario ran like a movie in my head from the night before at our son's first tee-ball practice. I had started talking to a woman whose son was also on the tee-ball team. We had an in-depth conversation in the first few minutes of our meeting, and halfway through the conversation I realized that I had already forgotten her name. Looking back on this situation I thought to myself, while still looking into the eyes of my daughter, that I could have turned to a tee-ball father and Karuk language speaker who was nearby and quickly said, "*Tanapshinvarivar pamuthvuuy*" (I forgot her name), and hope that he understood me enough to ask, "And your name is?" after I introduced him to her. The second part of the thought was, of course, fiction and all this ran through my mind in that half a minute while snuggling my baby. I am not sure why—it was totally out of the blue—but the significance to me is that I realized I was thinking in Karuk again. After all these years, the language that was buried deep inside me under the sadness and grief has started to return to the surface. I look down at my daughter while we are alone and softly coo and talk to her in that native tongue that I thought was lost within me. It has surprised me: the words and phrases that come pouring out of my mouth to soothe her little face are second nature and I have not heard them in the last four years since the fire. There is a new beginning, a new life within our family to bring our language back again.

nu'íimnih, nukshaha, káru araráhih nuchúuphi. We love, we laugh, and we speak Karuk.

4: Yuchi

FAMILY LANGUAGE WITHOUT A LANGUAGE FAMILY

Richard A. Grounds and Renée T. Grounds

What to do when you no longer have a fluent speaker in your near family? How to overcome not having a written form of the language, let alone having a teaching grammar or sequential curriculum for your language? Since Yuchi (also spelled "Euchee") is one of the rare language isolates, we do not even have related languages that we can look to for patterns of grammar. Therefore, we cannot draw on other members of a language family to recreate missing words in Yuchi. We cannot perform the family magic of transposing words out of a sister language—along some predictable shift in pattern—that would allow us to make those words reappear in a reliable Yuchi form.

What to do when the opportunity even to hear the beautiful rhythmic sounds, to hear the singing that is our language flowing down from ancient life-springs, is quickly ebbing away. With an ur-language that has been heard since the early beginnings of human history, we struggle with how to nurture such a rare gift and keep the language alive in our family, how to keep it from sinking into silence. And strangely, despite our unique language, our prospects for funding support are limited by the fact that our Yuchi nation is not recognized by the federal government. These are the challenges we have struggled with as we have worked to bring back the Yuchi language into our family and our Yuchi community.

dEzAt'ê O'wAdA:[*]
In my lifetime I have witnessed the decline of our Yuchi language from
the times of *dElaha*, my grandmother—one of seven sisters—and her
generation, who lived entirely in Yuchi, until today, when only five fluent first-language speakers remain to help us keep the language alive
in our community. *dElaha*, Ella Pickett, was thirteen and a monolingual
Yuchi speaker when she was sent to Euchee Mission Boarding School
in the town of Sapulpa. Ironically, this is the same town where I and
my young adult children live as we work to keep our language alive.
Although my grandmother was forbidden to speak her language at the
school and learned basic English language skills, *dElaha* did continue to
use Yuchi as her primary language of communication throughout her
adult years. She and her sisters lived on a cluster of nearby land allot-
ments and constantly spoke Yuchi to one another.

When we would take my grandmother to the Indian Health Service hospital in Pawnee, I remember that she could speak English well
enough—but only until the doctor entered the room. At that moment
she could only speak the Yuchi language. Her older sister, "Loshana"
(her name, Rosanna, was pronounced thus, because we have no initial
"R" in Yuchi), refused to ever use the English language. It was a political stance. She often said, *"zAnek'â'wAdA-ya, yUdjEhalA'wAdA"* (If you
want to talk to me, use Yuchi). We never really knew if she actually
had the ability to speak English but we thought she probably did and
had decided never to use it.

By the time of the generation following *dElaha*, the effectiveness of
the boarding school program had become abundantly clear. It was the
designated function of the boarding schools to undermine Indigenous
kinship, social, and governance systems by stopping the languages,
breaking up the continuity of ceremonial and medicine traditions.
Above all, the co-opting of Native children was designed as a long-term
strategy to force them to enter the economic system, to become lower-
rung wage earners and consumers. By interrupting the ancient flow of
songs in our community we have lost certain classes of songs. We do
not now know the old lullabies, women's work songs, or the songs for
administering the extensive variety of plant medicines.

Due to starting at an older age than the typical early start for children going to boarding school, my grandmother did not lose her

---

[*]   See chart showing the Yuchi writing system at the end of this chapter (Table A).

language. But the older boarding school survivors would not allow my father's generation to speak the language, even in the home. Despite a practice of washing out the mouths of children with soap at the boarding schools, they failed to wash the language out of my grandmother's mouth. Yet they did succeed in "brainwashing" her to think that the language should end with her generation. As a result, my father and his sister did not know enough of the language to hold a conversation in Yuchi. Instead, *dEz@ˆs'Ê*, my aunt Louella (whose name was drawn from *sAt'ê*, her father named Louis, and *sAzah@ˆ*, her mother named Ella), would always correct our English when she came to visit. She was constantly battling against our Okie-style English, trying to keep us kids from saying "ain't" and other slang terms. It had been drilled into her mind at boarding school that proper English was essential to be successful in life and she was passing that on to us. Instead of helping us speak Yuchi, our own family members had become the principal, hands-on enforcers of the new English-only regime. Our family was now being coerced into speaking a foreign language in the midst of our own homeland.

Accordingly, the opportunity to experience full services in the Yuchi language at the little Yuchi Methodist church south of Sapulpa has faded. As children we listened to long sermons that were delivered in Yuchi language and then translated into Muscogee and English that seemed to go on forever. Our services at Pickett Chapel are now marked by rousing songs in Yuchi and other tribal languages, but it is only in recent times that these fond memories have been revitalized with intentional use of the language, for messages by a few of the elders and more recently a message in Yuchi from Renée, my daughter, *dEzA'y@nE*.

dEzA'y@nE sA'wAdA:

I was about seven years old the first time I remember learning the Yuchi language. *dEzAt'ê*, my father, began taking *zOda'anA*, my brother, and I to visit *OhahanE Enû*, fluent elders, in their homes in the early 1990s. We no longer had a fluent speaker in our immediate family line but I began to feel like *OhahanE Enû* were my family. These face-to-face language sessions with Mose Cahwee, William Cahwee, Jim Brown, Maggie Marsey, Dimmy Washburn, and later Addie George gave me insight into a completely different world—the Yuchi world. We had no skills in the language or understanding of grammar, and had a hard

Richard Grounds (right) with son Alan Grounds and daughter Renée Grounds at the Yuchi Green Corn Ceremonies, 2012. Photograph courtesy of Renée Grounds

time even deciphering the particular sounds used in Yuchi. This often made for a humorous dynamic. I remember in one of our early sessions with William Cahwee we spent almost an entire class trying to say one phrase correctly: "*w@ wat'A nesha*" (year-how many-you do / how old are you?). We kept saying gibberish, like *w@wawansha*. All of us were rolling in laughter, trying so hard to say the simplest phrase but talking like babbling babies instead. We had our first introduction to what our elder Mose Cahwee often referred to as Yuchi jawbreakers.

At that time there were only a few recordings of Yuchi and no learning materials, so we had to create our own. We started by learning everyday phrases. When we wanted something from the bubble-gum machine we learned to say *s'at'A dEt@* (quarter-I want) and we learned to say *dE'yuhûnlA* (I am hungry). We focused on the rhythm of the language and accurately pronouncing the few things we knew. Those language sessions gave me a foundation for Yuchi grammar and prosody at an early age, which I continue to benefit from today. There were certainly times when *zOda'anA* and I protested visiting the elders because we wanted to play video games or visit friends. Sometimes we struggled because even though Yuchi was a priority for our family, the kids around us spent their time doing more typical kid activities. *dEzAt'ê* gently guided us in appreciating the time we spent with *OhahanE Enû* and helped us balance our interests. Now I am grateful for the time I did spend with *OhahanE Enû,* since many of them have passed away and there was a very short window of opportunity to get to know them. As a family, *zOda'anA, dEzAt'ê* and I grew closer through the pursuit of learning Yuchi. In contrast to our monolingual English-speaking friends, we had our own family language.

dEzAt'ê also reinforced our learning at home, which made a huge difference in my language development. He began making *zOda'anA* and me ask for things we wanted in Yuchi. For instance, if we wanted candy we had to say *zOsOdEgû dEt@* (candy-I want). One day *dEzAt'ê* raised the bar even higher to show us how much he valued our learning Yuchi. As a boy, *zOda'anA* particularly liked wolves, so *dEzAt'ê* said he would buy him a real, live wolf if he could ask for it correctly in Yuchi. *zOda'anA* and I were both shocked by this offer because we were confident we knew how to ask for a wolf in Yuchi: *dathla dEt@* (wolf-I want). *zOda'anA* was crushed when he learned that we had left out an important part of the phrase: it should be *dathla wAdEt@.* The *wA* particle is always used to refer to a living non-Yuchi person, in this case, the wolf. Believe me, we never made that mistake again!

zOda'anA and I soon realized that we could use Yuchi as a secret code in front of other people. We learned childish phrases like *nethl'@'lA* (Did you fart?). When we used such expressions we would really laugh, especially because no one else knew what we were saying. We got a puppy and trained it using Yuchi commands like *ahAgû* (come!), *aKAchE* (stay there!), *s'@chE* (sit!), *wAthla* (go!). When the dog went running down the street, our neighbors were surprised to hear us yelling "*ahAgû!*" We were proud of our "bilingual" family dog.

dEzAt'ê O'wAdA:

One of the basic strategies in developing ownership of the language for our family was to completely replace commonly repeated English phrases with Yuchi. Once I learned to ask *sOdEt@ha wahAha?* (your shoes-where are they?), then I never said it in English again. As a parent my use of the language focused on parent survival language. I became very quick with *n@ KAê thla* (Don't do that!), or *s'@hA wE* (Get down!). Of course, there were other parenting essentials, such as *n@zAKw@ˆthl@ˆ* (don't hang on me!). As we went along, there were an increasing number of phrases that I, in fact, had never translated into English, but the kids began to learn and use them simply because of the context.

A surprising realization that has become clearer to me over the last few years concerns the benefit of exposing *dEzA'y@nE,* my daughter, and *dEzAs'@nE,* my son, to the language at an early age even though, at the time, I was quite aware of my own limitations in the language. (For an embarrassingly long time I was forced to read off a card on the refrigerator door just to call the kids to eat, *k'agOthl@nE hElA sh@ˆsh@ˆ, a @gû k'a@thl@nô.*) My concern was that I was not better able to give them exposure to more advanced forms of the language and therefore the advantages growing from our efforts would have a minimum long-term effect. Yet to my surprise *dEzEOtOtOhAnû,* my children, did develop the ability to hear and understand the language in an immediate, direct way in spite of my limitations. I think this is promising for those who are forced to launch into a family learning program for all the family members at the same time. Due to the urgency and paucity of access to our original languages most of us cannot now afford the luxury of a two-stage learning process wherein the care-givers develop fluency in the language first and then begin to teach their children. Our approach was to make sure that what was being said—even though given in limited quantities—was said with the correct rhythm and with precise pronunciation. By ensuring a high quality of exchange in the language, the children were indeed enabled to develop a natural "ear" for the language as they continued with their learning.

The funny side of our naturally flowing questions and proper-sounding comments was that elders often overestimated our abilities in the language. By focusing on the fluid singing of our language, the elders now seemed amazed by our apparent facility. It sounded right to them and they presumed that we would, therefore, be able to understand everything that they said to us. So, we might start a conversation with a simple but properly delivered question that would then lead to a long response that was way over our heads and left us swimming in deep and fast Yuchi waters.

Prior learners had followed a typical English reading model for learning—that is, attempting to write down the words, then laboriously sounding out the individual syllables of each word and methodically

piecing together longer phrases. The elders had been stumped at trying to understand the language from new learners that was delivered
without the beautiful musical quality that is essential for understanding our language. Despite the fact that a new learner had seemingly
pronounced properly all the individual pieces of the words, the elders
often were quite baffled by what was being said. In turn, learners were
often frustrated at the seeming lack of comprehension of something
that they were sure had been said correctly. We eventually realized that
the elders were not posturing in order to drive home the point that our
rhythm was a bit off. They really could not understand anything that
was delivered without the proper musical score for the Yuchi language.
That was the only way they had ever heard the language spoken since
before they left the wombs of their mothers.

It is not surprising, then, that we sometimes refer to our elders as
walking dictionaries or as living encyclopedias. They are the living
source that embodies our culture, drawing from ancient times. No book
written about Yuchi could ever compare to the vast, quickly accessible
knowledge of our elders. The elders often remind us that our language
is a gift from the creator. In turn, our efforts to keep our language alive
center around our elders who gift us with their beautiful presence and
deep knowledge on a daily basis.

dEzA'y@nE sA'wAdA:

The family terms are an especially complex and rich part of the Yuchi
language. We continue to glean new information from the remaining
elders about the nature and usage of words for familial relations, even
after years of learning the language. In the last few months we have
started working more with Martha Squire, a fluent elder, who lives far-
ther away than the other elders (fifty minutes one-way via turnpike). I
am struck with how fortunate we are to be learning new aspects of family terms from Martha Squire. For example, when Martha Squire talks
about her grandmother she says *"dElahA shÂ Ânû"* (my grandmother-
deceased). The *-Ânû* ending is new to us because it is a kind of honor-
ific ending used only by women about their grandmothers or mothers.
I had been referring to my grandmother all wrong, using the generic
female *-sAnû* ending! (e.g., *dElaha shÂ sAnû*). Working with Martha
Squire was literally the very last opportunity to learn this important
aspect of the language. By virtue of this dramatic connection with the

living past through Martha Squire we will be able to pass these special forms of respect in the family to future generations.

When I was little, there was a transitional period in which *dEzAt'ê* demanded I stop calling him "dad" in English and instead refer to him only as *dEzAt'ê*. It was difficult for me to break my English habit of saying "dad" but I have come to appreciate the significance of using Yuchi family terms to identify each other. Yuchi family names continually reinforce our connection as a Yuchi family, in the midst of an English-speaking culture. *dEzAt'ê* calls me *dEzA'y@nE* (my daughter) and he calls his son *dEzAs'@nE* and it has strengthened our Yuchi identity. In the writing of this chapter, *dEzAt'ê* and I have implemented this strategy of identifying family members in the Yuchi language. I introduce sections written by *dEzAt'ê*, saying *dEzAt'ê O'wAdA* (my father, he speaks). *dEzAt'ê* introduces me, saying *dEzA'y@nE sA'wAdA* (my daughter, she speaks). The deeply relational aspect of the Yuchi language and culture is reflected in that there is no way of saying "daughter" or "father" in Yuchi without saying whose daughter or father it is. Therefore, there is no way to say "the father speaks"; I must say *dEzAt'ê O'wAdA* (*my* father, he speaks). The charts in Table B at the end of this chapter go into detail about the complexities of family terms in the Yuchi language.

dEzAt'ê O'wAdA:
One of the seemingly radical steps we took to help ensure the progress of *dEzA'y@nE* and *dEzAs'@nE* in the language was to take them out of public school to do homeschooling during some of their school terms. In addition to a focus on the language, a second part of the rationale for making these moves was to create an opportunity to educate *dEzEOtOtOhAnû* against the kind of anti-Indigenous brainwashing that seems to be built into the public educational system, particularly in a state where the schools still conduct annual celebrations of the so-called "Oklahoma land run." We drew from our elders for language and historical information and also used such books as James Loewen's *Lies My Teacher Told Me: Everything Your American History Textbook Got Wrong*. We tried to work against the intrinsic bias growing out of the older colonial perspective that continues to pervade not only the telling of the history of this land and predetermines outcomes in the judicial process, but is expressed in the structuring of the educational curriculum that is

inherently dismissive of Indigenous knowledge, history, religious rights, and governance systems.

While it is, perhaps, possible to learn to use our original Indigenous language to parrot the life-denying knowledge systems that grow out of Western epistemologies, we wanted to go through the Yuchi language to connect to the older understandings of the world—a world both created by our language and reflected within our language. We began to understand the remarkable relational aspects that are built into our language. The language is constantly situating the speaker in physical relation to the earth. The intrinsically non-hierarchical nature of Yuchi language trains us to live within a Yuchi understanding that does not have a separate word to refer to animals, making it hard to elevate humans above the beasts of the field. In fact, all non-Yuchi persons—including animals—are grammatically marked coequally. Our language speaks of life-affirming participation within the cycle of life, maintaining proper relations with the created order.

Our language also carries much from our unwritten histories. Many of the atrocities of the past were only spoken about in the original language, not in the language of the colonizers. It was telling to learn from one of our elders, Mose Cahwee-shAnû, that his grandmother who raised him did not know the English language but she did know the name of president Andrew Jackson, who was responsible for the so-called Trail of Tears, the death march of Yuchis and others to what is now the state of Oklahoma. We were reminded that these past historical actions are not ancient history. We are still dealing with the consequences today as we struggle to keep our language alive. Indeed, many of the racist attitudes of the past are becoming reinvigorated. Present-day community children who are learning the Yuchi language at the Yuchi House in Sapulpa are now seeing overt discrimination coming from teachers in the public schools because of using their language.

dEzA'y@nE sA'wAdA:

When I was in tenth grade, *dEzAt'ê* took me and *zOda'anA* out of public school so we could focus on learning Yuchi. I believe that year was a pivotal point in my Yuchi language acquisition because we started a master-apprentice program in which we visited *OhahanE Enû* every morning for two or three hours. Our master-apprentice teams were separated by gender because men and women speak differently in Yuchi.

Notably, the pronouns and family terms are different (see charts of family terms). *dEzAt'ê* and *zOda'anA* visited K'asA Henry Washburn in his home and learned to do typical "man" activities in Yuchi, like repairing cars and doing yard work. Meanwhile, I went to the home of Josephine Keith, a fluent speaker in her seventies at that time. We used daily activities, such as cooking, shopping, and cleaning, to learn Yuchi in an immersion setting. My favorite part of the master-apprentice program was the security and warmth of the home environment, which made it easier for me to learn the language than a classroom. Josephine always had something tasty for us to snack on and soon it felt as though I was going to visit *dElaha* every day. Josephine is a very fluid and fast Yuchi speaker. At first I felt overwhelmed by how much I did not understand. By the end of the year, however, I could decipher what she was saying in Yuchi most of the time and we held conversations in the language. Spending time with Josephine trained me to use women's speech in a natural way (after having been mostly around male elders) and significantly limbered up my speaking overall.

In the afternoons, *zOda'anA* and I completed our English home-schooling curriculum so we could get academic credit for the year. At an early age, the tension between the public school system and our Yuchi language learning was evident to me. By law, we had to complete an English-based curriculum but it took us away from *OhahanE Enû,* like Josephine, who taught us our own Yuchi history, philosophy, science, mathematics, religion, and language arts. I believe when I turned in my course work to the school board that year, I was awarded one "extracurricular" credit for my Yuchi work and about six "core" credits for my English studies. This experience showed me that Indigenous ways of knowing and learning are fundamentally devalued by the American school system. Throughout my English education process, I was told, directly and indirectly, that English is the only way to a successful life and that Yuchi simply does not count. This form of "brainwashing" is a carryover of the process *dElaha nahalA* underwent at Euchee Mission Boarding School. Fortunately, *dEzAt'ê* was intent on counteracting the systemic pressure to believe Yuchi is less important than English. However, I have seen that some other Native American children are not so well equipped to handle these demeaning messages to their identity, i.e., high rates of dropping out from school and suicide. In my case, learning Yuchi in a community context has fed my need for a deeply personal and genuine way of being in the world. To the extent that my family is a part of me, so also the Yuchi language is a part of me. I hope for a day when the English school system will not try to separate other Indigenous young people from the fulfillment of being connected to their identity, language, and community. *aKAê s@nlA TÂ.*

dEzAt'ê O'wAdA:

We faced many challenges in getting the language to *dEzEOtOtOhAnû* when they were growing up, with limited active support for the language within the community at that time.

We were able to garner hands-on support from individual elders—who nonetheless held long-standing, experienced-based doubts about the prospects of anyone learning to speak the language that was their birthright. However, the interest level of the community was at a low ebb and only enough to support a children's class operating once a week.

I remember how radical the idea seemed to the community when one of the young Yuchis, David Skeeter, then a graduate student in linguistics, proposed an immersion day-school for young Yuchi children. Unfortunately, there was not the level of commitment within the community at that time to take on such a large project even though we had, of course, many more speakers of Yuchi than now. We even had some who were fluent and still in their sixties who could provide instruction in the language. Looking back, the speakers during that time seem so young compared to today, when our youngest first-language speaker has already turned eighty.

We became involved early in a small-scale children's class started by elders and community members. For *dEzAs'@nE*, my young son, these community children's classes were critical for his acquiring broad knowledge of the Yuchi language. We played many games and conducted activities in the language during the children's classes that kept him engaged. Away from the class we tried to provide lots of exposure to the language by visiting elders, using the language at home and playing language tapes in the car that we had prepared with the elders. One of the remarkable successes was when *dEzAs'@nE* learned to count in Yuchi when he was still too young to count much in English. He listened to a Yuchi tape during a long, overnight trip while he was sleeping in the car. To our surprise he woke up the next morning and had learned the entire base-sequence of numbers all the way to twenty.

When *dEzAs'@nE* entered his mid-teens he was to become less interested in learning the language and some tension began to develop around using the language in the home.

I had made it a practice to use the Yuchi language in real-life situations. I did not want the language to be used only during class time or limited to some contrived language-learning routine. I wanted to be able to use our original language when communication mattered.

When there was a loss in the larger family I always spoke about it first in the Yuchi language to *dEzEOtOtOhAnû*. Even though my language abilities were limited I had developed a habit of always putting the kids to bed using the language and waking them up in the language. This meant that I told them that I loved them in Yuchi. I wanted our language of heritage—that we were now having to learn as a second language—to carry the full weight of heartfelt communication. At some point this became unacceptable to *dEzAs'@nE*. He demanded that I tell him that I loved him in English. I tried to explain that when I say it in the language it carries more meaning, has an even greater depth. We had one of those long family showdowns that are all-too-familiar to parents and teenagers alike. What was unusual about this verbal tug-of-war was that we were arguing about the very manner of expressing our love for one another. While I did not want to disappoint *dEzAs'@nE* I did want him to learn to value our language. My difficulty was that I had painted myself into a Yuchi corner, since I was already committed to a standing practice of displacing English with Yuchi wherever I could. Though the event has now entered family lore and is remembered at this distance with affection it was quite agonizing at the time.

My two children seemed to be on two different tracks with different styles of learning. *dEzA'y@nE* was independent in her learning style, carrying forward her effort regardless of whether her cousins or others in her cohort continued their progress in the language. *dEzAs'@nE,* on the other hand, was more extroverted and more of a "social learner." For him the larger community support was very important. *dEzAs'@nE* progressed well as long as there was a group of learners with whom he could participate. However, because of support for the language in our home he soon outpaced the other children attending classes. Eventually, this imbalance seemed to undermine his motivation to advance his knowledge of the language. During his later-teen years he seemed to make only small gains, due to his unenthusiastic effort. However, his effort toward language learning was reawakened when we finally were able to get both enough community engagement and the requisite funding capacity to develop a viable immersion program on a daily basis within the Yuchi community. Surprisingly, he was then able quickly to catch back up with those who had been doing daily immersion in the language for over two years. This highlights for me the value of community support, when it can be developed, for family language. However, there are trade-offs in developing community programs, as my own personal language growth has been constrained due to the demands of running a community language program. In the program we continue to search for a balance between servicing the larger community and effectively developing the language within family units who are most involved at the Yuchi Language House. This is a real challenge, sharpened by extremely limited financial and other resources that we face again and again. It is the children of the second-language learners who must be empowered to carry the language into the future—a goal that cannot be lost in the effort to provide general knowledge of the language to the broader community.

The other lesson I draw from reflecting on these years of experience in family language learning is the value of consistency over time in our effort to learn a language without textbooks. It is now extremely rewarding to hear *dEzAs'@nE* again pursuing fluency in the language, to hear him say—as the elders themselves have often said—that he prefers to use the language when he prays because it makes it stronger and more real to him. That is using the language when communication matters.

dEzA'y@nE sA'wAdA:

Even before our family intentionally began learning the Yuchi language, we were exposed to it at *s'@ˆs@ˆhA,* the Yuchi Ceremonial Grounds. As soon as I could walk, I was dancing around *yaTE-chE,* the ceremonial fire, as part of the Yuchi community, with the other children, youth, adults, and elders, who would later teach me the language. The Yuchi language is at the heart of our ancient traditions and is still used to conduct the ceremonies. However, English is the primary language of communication among the Yuchi members and the majority of them do not understand the Yuchi that is used in the ceremonies. Due to this loss of language, one of my fluent Yuchi elders tells me that the medicine is weak among Yuchis today compared to when he was growing up and everyone spoke the language.

When I was little there were at least a few dozen fluent Yuchi speakers at *s'@ˆs@ˆhA.* Now there are only a couple of fluent speakers at the grounds. In spite of this decline, my generation is starting to revive the use of Yuchi at the ceremonial grounds after a gap of about three generations of monolingual English speakers. We talk to each other in Yuchi at *s'@ˆs@ˆhA* and now Yuchi language phrases are used widely during ceremonies even by nonspeakers. Through the Euchee (Yuchi) Language Project, the young people and children are learning the language from *OhahanE Enû,* fluent elders, and are breathing new life into our severely endangered language. I have heard many of the elders say, in a state of wonderment, that they never thought they would hear a child speak Yuchi again but today they are greeted by toddlers in their language and they hear them offer prayers in the Yuchi language. Our Yuchi community is growing in strength and hope through the progress of the young people in learning the language.

I think of *gO'wAdAnA-A,* the language, as analogous to *yaTE-chE,* the fire, which is at the center of our ceremonies. When a fire is about to go out, we say, *yaTE-chE s'EhA galA* (the fire has almost turned cold). The elders tell us that at one time there were very few members at *s'@ˆs@ˆhA* and the Yuchi ceremonies almost died out, but a few families kept it going. Today two thousand people turn out for *EaPAnE* (Green Corn Ceremonies). In the same way that a fire can be relit even if there are only a few coals left, we are reviving our language even with only a few speakers left. I believe that if my generation continues to revive the use of Yuchi language—even if only by a few families now—we will one day again have strong medicine at *s'@ˆs@ˆhA,* like our ancestors.

TABLE A: Yuchi Pronunciation and Spelling Key

Vowels (a, e, i, o, u):
All capitalized vowels sound like the name of the letter:
A as in *Ate,*
E as in *Eat,*
I as in *Ice,*
O as in *Oat,*
Except that U sounds like the "u" in *rude* (that is, sounds like the name of "u" without the beginning "y" sound).

Lowercase vowels (or "little letters") are pronounced like short vowels:
a sounds like "a" in *all*
@ sounds like the "a" in *at*
e as in *eggs*
i as in *in*
o as in *boy*
u as in *sun*
v (less common) sounds like the "u" in *put*
The rooftop accent [ˆ] is used to show nasalized vowels.
<u>Underlining</u> is used to show stress or lengthening: wa <u>ha</u> IA

An apostrophe ['] is used to show a slight pause in the sound (when air is cut off deep in the throat); also called a glottal stop.

Consonants:
The consonants can generally be pronounced as they are in English with the following important exceptions:

thl   The front of the tongue is placed behind the base of the top front teeth (as if to make an "l" in English) and then the air is pushed over the sides of the tongue rather than straight forward. The result is a rushing sound.

"In-between" sounds are here represented by capital letters (after *Yuchi Tales* by Günther Wagner, 1931):

P   in-between "b" and "p," as in *P'a TA* (horse)
T   in-between "d" and "t," as in *TE* (yellow or brown)
K   in-between "g" and "k," as in *na K@* (three)
CH   in-between "j" in jump and "ch" in church: *CHU* (boat) (not pronounced like the word "jew" nor the word "chew"

TABLE B: Women's Speech and Men's Speech in Yuchi

dEzA'y@nE sA'wAdA:

Here are two charts that show the complexity of family terms in the Yuchi language and the grammatical differences in men's and women's speech. I created these charts through direct elicitation from Maggie Marsey shÂ sAnû and K'asA Henry Washburn. You will notice that there are many pronoun sets and therefore multiple ways of saying "my," "her," "your," etc. For example, the possessive pronoun "my" may be: *dE-, zO-, dEzO-, dEzA-, zEO-*, depending on which family term is being used. The particular form used for "my" in each instance is defined in the language and is not optional. So, *dE-chO'O* means "my grandfather" but *zO-chO'O* does not mean anything. A comparison of the "His" columns will also reveal drastic differences in the use of family terms by men and women. For "his brother," a woman would say *s'EOda'anA s'Anû* and a man would say *hÔdanE hÊnû.* (*s'Anû* and *hÊnû* can be referred to as noun class endings but for simplicity are not shown in the charts, except in the "Spouse" sections). Also, the –nA and –nE endings reflect regional variations rather than differences between men's and women's speech.

Chart A: Family Terms in Women's Speech by Maggie C. Marsey (2007)[*]

	My	Your	Her	His	Non-Yuchis
Grandfather	dEchO'O	nechO'O	sAchO'O	s'AchO'O	wAchO'O
Grandmother	dElaha	nelaha	sAlaha	s'Alaha	wAlaha
Father	(dE)zAt'ê	nezAt'ê	sAt'ê	s'At'ê	wAt'ê
Mother	dEzah@ˆ	nezah@ˆ	sAzah@ˆ	s'Azah@ˆ	wAzah@ˆ
Sister	dEzO'winA	sO'winA	sEO'winA	s'EO'winA	yÔ'winA
Brother	zOda'anA	sOda'anA	sEOda'anA	s'EOda'anA	yÔda'anA
Son	zOshashant'A	sOshashant'A	sEOshashant'A	s'EOshashant'A	yÔshashant'A
Daughter	dEzOs'@nt'A	sOs'@nt'A	sEOs'@nt'A	s'EOs'@nt'A	yÔs'@nt'A
Grandchild	dEzOjUnA	(zA)sOjUnA	sEOjUnA	s'EOjUnA	yÔjUnA
Aunt	dEz@ˆs'î	(zA)nez@ˆs'î	sAz@ˆs'î	s'Az@ˆs'î	wAz@ˆs'î
Uncle	dE(zA)'yû	(zA) nezA'yû	sA'yû	s'A'yû	wA'yû

---

[*]   In Yuchi, living persons are grammatically defined as either Yuchi or non-Yuchi. The category of non-Yuchi persons includes what English defines as animals, celestial beings, and non-Yuchi humans. Grammatically, non-Yuchi persons are not defined by gender and women and men refer to them the same way, using wA- or yÔ-. Yuchi persons are defined by gender, and men and women refer to them differently, as shown in the Spouse sections of the charts.

Cousin/ Relative	(dE)zOk'ala	(zA)sOk'ala	sEOk'ala	s'EOk'ala	yÔk'ala
Friend	dEk'aTE	nek'aTE	sAk'aTE	s'Ak'aTE	wAk'aTE
Sweetheart	dEzOdabEs@ˆ	nenzOdabEs@ˆ	sEOdabEs@ˆ	s'EOdabEs@ˆ	yÔdabEs@ˆ
Kid	zOgOtO	(zA)nenzEOgOtO	sEOgOtO	s'EOgOtO	yÔgOtO
Child	zOts'unA	sOts'unA	sEOts'unA	s'EOts'unA	yÔts'unA

Spouse	Non-Yuchi spouse*	Yuchi wife	Yuchi husband
My	wAdEk'aTOnû	———	OdEk'aTû Onû
Your	nek'aTOnû	nek'aTû sAnû	nek'aTû s'Anû
Her	sAk'aTOnû	———	sAk'aTû s'Anû
Non-Yuchis*	wAk'aTOnû	wAk'aTû sAnû	wAk'aTû s'Anû

Chart B: Family Terms in Men's Speech by K'asA Henry Washburn (2007, 2010)

	My	Your	Her	His	Non-Yuchis*
Grandfather	dEchO'O	nechO'O	sAchO'O	hÊchO'O	wAchO'O
Grandmother	dElaha	nelaha	sAlaha	hÊlaha	wAlaha
Father	dEzAt'ê	nezAt'ê	sAt'ê	hÊt'ê	wAt'ê
Mother	dEzah@ˆ	nezah@ˆ	sAzah@ˆ	hÊzah@ˆ	wAzah@ˆ
Sister	zEOw@'nE	zAsOw@'nE	sEOw@'nE	hÔw@'nE	yÔw@'nE
Brother	zEOdanE				
	dEzOdanE	zAsOdanE	sEOdanE	hÔdanE	yÔdanE
Son	dEzAs'@nE	nenzAs'@nE	sAs'@nE	hÊs'@nE	wAs'@nE
Daughter	dEzA'y@nE	nenzA'y@nE	sA'y@nE	hÊ'y@nE	wA'y@nE
Grandchild	zEOjUnE				
	dEzOjUnE	zAsOjUnE	sEOjUnE	hÔjUnE	yÔjUnE
Aunt	dEz@ˆs'Ê	(zA)nez@ˆs'Ê	sAz@ˆs'Ê	hÊz@ˆs'Ê	wAz@ˆs'Ê
Uncle	dEt(zA)'yü	(zA) nezA'yû	sA'yû	hÊ'yû	wA'yû
Cousin/Relative	(dE)zOk'ala	(zA)sOk'ala	sEOk'ala	hÔk'ala	yÔk'ala
Friend	dEk'aTE	nek'aTE	sAk'aTE	hÔk'aTE	wAk'aTE

Sweetheart	dEzOdabEs@ˆ	nenzOdabEs@ˆ	sEOdabEs@ˆ	hÔdabEs@ˆ	yÔdabEs@ˆ
Kid	dEzEOgOtO	(zA)nenzEOgOtO	sEOgOtO	hÔgOtO	yÔgOtO

Spouse	Non-Yuchi spouse*	Yuchi wife	Yuchi husband
My	dEk'aTOnû	dEk'aTû sAnû	———
Your	nek'aTOnû	nek'aTû sAnû	nek'aTû hÊnû
Her	sAk'aTOnû	———	sAk'aTû hÊnû
Non-Yuchis*	wAk'aTOnû	wAk'aTû sAnû	wAk'aTû hÊnû

Part III

FAMILIES AND COMMUNITIES WORKING TOGETHER

5: Mohawk

OUR KANIEN'KÉHA LANGUAGE

Margaret and Theodore Peters

Theodore

"What kind of an Indian are you?" I was asked this question by a nonnative fellow student at St. Lawrence High School in Cornwall, Ontario. I was in grade 9 and it was my second outing into the world outside of the familiar surroundings of Ahkwesahsne.

It was the 1969-70 school year and I had no idea who or what I was.

I was taken by surprise by this question. We were sitting on the curb having lunch and I had to think of an answer rather quickly. I thought back to the movie I had been watching the previous night and I remembered the name that the Indians in the movie had been called. "I think I'm an Apache," I replied. My fellow student replied, "Oh, that's cool."

Both of us were ignorant of the people living across the river from where we were sitting.

At least he had an excuse—he was nonnative, and probably watched the same movie I had seen about the Apache people. Many of my people grew up the same way I had, speaking our language without having the culture that goes along with it to make us whole. When you don't have your own identity, you will try to find a surrogate identity as a cloak in which to hide your shame, whether you realize it or not.

In my case I was lucky to have my Kanien'kéha language as my first language. When I realized what I was missing I was again lucky, and I was able to attend Longhouse events starting with socials and then actual ceremonies during the yearly cycle of ceremonies. I saw and heard the ceremony being conducted by my own people in our own language, in our own Longhouse. It was a very intimidating experience, letting go of one form of belief and starting to learn about my own. In a sense it was very confusing, letting go of something that I was raised with and learning about something that was there all along.

The foreign religion you know because that's all you ever knew or were told about, and your own belief/way of life was made to feel foreign and not your own. I consider the choice to start attending Longhouse a life-changing experience for me and my family.

Margaret

"Don't talk to me that funny talk! Talk right!" Teioswáthe yelled, glaring at me with her hands on her hips. She was only five years old and quite resistant to us speaking only Kanien'kéha (Mohawk language) to her, as the first language we had spoken to her in was English. Her father and I had only begun speaking more Kanien'kéha at home when our last child, Nihahsennà:a, was born. His first language was Kanien'kéha. By the time he was born we had decided to speak only Kanien'kéha to him, to see if we could produce at least one fluent speaker. He was born in July of 1989, Teioswáthe in May of 1987, and Kawennahén:te in June of 1986 and yeah, we got teased about that a lot.

It took a little time before the girls picked up the language, as we were more focused on getting our son to start speaking. We actually hadn't even realized that the girls would pick up the language the way that they did. We just spoke it more in our home, but Teioswáthe didn't always want to hear it. We would read books in the language to our son, and Kawennahén:te also enjoyed this, but her sister didn't always want to listen. She wanted us to read "real" stories, meaning books written in English.

It took some time for all of us to adjust to using the language in our home and even to begin using our children's Mohawk names. We also encouraged them to begin using the terms Rákeni (Margaret's father) and Ísta (Margaret's mother) towards us. It was a conscious effort on our part, and although it was natural for us to speak to our son in the language as we had decided to so even before his birth, it took a little adjusting to speak to our girls as we had started out speaking only English to them except for the baby talk in the beginning. However,

English was their first language. When the kids started to speak more Mohawk and we, their parents, would slip into English they would tell us, *"Kanien'kéha satá:ti"* (speak Mohawk).

I was in my first month of pregnancy with Teioswáthe when I received a call from the director of the Ahkwesáhsne Freedom School to go and teach. Apparently, a teacher they had hired didn't show up and they needed a teacher pronto. I said very clearly and indignantly, "No! I don't read or write Mohawk and I'm not a teacher."

"But you speak Mohawk," the director pleaded with me.

"Yes, but I didn't go to school to be a teacher. I can't teach!"

Two hours on the phone and a whole lot of pleading, and I finally and very reluctantly agreed to go and teach under the condition that I would go only until they found a replacement. Ha! or LOL, as they say these days. I ended up teaching at the AFS for over fifteen years off and on, going back to school to take language courses in between to learn to read and write Kanien'kéha and to learn language-teaching methods. I learned from good and bad teachers alike, using the good teachers as my role models and the not-so-good teachers to learn what not to do. And so began our journey into what we do today as parents, grandparents, and teachers of the Mohawk language.

When our son, Nihahsennà:a ("He has a small name") was born, his father, Tekahiónhake, and I made a conscious decision that when this child came into this world the first and only language we would speak to him in was Kanien'kéha. Our girls were two and three years old when Nihahsennà:a made his entrance into our world. Having worked at the Ahkwesáhsne Freedom School with Shakokweniónkwas (Thomas) Porter as director was a life-changing experience for my husband and me. Working at the AFS the teachers were expected to attend Longhouse ceremonies, and we were not familiar with our cultural background, and although both my husband and I grew up speaking the language fluently, we knew nothing about the clan system or the protocol of attending *Kanonhsésne tsi ioterihwaténkion* (Longhouse ceremony). We didn't know that you were expected to sit in a certain section according to your clan and gender or even that you entered the door from the east if you were male and from the west if you were female. Using our language was not yet an issue in our family, or most families for

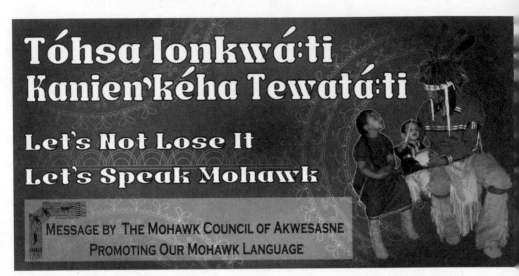

Tóhsa Ionkwá:ti Kanien'kéha Tewatá:ti

Let's Not Lose It
Let's Speak Mohawk

MESSAGE BY THE MOHAWK COUNCIL OF AKWESASNE
PROMOTING OUR MOHAWK LANGUAGE

Pictured on this Mohawk Council of Akwasasne billboard are Nihahsennà:a Peters with his children Iakokarí:io and Raniehtanawénhtha Clute. Takokari:io is a student at AFS and a fluent speaker, and the baby at one year old was an emerging speaker. Photograph courtesy of Margaret Peters

that matter, in our community of Ahkwesáhsne. Most of our people were under the impression that "White is right" and that our language wouldn't get us anywhere in the real world. Most parents, even if they were both fluent, were speaking English to their children because they believed that speaking our own language would only hurt their children academically. Some had been through some sort of residential school experience while others, like me, the offspring, didn't consider the language an issue at all. Language-wise, we were the "use it or lose it" generation, and to the detriment of our coming generations many chose to lose it while not being aware of the severe impact it would have on *tahatikonhsontónkie* (the coming faces), the future generations.

Having to attend Longhouse as part of my teaching experience, my perspective had started to change and language was starting to become an issue to me. I gave birth to Teioswáthe the first year I taught at AFS but even at this time we were still not speaking Kanien'kéha to the children. Something about speaking only Kanien'kéha to our children didn't quite feel right. When the girls became of school age we enrolled them in the English-based federally funded school system, as my husband believed that we wouldn't have to pay a thousand-dollar tuition fee and do fund-raising and mop floors like we would have to at AFS if we sent them there. I guess it was a guy thing. I was having mixed feelings as I continued teaching the language through the years. We still spoke only Kanien'kéha to Nihahsennà:a, and did not realize that our girls were acquiring and absorbing the language. Going to university later on in life, I learned that at that time our girls were at a stage in their cognitive development when they were naturally acquiring the language, meaning that at their age they could absorb not only one but many languages—but I hadn't known this was happening.

As Nihahsennà:a grew older and began to speak, he was speaking in Kanien'kéha. It was amazing to hear him begin to speak Kanien'kéha, and although I can't seem to remember his first words, I fully recall that any words he spoke were all in the language. The girls were picking up the language through osmosis, but as I stated, we still enrolled them in the federal school. We could send them on the bus and we would not have to do the kind of work that would be required at AFS, the independent school, which was even a little run down—we had to go tippy-toeing across the hallway there whenever we had yet another flood. Parents would take time from work and come to the school and mop up the floors. We didn't cancel school; we just worked around the mayhem. The students were used to it.

Theodore

My grandparents spoke very little English. My aunts and uncles all spoke English and were able to be part of the dominant society in various forms of employment. I believe that a person's experiences on the outside of our territories will determine their view on the importance of our language. If the language is seen as a deficit, then the individual will be of the opinion that we should educate our children in the languages of the dominant society. For a while I was a part of this group. Because of my experiences at work outside of Ahkwesahsne I started to believe that our children would be better off learning French in order to get along in the dominant societies next to our territory. When an acquaintance came to our residence with a survey on whether our schools should offer language immersion, I was of the opinion that they should offer French immersion instead. I explained the reason for my opinion: when I worked with men that were able to speak English, while we worked together they would speak in English but at breaktime they would switch to French. I did not speak or understand the language, so I felt that they were just being rude. So my point of view was that we should teach our children French to help them get along in Canadian society if that is where they ended up working. At this point in time I had my language, but I didn't have my culture. I was missing a large part of my identity but I didn't know.

The main thing was, I had my language and I could learn everything else in order to complete or restore my identity. For this I am grateful to my family. In the end I became an advocate for the Kanien'kéha language and I am doing my share to ensure its survival by making sure the language is used in our family as much as possible and will be passed on to the next generation of our family. Five speakers so far and counting.

Margaret

During my first few years of work in bilingual education, I was having very mixed feelings because I had the language but spoke English to my girls. One day we were getting ready to go on a family outing. Kawennahén:te was five years old and enrolled in the 50/50 program the easier school had now implemented. I was helping her get ready, and as she was putting on her jacket she said, "*Wa'kakiá:tawi'te*" (I put my coat on). One simple line, nothing out of the ordinary, but for me it was like a slap in the face because I realized she hadn't learned it from me, her mother, who spoke the language. It was her Mohawk teacher at school, Kaia'taiésha (Mildred) White, who had taught it to her. I began to cry softly and continued to help her get dressed. I felt very ashamed. The parents at the Ahkwesáhsne Freedom School were paying me to teach their children because they so desperately wanted their children to learn their inherent language, and here I had it and wasn't teaching it to my own, except for our little experiment Nihahsennà:a. As I went out to the car I told my husband, Tekahiónhake, that we were going to send our girls to the freedom school and I would do it alone if I had to. I would pay the tuition and mop the floors and do the fund-raising with or without him. Fortunately, he came on board because he was also at a point where he was captivated with our son speaking Kanien'kéha. We were going to do this together, and so for the new school year in the fall of 1993 we enrolled our girls in the AFS.

Theodore

Once we decided to speak nothing but Kanien'kéha in our home to our son, everything kind of naturally fell into place. At that time we were hoping to get one of our children fluent in our language, but what we didn't realize at that time was that our daughters were still young enough to acquire their language. There was a minor protest from Teioswáthe when we switched from her first language, English, to Kanien'kéha. Her sister, Kawennahén:te, didn't mind, she just went with the flow. For Nihahsennà:a, our son, it was a natural way of acquiring his language. Later on they had no problems learning to speak, read, and write in Kanien'kéha and English. They just transferred the things that they learned in immersion to learning the English language.

Margaret

There was no magic formula that we had for passing the language on to our children. We just spoke it to them, and not at them or around them, but directly to them. We spoke it to them in the house, in the car, at the restaurant, at the lacrosse games, at the movie theatre, at the laundromat, in the shopping malls, at the park, and the occasional times we attended church services, such as funerals and weddings, and just everywhere we went we spoke it to them. We didn't break it down or use baby talk. We just spoke it to them naturally and that was how they responded. When we tried to use Kanien'kéha as a code language on occasion, like so many parents have done, so our girls wouldn't understand what we were saying, to our dismay and delight they understood everything. We joked that we would have to learn French but Teioswáthe said she would learn French also. By now she had accepted speaking her own language.

I remembered Tommy Porter, the former AFS director and great orator, saying that we gotta teach the real language, like about going to the bathroom, and even the word for toilet paper that was so descriptive. "The kids should be taught how to say *Ionni'tokewáhtha*" (an item with which to wipe shit off). "It's real language." Tommy just seemed to have a way with words. He also referred to a high school that many of our kids from Ahkwesáhsne attended which was supposed to benefit language- and culture-wise from the various title programs that were provided to all native students. "Millions of dollars is put into teaching the Mohawk language from the Title VII program and [name of school withheld] hasn't produced one stinkin' fluent Mohawk speaker!" Sad but true. But the reality is also that the parents who are fluent are not passing their languages on to their children in the home. A parent of the same school was complaining to me that his daughter was not learning anything in her Mohawk class and I dared to question him about why he and his wife hadn't taught her the language, since they were both fluent speakers themselves. He stammered and sputtered a bit and didn't really have a valid response. I guess the fluent speakers didn't even realize the role they played in the continuance of language.

Only in the present day did the program change when my very good friend Katsitsión:ni Fox started working at the school under the Title VII program. She first began as the cultural specialist and she was also a parent of children who attended the Ahkwesáhsne Freedom School. She wasn't a fluent speaker but her children reached a functional level of fluency, so much so that her son Iohè:rase was starting to be able to assist with basic ceremonial speeches at various cultural events. She also dabbled in filmmaking. She was self-taught and became skilled to the point of eventually expanding her position to include teaching a Native Film class. Parents actually wanted to send their children to the school because of the great language and cultural expansion the school underwent as a result of Tsión:ni's aspirations—my own children included. Tsión:ni knew how to use the students' current language that they had when they went into her classes and expand their language usage by working on a variety of film projects. The more fluent students were able to use and increase their language skills and those who were at a lower level were motivated to want to learn and use the language. Tsión:ni and I did a lot of networking between our schools. I worked for the Ahkwesáhsne Mohawk Board of Education as a Kanien'kéha specialist and she worked for the Salmon River Central School. Eventually our networking led to us hosting a film program at the Galaxy Theatre in Cornwall, Ontario, to showcase the array of language resources we had produced. I wasn't as skilled as Katsitsión:ni but I always carried around a video camera in school, ready to film the children speaking the language. One of the first projects we worked on together was a no-budget film using dollar-store hand puppets and a script from the book *Brown Bear Brown Bear, What Do You See?*. Ours was called *"Kahón:tsi Ohkwá:ri, Kahón:tsi Ohkwá:ri, Ónhka Shé:kens?"* (Black Bear, Black Bear,

Who Do You See?). The students did the bulk of the production in front of and behind the cameras. Katsitsión:ni was a great director from the start and only improved throughout the years. Two years ago we celebrated our fifth annual Native Student Film Festival at the Galaxy Theatre. It was a great motivator for our students to speak Mohawk and to work on projects that would later be seen on the big screen, Hollywood-style.

Our own families didn't speak Mohawk to our kids, and it was Kawennahén:te who asked her paternal grandmother to speak to her in the language. *"Tóta, enwá:ton ken Kanien'kéha enhsekthahrháhse?"* (Grandmother, can you speak to me in the Mohawk language?) In fact most of our family members from both sides seemed to find it difficult to speak to our children in the language.

Theodore

If you have relatives that still speak Kanien'kéha, ask them to speak to your children in the language. If they forget, remind them, train your children to remind speakers to speak to them in the language. "Use it or lose it" is the simplest way to put it. I have found that our elders have been conditioned to speak to children in English. It has become automatic for them. They are like the people that work at fast food places and coffee shops: as soon as you order a soft drink they automatically fill your cup three-quarters full with ice and give you regular cola, even after you order diet cola, no ice. At the coffee shops they automatically give you regular coffee with cream and sugar, even though you have just asked for decaf coffee with milk and sweetener. Our elders have to be constantly reminded to speak to the children in our language, because most of them are in autopilot mode when it comes to speaking our language. It will work but you must do your part and remind them. When you hear the children speaking in your language and you are able to have a conversation with them, you will become very proud and happy.

Margaret

I grew up in a family that only spoke Mohawk to each other. My mother and father spoke Mohawk and my maternal and paternal grandparents spoke Mohawk. My paternal grandparents did not even know how to speak English.

My paternal grandmother kind of reminded me of the granny character on the old TV show *The Beverly Hillbillies*. She was old but very spry. I remember her always wearing a plaid housedress, her knee-high stockings tied on each side of her knees, with her long gray hair always up in a bun. My aunt told a story about the time my grandmother was in the hospital and the doctor had wanted to keep her from getting out of bed, so they put the side railings up. They informed my aunt that her mom should stay in her bed and use a bedpan if she needed to go to the bathroom. My aunt said she thought her mom was asleep, so she left to go and get a cup of coffee, and when she returned she found her mother climbing over the railing. My aunt ran to try and keep her in bed and told her the doctor had said she had to use the bedpan, and my grandmother replied angrily, *"Kiakotkáhtho kenh ne káksakon akaniskiá:ke?"* (Can you see me peeing in a dish?). These are the kinds of stories I pass on to my kids about their past generations. There may be no morals or grandiose cultural significance to the anecdotes but language still played a significant role and my kids enjoy hearing them.

Tekahiónhake and I were a blended family, as we both had children from previous relationships when we got together. We were in a different mindset when we had our first children and were not at all aware of the fact that our Rotinonhsón:ni Confederacy was so very close to losing our Six Nation languages of Mohawk, Oneida, Onondaga, Cayuga, Seneca, and Tuscarora. We didn't know that as a confederacy we had such a connection to the language and that if it ceased to exist, our spiritual and political protocols would cease to exist. We could no longer conduct ceremonies without the language and our political status would be affected, as the significance of the matters would be lost in translation.

Theodore

When we first started on our language quest we made the choice of putting our children in the Freedom School so that they would be taught in the Kanien'kéha language. We had to pay tuition and take our turn to clean the school and also to help at the fund-raisers. It was something that came with the territory. For a while our children were teased about attending the Free To Be Dumb School by some of their relatives. I remember the day we went to visit my mother, and their uncle said, "The Indians are here." Without missing a beat our daughter Kawennahén:te answered, "Indians are from India, I am Onkwehón:we."

She was quite young but she was already able to stand up for herself. With the language come identity and pride. Today she and her man have a baby girl who speaks the Kanien'kéha language and English, all self-taught, so to speak. She is three years old.

Some financial hard times and some elbow grease and we made it through.

Margaret

As our children grew we continued speaking the language to them. Not a hundred percent but enough to get them to a level of functional fluency, which meant they could converse in the language, understand the ceremonial language used at Longhouse ceremonies, and pass the language on to their own babies when our daughters became mothers. Teioswáthe was the first to have her baby. She became a young mother at the age of seventeen, and although at first I had felt that she wasn't ready to be a mother she proved me wrong by being a loving and nurturing parent to my first little grandchild. He entered our world on March 20, 2004, exactly eight minutes after midnight. Eight minutes after his grandfather's birthday on March 19.

It was extremely emotional for all of us who had the privilege of being present when Rarennenhá:wi made his grand entrance. We tied the piece of leather to his little wrist that would bind him to the physical world and his grandfather spoke the words of the welcoming speech to him to introduce him to his family and to the elements of the universe that would help guide him on his journey throughout this world. The first language he heard as he entered his realm was Mohawk. That was our way as Rotinonhsón:ni (people of the Longhouse). He was born ready to be given a Mohawk name and he was introduced to the natural elements of the environment that he may have to rely on someday for medicinal purposes. Rarennenhá:wi means "He carries a song."

We watched him grow from a newborn into a toddler and we learned that this age was crucial for his language acquisition. When I would play with Rarennenhá:wi during his first few months I would always say to him, *"Tóta, tóta,"* which refers to a grandparent. At eight months I actually heard him say the word *"Tóta."* His first word was in Mohawk and was an endearing term that I was convinced was directed to me, his grandmother. I was even able to record him, using a little recording device that was intended for the inside of a teddy bear. I carried around the recording and made people listen to it whether they wanted to or not, and although Rarennenhá:wi had a bevy of grandparents, step-grandparent, and great-grandparents, I knew his first word was for me and I told people that.

As he grew we continued speaking to him in Mohawk and he would amaze us with the vocabulary and phrases he began using. His mother, who had been most resistant to speaking Mohawk, was now using only the language with her son. His aunt Kawennahén:te and his uncle Nihahsennà:a spoke only Mohawk to him. His father, Blake, was not a fluent speaker and was a little resistant in the beginning about his son learning only Mohawk, and made a comment that if his boy spoke only in the language, "He might talk shit about me and I won't know what he's saying!" However, as he noticed his boy was beginning to speak Mohawk he also began learning a little himself. He said that he didn't always know what his son was saying to him but he would watch what he would do and figure it out through his actions.

As Rarennenhá:wi grew older we continued speaking Mohawk to him all the time. I also sang to him often, using the little water drum I had made especially for him. As soon as he would arrive at our house he would walk in, point to his drum on the shelf and say, *"Tsió:wi,"* which was meant to be *Kana'tsió:wi."* *Kana'tsió:wi* is a water drum that we use as our main musical device as Rotinonhsón:ni. I would sit with him on the couch and sing a variety of social songs with him as we would take turns using the *kana'tsió:wi* and a rattle made of a cowhorn attached to a wooden handle with little corn kernels inside that rattled when it was shaken. As he grew, his language usage expanded into phrases and sentences. He had me help him look for his favorite DVD and he told me, *"Ohwentsió:kon tká:ien"* (It's in the basement), where his old bedroom used to be. His terminology was that of an advanced speaker. We went down to the basement to look and he said to me, *"Toka' nòn:wa kanaktó:kon tká:ien"* (Perhaps it's there under the bed). He was only two years old and he never failed to amaze all of us with his language abilities. This was just from us consistently speaking to him in the language. All of our family members who were fluent spoke to him only in the language and friends and acquaintances who were not fluent attempted to use what little they knew. Rarennenhá:wi actually motivated people into speaking without us having to tell anyone to speak to him in Mohawk; everyone did so automatically. He is so precious. To see him one would not even realize he is native. He is fair-skinned and a little blondie, but he is bilingual, with his own language being his first. He was especially a big hit when we took him to the lacrosse games. There was a section where the older men would always stand, and their banter was delightful to listen to. They were the remaining fluent speakers in our community and little did they know what a valuable resource they were. They would speak to our grandson in the language and they were visibly amazed when this little blond kid would respond fully in the language. That was rare among our entire confederacy that a child so young could speak the language.

Then there was Iakokarí:io ("She has a nice story"), the beautiful little girl born on October 24, 2006, to our daughter Kawennahén:te. I watched as she entered into our world, and seeing your grandchild being born is the most beautiful experience in the world. We had requested that the medical staff not speak until the words of the welcoming speech were conveyed to Iakokarí:io so the first words she would ever hear would be in the Mohawk language. She didn't cry once as her grandfather introduced her to her family and to the elements of the environment. She just stared at him, blinking, and we were all convinced that she could understand what was being said to her. Once again, all we would speak to her was Mohawk. Everywhere, just everywhere we were, we would speak only the language to her. Her dad was not a fluent speaker but because Kawennahén:te was speaking so much Mohawk he began to pick up the language slowly but surely. Tehanónsake ("He is two houses") was an identical twin. While his brother questioned why Iakokarí:io didn't speak as much as their niece who was the same age, his brother told him that she could speak two languages and that her first was Mohawk. She didn't speak English as well as her cousin but she was becoming bilingual, with Mohawk being her first and more fluent language. She is a little beauty and, unlike her cousin Rarennenhá:wi, she has dark skin and long dark hair and she looks very native. But when they conversed with one another it was always in the Mohawk language, as that was the language they were accustomed to using from the onset of their ability to speak. Both children could switch languages depending on whom they were speaking to, and they were both aware of who could and couldn't speak Mohawk. If they encountered a nonspeaker they automatically knew to speak English. When they spoke to certain people who were fluent they would speak Mohawk. This was rare, for children their age in the present day to be speaking their inherent language. Inherently, we are Onondaga nation because of their clan lineage, but our ancestors migrated from the New York area of Watertown near Syracuse. As Ahkwesáhsne was not historically an original territory of the Mohawk nation, it was eventually settled and became the land base for the Mohawks who had migrated from the Mohawk Valley. The three main clans of the Mohawk are Wolf, Bear, and Turtle, and we are Snipe clans of the Onondaga nation. Snipe clan people were more common and in fact were the clan who maintained a high amount of fluent Mohawk speakers.

It was not only rare across the confederacy for children to speak their language but also exceptional for them to be aware of their identities or to possess any kind of indigenous knowledge. It made us very proud to be able to speak to our grandbabies in our own language, Hotinonhsón:ni language, and to have the privilege of providing them with their cultural identities to the best of our knowledge.

Iakokarí:io is an exceptional child. She is very intelligent and has the speaking skills of an advanced learner of the Mohawk language. *"Konnorónhkwa Tota"* (I love you, grandparent), she always tells her grandfather and me. *"Ha' káts tho sákien"* (Come on, go and sit there), she would direct when we would go to visit their home. Or *"Íkehre akatá:wen Tota"* (I want to take a bath) whenever she would come to visit our home. It was a ritual. Once when she slept over, her mom tried to give her a bath when she went home and Iakokarí:io told her, *"Iah entà:on'k. Ó:nen tota iakonóhare ne ohò:kwa Satéswat."* (I don't have to. Grandma already washed my butt. Smell it.) That was her logic in her language.

In the present day, my time with my grandchildren has become more limited since I accepted the principalship in the Grand River territory of the Six Nations. My position for the past several years was with the Ahkwesáhsne Mohawk Board of Education as Kanien'kéha specialist, but I was granted a one-year leave to work for the Kawenní:io Private School, where I was encouraged by my friend and colleague Amos Key Jr. to apply upon the retirement of the principal, Isabel Jacobs. Amos was known for advocating that a school principal could influence the atmosphere of an immersion school environment. I was hesitant to apply but he told me that the school needed some new direction, as

Isabel had struggled for the past few years dealing with a school system that had acquired a not-so-positive image among its own community members. I had been involved with the school for many years because my friend Candace Squire worked there as a teacher and was one of the founding parents of the school when it was in its grassroots stages of becoming established as a private school. The Ahkwesáhsne Freedom School has trials and tribulations, but it has the advantage of maintaining its autonomy from government rules, regulations, and bureaucracy. The Kawenní:io/Gaweni:yo school operates under the umbrella of Indian and Northern Affairs Canada where they receive their funding, which creates its own problems. Nevertheless the school serves as a true model for a culturally based language program. I guess as an outsider I could see the positive aspects of the school when many community members could only see its flaws. Establishing immersion programs is the most crucial measure a community can execute if they are truly serious about saving even a portion of their language through their children. The grassroots people of the Six Nations territory decided to save their languages by implementing a Cayuga and Mohawk immersion school and have faced, and are continuing to face, harsh criticism, which unfortunately comes most often from their own community members. It is the same story among many First Nations. We become our own worst enemies. Internal strife within the community and inside the schools occurs and sometimes supersedes the objective, which is to build our children's cultural identities through the acquisition of their inherent language.

Kawenní:io/Gaweni:yo is a prime example of an immersion school that shows its success in the teachers it retains. The majority of the young teachers are the inaugural students of the Kawenní:io/Gaweni:yo school. Russ Davis, Esenogwas Jacobs, Alisha Thomas-Hill, Connie Johnson, and Andrew Thomas all returned to the school because they truly believed in the survival of their culture through their language. Tamara Jonathan, although not a graduate of Kawenní:io/Gaweni:yo, worked for years as a teacher's assistant and learned Mohawk as her second language. These are a bevy of the most talented teachers I have ever encountered, first as they struggled to learn the language themselves and now that they have returned to teach. My thought is that they are the most appropriate teachers because they have the ability to identify with their students' learning process.

In any case, if all the nations can become strong again in their languages, the better the chances my grandchildren will have to encounter speakers wherever they travel to.

Theodore

Problems along the way: not enough support for the immersion program from those that could have provided these things, not enough teachers for all of the things that we wanted to do. I think every community that wants to revitalize their language encounters the same obstacles but we are slowly turning things around. The young people that have gone through the immersion programs are now returning to become the leaders, teachers, and decision makers. There is a changing of the guard and this is a good thing because these are now the parents and they want their children to have a better experience than they did.

I guess there will always be challenges when you are trying to do something good, and the revitalization of our language is as good as it gets. Remember, it is your language that is the key. In our language we will remember who we are, where we came from, and where we are going. Our Creator told us, "When you come back to the Skyworld, make sure you speak the language I gave you, have your Onkwehón:we name, have your personal song, have your clothing, and know your ceremonies." If you don't have these things then you will really have "problems along the way."

If you as parents are fortunate enough to have your language, give this most precious gift to your children, and if they do the same for their children we will not lose our identity. Everything that we are as a people is stored in our language. It was given to us by the Creator and man tried to take it away from us. To your last breath, do not let this happen. Learn your language first, then you can learn as many languages as you want or are able to. It is up to every one of us, our choice, but you have to make it.

Postscript

Margaret

In the federal school, immersion was implemented in 1995 and is continuing to this day. The program began as a grassroots effort of parents who felt the federal government and education system had taken away our language and should be responsible for giving it back. The AMBE parents pushed the school system for a full immersion program and it was implemented with some apprehension on the part of the AMBE leadership and board, as there was no plan or formal curriculum. And so it began, and I was encouraged to apply as a teachers' aide. That was when I got introduced to what I considered the best class I ever had in my teaching career. Shakohawitha Lazore, Ahnekate:ni Adams, Ohnawa:ke Edwards, Tekarihwakhen Herne, Wahsonti:io Jacobs, Kahriiohsta Benedict, Konwathara:ni Johnson, Wahioronko:he Oakes, my niece Taioron:iote McDonald, Wahe:shon Lazore, and my son, Nihahsennà:a Peters, became my students and little family unit for two years. We had originally enrolled our son in the Freedom School, but for some reason he was not doing well. His first language was Mohawk but we kept getting bad reports from his teacher about his behavior, saying he didn't work, couldn't read or write, and just was not doing well. AMBE was entering its fourth year of immersion and Joyce Sharrow was the teacher. I knew her reputation as an effective language instructor, so we enrolled Nihahsennà:a into the AMBE immersion program. Although he belonged in the third grade we had to put him into the second grade because that was the highest grade level at the time of his enrollment. At this time I was at SUNY Potsdam, majoring in elementary education. He had a great year and when we sent him back for the next school year we were informed on the first day of school that there was no third grade immersion class.

Well...this would not do. A group of us parents demanded that the school continue the immersion program, and although there was a struggle as there always is with immersion programming we, the parents, were able to continue the program with the reluctant agreement of the school leadership. The only problem was we couldn't find a teacher. And so...I withdrew from my second year at SUNY to go into the classroom to teach, and although I was reluctant to withdraw, it was the best decision I ever made in my teaching career. I spent the next two

Margaret's former student Ahnekate:ni (Myan) Adams, graduate of
the Ahkwesáhsne Mohawk immersion program and current student
at Cornell University, pictured with his grandmother Sally Ann
Adams, a fluent speaker. Photograph courtesy of Margaret Peters

years with the group and we did a lot of activities that brought attention to the immersion program. I recorded my students and had them
speaking on the radio, they were learning to recite ceremonial language, they were singing traditional songs...our class became a strong,
culturally integrated program that exposed some of the students for the
first time ever to their identity as Rotinonhson:ni (people of the Longhouse). I brought into the program my experience from having taught
at the Freedom School and from attending Longhouse ceremonies. We
even had two of our students act as youth ambassadors when Trent University asked for Mohawk-speaking representatives for an elders' conference they were hosting. I recommended a student who had achieved
a high level of functional fluency although he came from a non-speaking home, but with a parent very supportive of immersion. Ahnekate:ni
(Myan) Adams, now a student at Cornell University (just to mention
that for people who believe that students in immersion programs won't
succeed academically), wowed the conference attendees with his language and leadership qualities. He asked a friend, my son Nihahsennà:a,
to accompany him and to assist him, and although Nihahsennà:a had
the language as his first and also knew the cultural teachings, I felt the

best choice was to send a student who succeeded in immersion pro-gramming in spite of coming from a non-speaking but supportive home environment.

That was the entire class. Each of the students had a strong leader-ship quality and I didn't focus on their literary abilities but on the oral language skills which they all possessed. Taioron:iote (Kate) McDon-ald received the best reader (English) award in the seventh grade when she went on to Salmon River Central School. Shakohawitha Lazore received the Best Kid award in the seventh grade, awarded to students who are courteous and academically stable. Wahe:shon Lazore was recently chosen as the Mohawk Pageant princess at the New York State Fair. Tekarihwakhen is well on his way to becoming a great chef. Nihahsennà:a spent time as a language teacher at the AFS. Ahnekate:ni is at now at Cornell and is on the Cornell and Ahkwesáhsne's Lacrosse team, the Braves, very well known for his skills in the traditional sport. These are just a few examples of the successes that students can obtain if an immersion program is properly nurtured and supported.

We recently lost Shakohawitha at twenty years old, and as he makes his journey back into I:si Na'karon:iati (the spirit world) I am convinced that he was here for a reason and that we may not all know exactly what his duty was. The Creator felt it was time to call him home, where we will all join him someday. It offers me serenity to know that Shakohawitha was able to meet our Creator and speak in his original language.

This chapter is dedicated to the memory of Shakohawitha (Richard) Lazore, 1990–2010.

6: Māori

MY LANGUAGE STORY

Hana O'Regan

I am thirty-nine, I am fair-skinned, with brown hair and hazel eyes. There is not much of my physical presence that speaks of my Kāi Tahu, Māori ancestry. In fact the biggest indicator of my Māoriness is probably my Irish surname because of its association with my father, who has a public profile within Māori and mainstream society in New Zealand. My identity as a Māori has always been an issue to me and significant others around me.

I recall being teased as a young child at primary school and at times called derogatory names associated with race, like "nigger," even though I had no comprehension of its meaning. From an early age I was challenged by my peers and adults alike about my right to call myself a Māori. I was defined by fractions, my percentage of Māori blood, and this was somehow meant to disprove any validity or authenticity I might have as a Māori.

I recall acutely the fear and apprehension I felt as a child at the age of six when I woke up from surgery after an accident that resulted in the complete severing of my right hand. I was still recovering from the anaesthetic. I couldn't feel the hand that they had reattached and I overheard my parents and doctors talking about plastic and microsurgery. I remember sobbing profusely, and as my mother moved to comfort me I told her I didn't want a plastic hand, I wanted my real one back. She explained that I still had my real hand but I was just unable to feel it at that moment, and that reassured me somewhat before I burst out into tears all over again. It took some time before I could explain to her that my distress was because I could recall the blood that I had lost. I knew I had lost a lot—and I was concerned that I had lost my Māori blood. I wanted to know how I might be able to get it back, or if that meant I couldn't be a Māori anymore. People had talked about how much of my body would be Māori if it was dissected—my little finger, my right leg—all in jest, all to make a point. But in the mind of that six-year-old girl, it meant her very sense of self had been lost.

I want to now fast-track thirty-one years, to when my own daughter, who is now aged nine, was six years old. Manuhaea is fairer than I, with blonde hair and blue eyes, finer features than mine, and of a small stature. I have been concerned since the day she was born about issues of identity—wanting with all of my heart to shield her from the taunts and negative perceptions I experienced growing up. I didn't want my beautiful baby girl—or her beautiful little brother, Te Rautāwhiri, born a year later than her—to ever have to question who they were or be questioned by others. For nine years now, I have waited to hear the questions about identity and colour that preoccupied my childhood mind, but they haven't come. I've watched her in Māori environments running around with other Māori children, even talking about those very same identity and ethnic marks, but never has she raised with me questions as to how Māori she is. In fact, the opposite has occurred.

On a number of occasions of late, she has asked about the ethnicity of others who are, in terms of their physical characteristics, identifiably Māori. When she was six, as I was talking to a painter at our house who was Māori, my daughter asked me over to her and asked in Māori, "*He Māori rānei tērā takata Māmā?*" (Is that person a Māori or not?) I was shocked that she needed to ask, but responded with another question: "*Tēnā, he aha ōu whakaaro.*" (Well, what do you think?)

She responded, "*e Aua, tērā pea ekari kāore au i te tino mōhio.*" (Well, I guess he could be but I don't know.) On further questioning she disclosed the real basis of her confusion: "*He āhua Māori ia ekari kei te kōrero Pākehā ia!*" (Well, he looks a bit Māori, but he can only speak English!)

Being raised with Māori as her first language and her brother's has given her a completely different sense of identity as Māori from that six-year-old girl waking up from her surgery thirty-three years ago. What's more, people have not questioned her in the same way as they did me. She looks into the mirror and sees a Māori face look back at her. I used to look into the mirror and imagine what it would be like if I looked like a Māori, and what that would then mean. I didn't stop, back then, to consider that what I heard, as opposed to what I saw, might define my Māoriness in time.

The Kāi Tahu Language Story

To put my own personal *reo* (language) and identity journey into context, it is first necessary to understand the historical experiences of my people and the impact of those experiences on our heritage language and culture. My people, the Kāi Tahu, are of the South Island, and our tribal territory is the largest of any tribe in New Zealand, extending over more than 80 percent of Te Waipounamu, the South Island, or approximately 49 percent of New Zealand.[1]

Kāi Tahu were traditionally a seminomadic people who migrated seasonally from their base settlements to exploit the many and varied food resources of the main island and neighbouring islands in the Southern Ocean. Their ancestors had migrated from tropical Eastern Polynesia into a land that ranged from pockets of warmer microclimates to the sub-Antarctic environments of the far south. They traversed the Southern Alps—Kā Tiritiri o te Moana—which host the country's highest mountains, on an annual basis. They did this to harvest the *pounamu,* or greenstone, from the West Coast—Te Tai o Pountini. Greenstone was the prized jewel in pre-European Māori society, used extensively for tools, weaponry, and adornments. This treasure was exported to the North Island over many centuries and remained an important commodity well after the introduction of iron and steel.

Unlike the Northern New Zealand Māori, the culture that had developed in the South as a process of adaptation to this harsher environment was not based on the cultivation of the *kumara,* the staple brought with the ancestors from Eastern Polynesia. The southern experience required them to travel the width and breadth of the island, interchanging and trading with their related subtribes across the land in order to achieve a sustainable existence. This also meant that when the tide changed and European settlers started arriving as a part of the colonisation process, the South was in most respects easy pickings, with great tracts of land impossible to systematically defend and susceptible to squatting and a range of land alienation tools.

Not only had Kāi Tahu suffered poorly after the introduction of foreign epidemics that had effects similar to those of the Black Plague in Europe, we were also plagued by inter- and intra-tribal warring fuelled by the deadly gun, which had devastating effects on the population. By the mid-1830s we were a people of few elders or children and were sentenced in the literature and public record of the time to the fate of racial extinction. It is with great wonder, as a descendent of those survivors, that I can look back at our history now and exclaim that we are here at all.

My ancestors not only survived those odds—the death, the impoverishment, the humiliation of being alienated from tribal lands and resources, forced assimilation, social and economic deprivation—they persevered in such a way, over generations, that the tribe was eventually able to reassert itself in the economic, political, and social landscape of the South Island and the country.

One reason for this "re-emergence" has been an inherited tribal legacy dating back to 1849, the Ngāi Tahu Claim. It was in that year that one of our leaders, Matiaha Tiramorehu, first wrote to the Crown protesting the Ngāi Tahu position in terms of broken promises of the Crown and Government, underhanded dealings, and the poverty afflicting his people. That was to be the start of 149 years of unbroken protest that would end with the Ngāi Tahu Claims Settlement Act in 1998.

Generation after generation of Ngāi Tahu found ways to support their leaders to petition Parliament, protest in the Māori Land Courts, present at Commissions of Inquiry—whatever legal and judicial means they could. I saw as a youngster the impact that this struggle had on my immediate family and relations. It was an ever-present part of our lives, be it at tribal gatherings and meetings or discussions at the dining room table. Families mortgaged homes and took out personal loans to fight for the Claim, as their parents and great-great-grandparents had done. It had been a tremendous personal and collective commitment and it paid off. In 1998 the Claim was settled and Kāi Tahu received compensation for their loss and other rights and assets, and the tribal economy, which had been developed and built on the minimal monies available over the previous twenty years, was able to reassert itself once again.

I often wonder whether Matiaha Tiramorehu and his peers back in 1849 foresaw the death of our language and culture as a result of the displacement of their people. I also wonder whether or not it was believed that the language and culture could be brought back once the Claim was settled. Whatever the case, my people became one of the earliest of tribes to show dramatic language decline. This was contributed to by the breakdown of communities through loss of land, assimilation into

Pākehā culture, the high rate of intermarriage that itself was promoted in the mid-to-late 1800s as a strategy for survival, and the national policies and laws that sought to devalue and destroy the Māori language.

Kāi Tahu are now the fourth-largest tribe in the country, with a registered population of over 40,000 and a census population of 49,185.[2] We are now a major player in the South Island economy, especially in the areas of fishing, property development, and tourism. But despite the successes, all this has been at a cost, and perhaps one of the biggest costs has also been the most silent—our *reo,* our language.

My *Whānau* (Family Story)

Intergenerational transmission of *te reo* ceased in my *whānau* (family) approximately 110 years ago. My great-grandmother Rena Harawata was born around 1870 into a Māori-speaking family who were also competently bilingual in English. It is believed that she was raised with both languages in the home but was strongly encouraged to learn and master English as the perceived language of success of the time. When my *taua* Rena Ruiha was born in 1900, she was raised in English and was not therefore a speaker of *te reo.*

My father, Tipene O'Regan, can recall as a child sitting and listening to his *taua* and his Aunty Ngawara, of Te Arawa tribal descent, talking in Māori, although by this stage her language was not as fluid as that of her daughter-in-law.

My *taua* (grandmother) knew only a few words and commands but used these with my father. She died well before I was born. My father studied Māori at university and spent many years immersing himself in the culture and its history, but his language learning took a second place to his political role: leading our tribe in our Claim against the Crown. He used a little of what he knew with us in the home, but again this was restricted, to commands and a few basic sentences.

I was fortunate, however, after the accident with my hand, to have the opportunity to spend a great deal of time with a learned elderly lady, Te Aue Davis, from the northern Ngāti Maniapoto tribe. She was a weaver and a fluent speaker of the *reo.* She would take me with her as she travelled the country and my own *marae* in the South Island as she taught the art of weaving. She fostered my love of the language and culture, and at age thirteen I became the first of the five children to go to Māori boarding school in Auckland, where Aunty Te Aue lived.

Hana O'Regan at age twelve, Roseneath Primary School, Wellington

Te reo Māori was compulsory at school until the age of sixteen. It was all around me in performance, in class, and in our daily lives. I didn't like the school much at all—in fact, I was pretty miserable for four years—but for the opportunities it gave me in the language, I remain extremely appreciative.

I had grown up knowing I was Kāi Tahu, knowing who my relations were, visiting our *marae,* or traditional meeting houses and villages, as well as those of numerous others around the country. I had always thirsted for the language and culture and sought out whatever little there was around me, and I was always fiercely proud of that identity, which is why I was sent off to Auckland to Māori boarding school at the age of thirteen. So it hurt when people laughed at me and belittled my people. This had a significant personal impact on my desire to learn the language and by the end of my fourteenth year, I had written in my journal whilst at boarding school that I would dedicate my life to helping my people find their language again, to give them back their voice.

I worked hard at learning the language although it was by no means easy for me. As in most of my studies, I had to invest a lot of time and effort in order to achieve a slightly better than average grade. But *te reo* for me was a joy. I found it easy to dive into its poetry, I loved the way it sounded, and I treasured it for the world it opened up to me. At age seventeen I left for a year in Thailand as an exchange student. After three months my competency in Thai had overtaken my Māori, and after eleven months I returned to New Zealand feeling like I had to start all over again. It frustrated me to think I had learnt in three months, in an immersion Thai environment, what had taken me four years in New Zealand to achieve in *te reo*.

I continued on in my study of *te reo* at University in Wellington, graduating with a degree in Māori language and political science. Before too long, at age twenty-one, I was to shift to Dunedin to lecture in *te reo* at the University of Otago, where I taught for four years. I had finally moved into my own tribal territory and was starting to do what I had dreamt of doing all those years before, teaching *te reo* in the South Island, yet I wasn't anywhere near prepared for the enormity of the task at hand.

Turning the Tide—The Start of the Kāi Tahu Language Revitalisation Movement

In 1993 I became involved with a handful of other young Ngāi Tahu speakers associated with the University of Otago who were running weeklong, total immersion Māori language courses during the holiday breaks. We started to look at the bigger picture of the state of the language within the tribe and ways of addressing its continued decline. As we delved into international literature on language revitalisation and language planning by the likes of Professor Joshua Fishman, we became acutely aware of the precarious position we were actually in, and an anecdotal environment scan of the tribe's language health was alarming.

There were little or no educational opportunities in *te reo* available to most of our children, unlike in many areas in the North Island. A lack of fluent speakers also meant a lack of competent, fluent teachers to service the demand throughout the region—and that was where there *was* demand. We had few or no high-density areas of language speakers anywhere in the entire territory that could be used to support community language development. Isolation, lack of accessibility, and lack of exposure to the language all contributed to its poor health.

We were able to count on one hand the number of native speakers of our language left, and those of our distinctive southern dialect were even fewer. Of that handful of elders, there were no practicing speakers at that time; that is, they were all raised with *te reo* as their native tongue but had not spoken it in a native context for decades. Although they no longer had native competency, they were still a rich source of phrase, vocabulary, and associated cultural knowledge.

In some areas, *te reo* had not been the language of intergenerational transmission for over one hundred years, and therefore, there were even limited "remembers" of the heritage language. Although a few words and phrases had proved to be linguistically persistent, like terms for grandmother (*taua*) and grandfather (*pōua*), and names of flora and fauna around transitional *mahika kai,* or food gathering places and practices, we were essentially dealing with a language that Fishman's language scale would have classified as being past the point of no return.

Within the Kāi Tahu tribal territory, of the 62,300 Māori recorded in the "Health of the Māori Language" report, 2006, only 16 percent were able to speak *te reo* Māori to some degree, with the national average being around 25 percent.[3] This number, however, includes all Māori living in our territory—the picture gets worse when we break it down to tribal affiliation. Although official statistics record approximately 13 percent of Ngāi Tahu as having an ability in *te reo,* those of us Ngāi Tahu within the *reo*-speaking community believe the number to be significantly lower; we believe the self-assessment in the survey fails to adequately address those who have an inflated perception about their own language competency.

Although this assessment may seem a bit harsh, it actually derives more from a position of desperation than criticism, as I am one of the small number of Ngāi Tahu who are actively involved in our tribal language revitalisation effort and attempting to raise our children in *te reo*. The reality is that we are faced with a severe shortage of competent speakers at our tribal gatherings, during our cultural rituals, and even within our leadership. This language loss has had a profound effect on how we see ourselves as a people, and also on how others see us. Nationally we have been the subject of many taunts and jokes by other Māori and at times academics and journalists over the years equating us to something less than real Māori.

As a child and teenager growing up in the North Island, I would hear my people being referred to as plastic Māori, fake Māori, or try-hard Māori. Some would argue that there were no Māori in the South Island anyway, so claiming you were from a southern tribe wasn't even plausible, let alone possible.

By 1995 we had developed the bones of our Kāi Tahu language strategic vision, *Kotahi Mano Kāika—Kotahi Mano Wawata:* A Thousand Homes—a Thousand Dreams. The goal was to have at least one thousand home-speaking *te reo* by the year 2025, and that would then be the realisation of one thousand aspirations. We were immensely proud of this vision and lobbied our tribal political body for support, which they duly gave, and soon we had a language officer working in the education unit of the tribal organisation. The milestones were many and significant but in the scheme of things, when we considered what was actually required to achieve a language shift, they succeeded in only creating opposing ripples against a receding tide. Our biggest obstacles were the people themselves and perhaps the most crippling of conditions afflicting language revitalisation movements worldwide, apathy.

Our people told us they wanted *te reo,* they wanted their children to have the opportunity to learn it, but they didn't necessarily want to have to do anything themselves to achieve it. They were also not really interested in hearing about the rate of language loss worldwide and the numbers of endangered languages that died every week somewhere around the globe. These conditions, of apathy and its close relative ignorance, continue to present the biggest challenge in our language revitalisation efforts today, and unfortunately, the beast looks like it is just getting bigger.

For the best part of fifteen years I have continued to work with my peers promoting and contributing to the Kotahi Mano Kāika initiatives, whilst teaching in our tribal *hui* and lecturing in *te reo* at Otago and then at Christchurch Polytechnic Institute of Technology in Canterbury. However, twelve years on from the strategy's official launch, although we had started to make inroads into areas of critical awareness and language planning, we had only managed to grow the Māori-language-speaking homes by a couple of dozen; we were a long way off our one thousand.

I had hoped to support the plan by having a dozen children of my own, who I could raise speaking Māori, organise planned marriages for (without their knowing, of course) to other Māori-speaking people, and ultimately have numerous fluent grandchildren running around me. A slight hiccough to that plan happened when my specialist told me at twenty-five that I was unlikely to be able to have children, because of endometriosis. At age twenty-nine, after a set of unfortunate circumstances, I reassessed my personal contribution to the Ngāi Tahu language effort and devised a five-year plan that would have me fostering Ngāi Tahu children and nurturing them in a language home environment. I gave myself five years to achieve this and explained the macroplan to my then partner when we began our relationship in September that year. By October I was pregnant with our baby girl, Manuhaea Rena Mamaru O'Regan, who was born on July 3, 2003.

A New Generation Is Born

All my years of lecturing, writing poetry in Māori, composing songs in Māori, and debating in public and on national stages in Māori didn't prepare me for the moment I first held my precious baby in my arms. Or, for that matter, the many more moments after as I learnt how to bathe her, change her, burp her, and feed her. I had made a promise to myself and to her that I would raise her in *te reo* and ensure that she did not have to struggle or fight for her language as I had done. I made a commitment to only speak Māori to her, and I had lectured her father to make an effort to learn so that he could support the *reo* in the home even though he could not speak Māori himself.

Yet when the time arrived, I learnt very quickly that I didn't have at my disposal the language I needed, and it wasn't just the vocabulary; it was the idiom, the turn of phrase, the terms of endearment. I didn't know the term for winding or burping a child, or how to say, "Let's put your legs up so I can clean you up"; these weren't structures or sentences I had ever had to use in the lecture room or with my peers!

Clockwise from front left: Manuhaea Rena (age four), Sandra O'Regan, Hana O'Regan, Tipene O'Regan, Te Rautawhiri Mahaki (age three)

It was also a revelation for me in terms of what I had expected my tribal relations to do. I had lectured and preached about the importance of speaking to their children in the home from birth, to make the commitment and stick to it—yet I had little appreciation of how hard that would be on a daily basis. I had written books on language in the home with appropriate phrases and structures, but the practicality of referring to those books to find a word mid-nappy-change had not even been remotely in my consciousness.

I also considered, from the privileged position of language competency I had been lucky enough to acquire, how much harder it would be for those without that exposure. One thousand Ngāi Tahu homes speaking *te reo* seemed further from reach than ever.

I struggled daily with my commitment to only speak Māori to my children. My Māori language exposure during childhood, as a second-language speaker of *te reo,* consisted of a set use of commands, basic counting, and a handful of songs. I was an adult (early twenties) before I started learning to speak Māori as a vernacular in informal contexts. Our household also presented its challenges. The children's father only spoke English, so we adopted the OPOL (one-parent, one-language) practice of bilingualism, although in fairness there weren't many other options available to us. Despite the challenges, our two children were raised as fluent speakers of both Māori and English.

Both children spoke Māori first, and this remained their dominant language until the age of about three. Their first words, their first sentences, and first songs were all greatly celebrated milestones—but the fact that they were also all in Māori added to the excitement and joy. The joys and milestones kept on coming, year after year, but they started to be tempered by anxiety as the influence of English on the home language began to increase. The challenge we collectively face in our home now is maintaining *te reo* as the main language of communication between the three of us.

To date, the record is as follows:

- I have not yet spoken English to the children (with the exception of four protest sentences).
- Māori has been the dominant language of communication and engagement between mother and children for the last nine years.

- When aged 4½ and 5½, the children started to introduce English words into their speech between themselves, and that aspect of the language interaction has continued to increase.
- Since the age of 5½ my son has, on a number of occasions, said short sentences to me in English as a form of protest or teasing.

In all honesty, I hear my children struggle daily—as do I. English is that much easier for them now in so many contexts: it's what they hear the most, it's what most of the people around them speak. As their main example of *te reo*, I struggle to impart what is required for them to use it functionally all the time, and I fear I am losing the battle.

The Battlefield of Language Maintenance

Our family dynamic changed significantly in late 2011 when the children's father and I separated; since early 2011 the children and I live as a unit of three within the family home. I remain committed to maintaining a Māori-language-speaking home where my children and I speak Māori to each other. However, the frustrations that I experience daily challenge this commitment and conviction, usually due to the limitations I continue to face as a second-language learner of *te reo* and the children's increased tendency to turn to English. I continue to struggle to find ways of expressing and explaining things in *te reo* that I have never had to explain before, for example:

> Where does the water go from the bath?
> It goes down the long round hole thing (pipe).
> What's a long round hole thing?
> The thing that can carry the water to another place.
> Who carries it?
> No, it just flows down it.
> To Pāpātuanuku (the Earth Mother)?
> …Arh, yes—but to big ponds where it can be changed back into good water again.
> How does it get changed?

At points like these I tend not to even tackle the process of oxidisation as a form of water purification, and some other strategy is sought to divert them from their questioning. Although I can typically "escape the moment" in such situations—so far—it does mean I limit the kind of interaction I might have with my children if the language used were instead my first language, English. These situations are compounded by the fact that I seem unable to extend my own language at the same rate that their language and education develop, and as the main role model and transmitter of the language on a daily basis, I become increasingly concerned about the long-term sustainability of *te reo* in our home environment.

The rate of language shift in our home increased significantly when Manuhaea started school in July 2008. I had chosen to put her in a bilingual unit within a mainstream school, as opposed to one of the two total immersion schools available to me. My choice to take the bilingual option was based on feedback from other parents who said the children in the immersion schools often reverted back to English in the playground and when outside of formal instruction. Research had told me that the single most important factor in language maintenance was language in the home, so I opted then for the school my best friend's child, Te Aotahi, was attending, to ensure my daughter would have a Māori language buddy. Te Aotahi is four years my daughter's senior and she had grown up only speaking Māori.

As the weeks passed, however, the temptations of the new English-dominant language environment would grow and Manuhaea would start exploring and introducing this new knowledge into the traditionally Māori-dominated home interactions. I would hear her telling her brother, "Did you know the Pākehā (English) word for *rorohiko* is 'computer'?" and so forth. I heard her start to compose and sing songs to herself in English for the first time, whereas this was previously a common pastime in Māori. Her new world was exciting for her and she was proud to impart this new knowledge to her little brother, Te Rautāwhiri, who was likewise keen to learn. Although Māori remained the main language of choice in the majority of interactions, more and more English words began to be incorporated into the Māori sentences and phrases, and this led on to complete English sentences and discussions.

My reaction to this change was not academic or informed by what the literature deemed to be best practice. I became progressively more anxious about the shift and corrective of their language choice at every turn, instructing them to *kōrero Māori* (speak Māori) at every opportunity. I wanted them to speak English and be competently bilingual, but I considered the home environment one of the sacred last bastions where we could control the domination of English. To see palisades that I had constructed in my own mind to protect our language start to crumble was disheartening, to say the least.

I was constantly on guard, quick to growl or correct, night and day. If I heard an English word in conversation I would bark out my reminders to speak *te reo,* with anger and disappointment. You need to understand that I did not like my behaviour in the slightest, and I would have nightly personal deliberations, scolding myself for my reactions. I wanted to be able to feel happy for them, to encourage their language development in both languages, but I was conflicted with my knowledge about language shift and the difficulties of maintaining a minority language against odds such as ours.

I questioned myself as to why I was so afraid of English. Was it its gnarling teeth with its vicious bite? Was it the breadth of its wings that eclipsed the light of day? Or was it its sheer enormity that scared me as it entered the doors of our house, lest I be thrown outside by its huge swaying hips? Or was I scared of its many friends taking over our safe haven with their noisy, loud, dominant mouths, drowning out my cries? This language I was so afraid of was, after all, my own native tongue, the language in which I had myself learnt about my world. So why had I become so threatened by it in my home? My only explanation was what I had experienced myself as a second-language speaker of Māori in New Zealand:

- It was easier to speak English in the community we lived in.
- There were many more resources available to support the development of English and to engage the children.
- English was the language spoken by the majority of those around them.
- English dominated all media and modern technology.

With traditional proverbs about determination, fighting against the odds, never backing down, and the like, I had long lectured my children about the need to be strong in their commitment to *te reo.* From a tender age they had been told about the need to keep our language alive and the threat of language loss. They would tell others from the age of three and four about their need to speak *te reo* lest the language of the tribe would die! These poor children had the weight of their language's survival on their shoulders before they could properly carry a backpack.

Te Rautawhiri Mahaki Mamaru-O'Regan (age five)

As their mother, I am not proud of the fact that I have inadvertently or otherwise burdened my children in an effort to ensure they did not suffer the burden of language deprivation and loss.

I am sure they have no real comprehension as to why this is such a big issue for their Māmā, they just know it's one of Māmā's big issues! They are personally not concerned if it is Māori or English that comes

out of their mouths, as long as they can communicate their message—
so why the fuss? Baker reminds us of the role of one's language (or languages) in this respect:

> For the child, language is a means to an end, not an end in
> itself...Language is a vehicle to help move along the road of
> information exchange and social communication.[4]

As long as they were still able to communicate in Māori, why should
I worry? I tested my assumptions and fears one night three years ago
as I prepared their bath. Once they were in the bathtub I pretended to
leave but instead hid quietly behind the door. I wanted to assess their
language of communication when I wasn't there. Twenty minutes I hid
behind that door, the paranoid, language-obsessed mother, spying on
her two young children.

My son, Te Rautāwhiri, asked his sister a question. *"Ko wai tō
whāiaipo Manuhaea?"* (Who is your boyfriend, Manuhaea?)

"Kāore ōku whāiaipo" (I don't have a boyfriend), she replied.

"Āe rā, he whaiāipo tōhou, e mōhio ana au" (Yes you do, you have a
boyfriend, I know), argued her brother.

After some time of intense and very informative discussion Manuhaea asked, *"Kai hea rā ā Māmā?"* (Where is Māmā?). And I was caught
in the act as a little head appeared from behind the door. Despite
my obvious embarrassment as I tried to find the words to explain my
actions to my then five- and six-year-old children, the fact was that I
had heard only one English word used during the interaction, and that
was the word "marry."

If they were still turning to Māori as a means of communicating in
this personal and informal context, were my suspicions about their
language preference right? Or had the work needed to establish their
native tongue already been done, so that it would naturally persist
and thrive without my constant nagging? Perhaps they were just truly
experimenting with their second language, English? My pessimism continued to nag at me as I thought of many others who I knew had made
such transitions and never returned.

As I mentioned earlier, when asked what will happen to our language if we don't speak it, both my children will readily be able to
respond with the answer: "It will die." The question remains, is this a
reflection of their comprehension of language maintenance and causes

of language loss, or a response to their mother's indoctrination efforts? Undoubtedly the answer is the latter of the two, yet that still begs the question, What else does one do? Is it right to leave one's heritage language to chance in a time of unprecedented global language decline? The question, for myself and my family and perhaps others attempting to revitalise an endangered minority language in their homes, is where the boundaries of language maintenance lie and how strict we need to be about protecting them.

> When they begin to assert their language preference, parents can only act as gentle gardeners. They can encourage, offer opportunities and possibilities, but rarely decide, direct or drive the language life of a teenager.[5]

> Mixing is typical and to be expected in the early stages of bilingual development. However, many parents do not like to hear children mixing two languages...Parents can help in the process of language separation by various do's and don'ts. The most important is to avoid criticizing, or constantly pointing out mistakes, revealing anxiety and concern.[6]

Well, I failed on every count in this regard. Not only were my children intensely aware of my concerns around the language loss of our people and within our family, they were also subject to an habitual correcting of language.

In a chapter titled "Stemming a Bilingual Rebellion," Kendall King and Alison Mackey put the struggle into perspective, reminding us how difficult it can be to get four-year-olds to behave how we want them to, and that it is therefore reasonable to suggest that it will be as difficult to control what they say. Their advice is this:

> Perhaps the most important thing is not to allow language to become a battlefield...don't let language become the stage for power struggles between you and your child.[7]

The home environment that I had created wasn't quite a *battlefield* but could probably be likened to a rather limited enclosure with electric fences on all sides and with the children's mother in a watchpost on guard around the clock, lest anyone attempt to breech the boundaries!

Te Rautawhiri Mahaki Mamaru-O'Regan (age seven) and Manuhaea Rena Mamaru-O'Regan (age eight)

Although my actions seem a far call from expert advice on the matter, the real issue for me now is whether or not the actions are indeed necessary.

For the moment my children, who just celebrated their eighth and ninth birthdays, continue to be functionally bilingual. They have a strong sense of cultural and personal identity that is informed by a Māori worldview. They still only speak Māori to me and a selected few others who are part of our close community of friends. They *can* still speak Māori if they choose to—so perhaps my anxieties are unfounded and exaggerated and I need to relax the boundary markers, or at least turn off the electric fences!

I do know where my anxieties derive from. I am aware that this development in our own family's language history—having a generation that speaks Māori as their first language—could change at any point. The risk, then, is that my twenty-four years of formal language learning and efforts at raising my two children in *te reo* hang on a very thin thread, albeit a tightly plaited one! All it will take for that effort to be undone is for my children to choose not to raise their children in *te reo,* and my grandchildren will have to start all over again, if indeed the inclination to do so exists at all. One generation's choice to not speak, promote, and transmit the language is a death sentence for that language. Any reprieve the *reo* might have lies in the hands and hearts of individuals of that time if they are willing and have the capacity to do anything about it.

In terms of my people, my tribe—our language continues to die and the majority choose to let it do so. My lament and those of my peers who are raising their children speaking *te reo* in the home are real, but faint against the dominant political issues that occupy our tribal discourse. My only hope is that they will be heard before it is too late.

I continue to hope that the efforts of my ancestors in fighting for the Claim and the sacrifices they made in their time will not be in vain—and that we will not become a tribal collective bound by shared lineage but without the language that holds our cultural heritage. I continue to hope that our people will once again be a people who want to celebrate and embrace our language as a core part of our culture and our heritage. I don't think we will ever get to the point where all Kāi Tahu are able to speak it again, although I would love to be proved wrong. But I hope and dream that all those who want to learn it have the ability to do so, and that everyone, be they speakers, learners, or nonspeakers, can support and value its continued growth and development.

On a personal level, I can't think of anything better than to be lucky enough to reach a good age and be sitting on the porch of my house or *marae*, sharing *reo* "war stories" with my best friend and fellow Kāi Tahu language advocate, Charisma Rangipunga. We would have our respective grandchildren and maybe even great-grandchildren playing around us, arguing, teasing, joking, playing, and singing in *te reo*. They would all know who they were and be proud of their identity as Kāi Tahu. They would have the language of their ancestors at their disposal as a natural and positive part of who they are and who they want to be. They would all be aware of the importance of language survival and language maintenance, and their role in ensuring that both are achieved.

As for the anxiety, the pessimism, the fear, and the pain of language loss? When the time came for me to go from this world, there would be no more anxiety or fear, as I would know I did all I could when I had the chance. I would chuckle with my grown-up children about my overbearing and overprotective ways in my *warrior days*. And hopefully they would understand and forgive me for my spying moments, my grouchy words, and my "War of the Worlds sermons." And as I slipped away, their last words to me in *te reo* would be as sweet to my ear as the first ones they ever uttered to me, and I would feel the same sense of pride, hope, and joy as I did back then. My language would have survived, its survival securely in the hands of the next generation. We would have learnt the lessons of our past, and we would know what is needed to ensure the future of *te reo*. No pressure, my darlings—the fate of our language is up to you! No pressure!

Notes
1. *Te Puni Kōkiri,* http://www.tpk.govt.nz/en/region/te-waipounamu (retrieved on April 5, 2010).
2. *Statistics New Zealand,* QuickStats About Māori, Census 2006/Tautauranga 2006, http://www.stats.govt.nz/Census/2006CensusHomePage/QuickStats/quickstats-about-a-subject/maori.aspx (rev. March 27, 2007).
3. *Te Puni Kōkiri,* 2008.
4. Colin Baker, *A Parents' and Teachers' Guide to Bilingualism* (Clevedon, UK: Multilingual Matters, 2000), 64.
5. Ibid., 65.
6. Ibid., 63–64.
7. Kendall King and Alison Mackey, *The Bilingual Edge* (New York: Harper Collins, 2007), 240–241.

7: Hawaiian

E PAEPAE HOU 'IA KA PŌHAKU: RESET THE STONES OF THE HAWAIIAN HOUSE PLATFORM*

William H. Wilson and Kauanoe Kamanā

E paepae hou 'ia ka pōhaku i pa'a maila ka hale e ho'olulu ai—'reset the stones of the platform and build upon it a house, a haven for our language and culture'—was a rallying cry of the 1970s. We and our two children, Hulilauākea and his sister, Keli'ihoalani, have experienced living in such a "house." The stones for the platform were there from earlier generations, but it took some work to reset them, build the house, and live comfortably in it.

A *hale,* a house, is treated as a living entity in Hawaiian tradition. It is something that is born of its builders and must be properly accepted into the world of human beings through the severing of its *piko,* its umbilical cord. That *piko* in earlier times was a tuft of thatch over the door of the new home, cut with an adze and a special blessing.

Today, in a modification of that ancient practice developed in Hilo by our strand of the larger Hawaiian language revitalization movement, we hang over the door of a new home a woven band of various plants symbolic of our hopes for its occupants. *Koa* for bravery, *liko lehua* for

---

* This quotation is taken from Larry Kimura's poetic call *Auē Nā Ali'iĒ* 'O Chiefs'. Other headings in this article are taken from Hawaiian tradition, much of it available in *'Ōlelo No'eau*, by Mary K. Pukui.

stalwartness, *kukui* for enlightenment, *laukahi* for unity. We cut the band—the *piko*—with an adze, and offer prayers and special foods to mark the occasion. Such *'oki piko* events secure happiness and hopefulness in our growing population of families in the Hilo area of Hawai'i who speak Hawaiian as the home language.

Approximately thirty-two years ago, we "gave birth" to the first such modern Hawaiian-speaking *hale* when we decided to speak only Hawaiian with each other in preparation for the impending birth of Hulilauākea, our first child. It was quite a challenge, as we were seeking to separate ourselves from our community's linguistic norms solely through the force of our own wills. In our late twenties, we spoke Hawaiian with elders every chance we could; we had even begun insisting that only Hawaiian be spoken by students in our university classes. However, in our own personal lives at home, we spoke English with each other, as was normal for our generation throughout the Hawaiian community.

It was rough that week at Hale Kāwili Adult Student Housing when we cut the *piko* that connected us to our dark, restraining, but highly familiar English-speaking womb. There were then no other young couples like us who had a Hawaiian-speaking *hale.* One of us would begin to speak only Hawaiian to the other; the uncomfortableness of it all would lead to frustration; and we would resort once again to English. So it went for a week, but by the second week, with much perseverance and discipline, we were okay, and we have continued to speak only Hawaiian with each other since.

Our speaking Hawaiian as a couple allowed our own two children to be brought up as fully first-language speakers of Hawaiian—something that had not existed in Hilo for at least two generations. It also became a key source of strength in efforts to build more and more *honua*, or landscapes, where Hawaiian-speaking *hale* could rise. Today, in Hilo, there are over fifty families where Hawaiian is the sole language used between at least one parent and a child. Many more families use some Hawaiian at home with their children. And the numbers are growing.

Ka Nohona I Kahi Hāiki—Living in the Place of Narrowness
The birth of our Hawaiian-speaking home involved a long period of gestation, in *kahi hāiki,* that is, in "the narrow place," as the womb is known poetically in Hawaiian. Over that time our two highly

(Left to right) Kauanoe, Hulilau, Keliʻihoalani, and Pila at a family gathering on Kauaʻi, 2009. Photograph courtesy of Kauanoe Kamanā

distinct identities developed in isolation. Yet they would later converge in young adulthood to focus on an expanded world of language revitalization.

One of us, Kauanoe, is Hawaiian—raised in a highly Hawaiian environment. Kauanoe experienced both the urban Hawaiian community of Honolulu, where she lived most of the year, and highly rural Molokaʻi Island, to which her family returned home in the summers. It was a rather idyllic life filled with loving parents, cousins, aunts and uncles, large lūʻau parties, church, music, and a uniquely secure educational experience in the all-Hawaiian Kamehameha Schools. Both Kauanoe's parents and all her ancestors were able to speak Hawaiian, but neither Kauanoe nor her much older brother spoke the language.

By the time Kauanoe was born, in 1951, the Hawaiian language had long been restricted to songs, certain usages in church, and occasional instances when grandparents used the language for specific purposes that did not involve children. However, Hawaiian words were all around. They were in the names of foods, flora and fauna, in family names, in street names, and in the informal vocabulary of everyday life embedded in the Native Hawaiian version of Hawaiʻi's distinctive

Creole English, known informally as "Pidgin." This use of the Hawaiian language through Pidgin sufficed then as a marker of ethnicity for Kauanoe. Pidgin still serves this purpose for many Native Hawaiians. However, things would change for Kauanoe later in life.

Bill is not Hawaiian. Although he was born in Hawai'i and lived in the islands until late elementary school, Bill later moved with his family first to Denmark and Germany, then to Kansas and Oklahoma. Bill spent his adolescence missing Hawai'i while gaining a wide range of experiences in multilingual and multicultural circumstances. He began to try to teach himself Hawaiian during that time. When he returned to Hawai'i in his senior year in high school, he took Hawaiian in night school. Yet his experience of Hawai'i was primarily through *haole*, or Caucasian, circles, rather than the Hawaiian ones in which Kauanoe lived.

Kauanoe studied French while at Kamehameha. It was a time when studying Hawaiian was not encouraged there. High school was a difficult time for Kauanoe, as her mother died when she was in ninth grade and both she and her father struggled to adjust to life without her. After high school, Kauanoe studied data processing at Kapi'olani Community College and worked in her cousin's Hawaiian-themed baby blanket factory.

Hihia Nā Makau O Ke Aloha—Our Lines Become Entangled
We eventually met through the Hawaiian language classes of the University of Hawai'i at Mānoa. Bill was there first. A biology major hoping to find a job as a geneticist with the sugar plantations, he was pursuing his interest in Hawaiian language "on the side."

After completing her studies at Kapi'olani Community College, Kauanoe had come to UH specifically to study Hawaiian language and culture. The 1970s were the time of the Hawaiian Renaissance, with young people of all ethnicities, but especially Native Hawaiians, rallying around the distinctiveness of Hawai'i. Kauanoe had been inspired to study Hawaiian while watching her father listening to a Hawaiian radio talk show put on by UH Hawaiian-language students and teachers. Soon she would be joining with Bill, or Pila, as he is known in Hawaiian, and others in bringing elders to appear on the show.

Both of us continued with the Hawaiian language classes through fourth year. It was a time of development for Hawaiian language, culture, and history studies. Kauanoe helped write up the official proposal for the Hawaiian Studies B.A. and was one of its first graduates. Bill abandoned biology and became a liberal studies major focusing on Hawaiian and Polynesian linguistics.

We found common cause in our interest in Hawaiian and decided that we would work together toward the promotion of the language. Although there was a fine dictionary of Hawaiian, the structure of Hawaiian was not well understood and teaching it was not very successful. We wanted to learn more, and opportunities opened up for us as graduate students in the linguistics department. Both of us obtained graduate assistant jobs related to Hawaiian—Bill teaching Hawaiian in the Indo-Pacific languages department and Kauanoe as a Hawaiian-language expert in a research project into the origins of Hawai'i Creole English under Dr. Derek Bickerton.

Outside our formal education, we continued to learn in the community. We went on trips with our Hawaiian-language teacher, Larry Kimura, to visit elders and use Hawaiian in places where it had formerly been the regular language of all interaction. Kauanoe joined Nā Pualei O Likolehua, a *hālau hula*, where Kauanoe's assumption of traditional cultural responsibilities and obligations grew. Both of us were active in the campus Hawaiian language and culture organization, Hui Aloha 'Āina Tuahine, and began teaching Hawaiian in night school and as volunteers at Punahou School.

Hawaiian music had become the rage of our generation. Honolulu was full of Hawaiian parties as well as nightclubs where our friends entertained, and impromptu performances by the audience of language and hula students were as much a part of the show as the musicians. More serious activities involved joining with Larry Kimura, Hawaiian elders, and other young teachers in the newly founded 'Ahahui 'Ōlelo Hawai'i Hawaiian language organization and other efforts to promote the learning and teaching of Hawaiian.

In 1976, we married. His doctorate nearly finished, Bill left his graduate assistantship for a permanent job with the state archives as a translator of old Hawaiian documents. Kauanoe completed her master's in linguistics and began to pursue further graduate work in American studies with a focus on Hawai'i, while teaching Hawaiian language at the University of Hawai'i at Mānoa laboratory school. These experiences and our expanded life as a couple gave us more and more understanding of the Hawaiian language, its role historically, and its potential role for the future. We became increasingly fluent in the language and also familiar with the ways of our respective, very different, families.

Hoʻokahi Aliʻi ʻO Hanakahi—Unity under Hilo's Chief Hanakahi (Single-Work)

Two years into our marriage, the dean of the College of Arts and Sciences of the University of Hawaiʻi at Hilo came calling. The students at UH-Hilo had joined with the community in calling for the development of a Hawaiian Studies B.A. there. The challenge was finding someone with a doctorate to teach in the program and thus give it credence in the academic community. This was a very sensitive issue at the time, as a Native Hawaiian faculty member working on developing the degree in Hilo had just been denied tenure for failing to obtain the Ph.D.

The problems at UH-Hilo seemed to be similar to problems at the Mānoa campus, where we studied. At Mānoa, Hawaiian-language faculty had had little say in the larger language department where Hawaiian was taught. We also felt that the methodology used there of teaching through English further placed Hawaiian in a subordinate position that worked against students really learning it. We told the UH-Hilo dean of our disenchantment with the denial of tenure to the Hawaiian studies professor in Hilo and of our belief that if UH-Hilo developed a Hawaiian studies program, it should have its own department and be taught through Hawaiian.

To our surprise, the dean agreed with us on the type of program and administration required to move Hawaiian forward. He encouraged Bill to consider at least coming to Hilo for one year to work on writing up the Hawaiian studies program proposal. Our teacher, Larry Kimura, counseled Bill to talk with the person we considered head of the UH-Hilo Hawaiian program, elder Edith Kekuhikuhipuʻeoneonāaliʻiokohala Kanakaʻole.

Aunty Edith, as she was known, had met Bill before through the ʻAhahui ʻŌlelo Hawaiʻi in Honolulu and in a meeting of the local Hilo Hui Hoʻoulu ʻŌlelo Hawaiʻi Hawaiian-language organization, of which she was president. Bill telephoned her and requested to meet with her at her convenience.

Aunty Edith and Bill met during the 1978 Hilo Merrie Monarch Hula Competitions, in which Kauanoe was dancing. Aunty Edith knew of Kauanoe and brought a bouquet of *lokelau,* the Hawaiian "green rose," for Bill to give to her, a gesture of *aloha.* In the meeting, Bill communicated up front to Aunty Edith that he would not go to Hilo if Aunty Edith thought it would not be a good idea. In addition, he told her that if he went, it would be under the condition that the proposed Hawaiian studies degree be taught through Hawaiian and that it have its own department. Aunty Edith was in agreement on the medium of instruction and administration of the program. She urged Bill to come to Hilo to help. Unknown to Bill at the time was the fact that Aunty Edith had cancer and would die within a year and a half of their meeting.

Bill came to Hilo in 1978 and Kauanoe came in 1979. It took until 1982 for the Hawaiian studies proposal to make it through the board of regents. During that first year, there were twelve majors, the two of us as faculty, and Aunty Edith's daughter Pualani Kanahele, a student of the program, working as a lecturer.

The development of the UH-Hilo Hawaiian studies major was intimately connected to our becoming a Hawaiian-speaking family. From 1979 until the birth of Hulilauākea in 1981, we were both teaching Hawaiian language and culture using Hawaiian as the medium of instruction—a new experience for both of us. It was during this time that we seriously considered what developing a Hawaiian-speaking family from second-language speakers would entail.

Bill had seen European children growing up with their national languages in the home, community, and school. Both of us had also seen children who were speakers of Hawaiian from the tiny community on the highly isolated island Ni‘ihau, where life continued much as it had been experienced by the remaining *kūpuna* generation of elders in Hilo. But what we would be doing was different. The closest thing to second-language speakers raising first-language speakers of Hawaiian were cases we had seen where a child responded in English to a second-language parent's Hawaiian. We wanted to raise our children with Hawaiian clearly being their first and dominant language.

As described earlier, our crucial decision was to speak only Hawaiian with each other. That change in our life allowed us to speak only Hawaiian to our children from the time of their birth. We also benefited from our language students' interest in helping to care for our babies between classes, using only Hawaiian. Hulilau, and then Keli‘i, grew up on campus in an environment where Hawaiian was the language of a growing community of second-language speakers and the elders who taught with us.

Hulilau and Keli'i at home before leaving for school on Lei Day, 1989. Photograph courtesy of Kauanoe Kamanā

Kū Ke Kalo I Ka 'Ohā—A Full Taro Develops When It Has Side Shoots

We always maintained Hawaiian as our own language within our little nuclear family and campus world. Around others, speaking Hawaiian required some tenacity and a readiness to explain our work in Hawaiian language revitalization, but people in Hilo became used to us speaking Hawaiian in local stores and other public places.

In retrospect, being somewhat isolated from our own families helped us maintain Hawaiian, as Hawaiian was not normally used in either of them. We interacted with various members of Kauanoe's extended family through sporadic trips to Honolulu and Moloka'i. In Honolulu, we generally stayed with Kauanoe's aunt— Tūtū Lini to the children. Tūtū Lini, could, and did, speak Hawaiian to the children, although she spoke English with us. Similarly, Kauanoe's father, who became known as Tūtū Kia'ipō, spoke Hawaiian with the children but English with us.

The real challenge was going back to Moloka'i for Ka'ai and Kamanā family events where there were huge droves of children and many younger adults who knew no Hawaiian, all interacting in parties several days long with hundreds of people. Our children were first carried around by older cousins, and then ran with the crowd. The fact that the children spoke Hawaiian was a matter of comment from many, in the form of gentle ribbing, but also of some amazement. People liked to hear the children talk to each other, to us, and to older family members.

The whole situation was a bit embarrassing for Bill, who felt somewhat uncomfortable speaking Hawaiian in the presence of Hawaiians who did not speak the language. It was always obvious in these big events that Kauanoe's family had a strong Hawaiian cultural identity that went beyond Bill's ability to speak Hawaiian. On top of everything was the rapid-fire Pidgin used as the everyday language on Moloka'i Island. Bill's knowledge of Hawaiian conversation styles came from quiet, one-on-one interviews with elders; it took time for him to get used to the informal Hawaiianness of Pidgin. Large groups of people sat in circles joking and teasing. The same person would be referred to by multiple names, and conversations circled through recent events and family history that everyone seemed to know. But after a while, Uncle Pila was part of the mix.

It was also initially somewhat uncomfortable for Kauanoe to be with Bill's highly nuclear-oriented *haole* family. There were just Bill's two parents and his brother and sister. Hulilau was the first grandchild. The Wilson tradition was for the family to be together for Christmas at the Kaua'i home every year. The family sat together at a large table in the dining room—just the immediate family, arranged boy-girl style, all eating the same thing placed in the same way on the same types of plates and engaging in conversation to which all were expected to contribute. This was very different from the Hawaiian style of little clumps of people eating informally, often around shared bowls of *poi* and choosing from a large number of different types of foods in side bowls. Most of the social interaction in Kauanoe's family occurred before and after eating—and generally in same-sex groups. Kauanoe not only adapted but also built strong bonds, beginning with a love of music shared with Bill's parents.

There were no elders in the Wilson family who knew Hawaiian, and so communication was a challenge at first, when the children were small and knew no English. As the children grew, our little side shoot of the Wilsons kept using only Hawaiian among ourselves at Wilson family gatherings, and English with Bill's family, even at Bill's parents' dinner table. Sometimes that would irritate Bill's dad, and we would respectfully explain to Tūtū Pā, as he was known, that we did not mean to offend him, but we and our children kept on using only Hawaiian with each other in front of him and anywhere else we were.

Bill's mother was also concerned that the children speak standard English. As an adolescent, Hulilau used to irritate her by purposefully responding to her in Pidgin when he knew full well how to respond in standard English. In spite of the differences between the two sides of the family, the children grew up very close to both. The large extended Ka'ai and Kamanā side and the nuclear Wilson *haole* side have both always been proud of our family's role in revitalizing Hawaiian.

Pūnana Ka Manu I Haili—The Bird Makes a Nest in Haili of the Hilo District

A distinctive aspect of the Hawaiian language revitalization movement is its interlocking system of indigenous-language medium schooling, the development of which we championed with a core group of Hawaiian language advocates through the 'Aha Pūnana Leo—the Hawaiian Language Nest organization. We believe that this system of schooling is what made it possible for us to maintain Hawaiian as our family language until today, and for the community of Hawaiian users to expand.

We were cofounders of the 'Aha Pūnana Leo in 1983. When it opened its Hilo preschool site in 1985, Hulilau was in its lead class. Keli'i joined within a few months, when she made two. The lead class of the Pūnana Leo O Hilo was then the catalyst for the 1987 opening of the Kula Kaiapuni Hawai'i O Keaukaha, the Hawaiian immersion program on the local Hawaiian Homestead. Keli'i was two years behind with a group of children that assured that the program was not a one-time experiment, but a permanent part of public education in Hawai'i.

We were heavily involved in these programs, not only as parents but also as board members of the 'Aha Pūnana Leo, developers of enabling legislation, writers of curriculum materials, and as the teachers of the second-language speakers who were the teachers. We were political activists who insisted that the education of our children be entirely in Hawaiian and that English be introduced as in Europe—at grade five. And we insisted that English be taught through Hawaiian.

The importance of schooling through Hawaiian had been made clear to us by *kūpuna* who spoke of the effect that closing Hawaiian medium public schools had during the process of the United States annexation of Hawai'i. We had also heard how some older native speakers had tried to speak only Hawaiian with their children at home in the territorial period, only to have the children lose the language after entering English medium schools. We ourselves had seen children of immigrants responding to the parents' ancestral tongue with English.

Kauanoe took leave from our Hawaiian studies program from 1984 to 1986 to develop the statewide Pūnana Leo schools. She used her early childhood training to combat a state ruling that Hawaiian was not covered by policies that allowed private Japanese and Chinese language schools to operate with native-speaker teachers who lacked early childhood credentials. When we succeeded in 1986 in getting the state legislature to pass a law to allow Hawaiian elders as Pūnana Leo teachers and to also remove an 1896 ban on the use of Hawaiian in the public schools, we thought that the system was ready to accommodate Hawaiian-speaking families. However, the state Department of Education did not open Hawaiian medium kindergarten programming for the children matriculating from the Pūnana Leo. Kauanoe therefore became the lead person for the 'Aha Pūnana Leo in developing the Papa Kaiapuni Hawai'i, a "public Hawaiian medium kindergarten" run free of charge at the Pūnana Leo Hilo during the 1986-87 school year as we lobbied the state public education system to live up to the new legislation.

We succeeded in the 1987-88 school year, moving our program into a parent-renovated storage room at Keaukaha Elementary School. Every year we added a new elementary school grade, spending much time helping the teachers and lobbying the public school administration for classroom space. Then Kauanoe took leave again in 1994 to 1997 when we and other parents of the lead sixth, seventh, and eighth grades moved the children into the vacant third floor of a business building in downtown Hilo. Our mission was to open the stand-alone intermediate–high school program promised by the state Board of Education. The state allowed the classes to be an offsite program of Hilo Intermediate School, but the rent was paid by the nonprofit 'Aha Pūnana Leo. Kauanoe was responsible for development of the program. The following year, we moved the children to a site purchased for the 'Aha Pūnana Leo, Inc. by the state Office of Hawaiian Affairs under the leadership of Clayton Hee, a key lawmaker who has been a great champion of the language.

The name decided upon for the downtown site was Ke Kula 'O Nāwahīokalani'ōpu'u, or Nāwahī for short. The name honors Josepa Kaho'oluhi Nāwahīokalani'ōpu'u, who was a nineteenth-century

Hawaiian leader from the Hilo area with connections to many of the families of the school, including Kauanoe's mother's family. In 1997, the state legislature mandated the transformation of our Hawaiian studies department into the state's Hawaiian language college, with Nāwahī as its laboratory school. Kauanoe's position was then integrated into the university as the college's head of the laboratory school program. With Kauanoe as head of Nāwahī, we could assure that it would be run completely in Hawaiian.

We knew that moving through intermediate and high school would be challenging. Adolescence is a time of great change, when young people develop an identity distinct from their parents. It is also a time when, in Hawai'i, distinct interests and talents of students have been traditionally addressed through large public and private intermediate and high school programs. Rather than compete with those programs, Nāwahī would pursue a concentrated college preparatory program for all students, with all students participating in aspects of traditional Hawaiian subsistence agriculture and traditional Hawaiian arts.

It was during adolescence that some children of the other initial families using Hawaiian experienced a switch to English—especially those families who used Hawaiian only part of the time, or who had taken their children out of Hawaiian immersion and placed them in English medium schools to provide them expanded academic, social, and athletic experiences. Within our own nuclear family, however, Hawaiian held strong. The children have never spoken to each other in English, nor have they used English at home with us.

I Mua A Inu I Ka Wai 'Awa'awa—Drinking the Bitter Waters Necessary to Reach Success

Our own family, however, was far from immune from the challenges of adolescence. When Pila volunteered to teach Keli'i's class a social studies course, she refused to respond to him as a teacher and actively promoted children speaking English in the class, to force her father to abandon teaching it. Her tactics did not work. Hulilau also rebelled against the rules of the school. Pila was seriously worried that his rebelliousness would drive off the young teachers and other families. Kauanoe held the line firm and Hulilau complied after a few incidents.

Our school faced challenges from adults as well as from students. One group of parents wanted Nāwahī to use English as the medium of intermediate and high school education. Some of them later split off from the

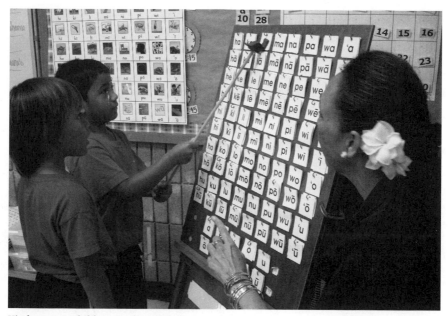

Kindergarten children reading Hakalama Syllabary with Kauanoe. Photograph courtesy of Kauanoe Kamanā

school to start their own English medium Hawaiian culture-based charter school. We were concerned that the loss of students through transfers to other schools would seriously threaten the school's reaching grade twelve. Yet Kauanoe refused to give in, and the remaining families became stronger and stronger linguistically, culturally, and academically.

The challenges at Nāwahī also affected the young college students who were majoring in our program and teaching with Kauanoe at Nāwahī. The use of English by Nāwahī students in the hallways and the challenge of teaching rebellious adolescents were very difficult for the idealistic students coming from our Hawaiian studies program. They were finding it hard to believe that it was possible to raise their own future children in Hawaiian.

From the opening of the Pūnana Leo, over a decade passed with no new young couples deciding to raise their children speaking Hawaiian at home. The tiny handful of older couples like us, either both Hawaiian speakers, or one a speaker and the other a supporter, were scattered throughout the state. As stated earlier, some of these families were actually switching to English in intermediate and high school. Some of these children would come back to Hawaiian after they went to college, but we did not know that at the time.

The final push through high school and into the early years of college for our children was also a period of decline in the growth of the Hawaiian-speaking community, not only among couples but also in enrollments in the statewide Pūnana Leo and Hawaiian immersion systems and in college programs. After the explosive growth when we had moved into preschool and elementary school, there seemed to be a reevaluation throughout Hawai'i of whether it was really possible to speak Hawaiian in the contemporary world. This reevaluation actually resulted in further growth later on when the academic and cultural strengths of our programming became more widely known.

In spite of their rebelliousness, our own children were highly supportive of Hawaiian, as were other Nāwahī students. Nāwahī students have always been very active in sports, playing under Hilo High School. Keli'i was on the girls' volleyball team and she and her Nāwahī schoolmates on the team developed a set of Hawaiian language cheers, which they taught to other teammates and supporters.

In the summer we sent her to Honolulu to stay with Bill's sister Betsy and play club ball. The girls in Honolulu were primarily middle-class students from private schools and spoke standard English rather than Pidgin. One memory of that period that stands out is Bill's leaving Hilo to attend a game and then socializing with the Hawaiian parents of one of Keli'i's teammates. The parents were telling Bill how much they enjoyed Keli'i and what a fine girl she was. They then began to tell Bill about this new development in the Hawaiian community where some parents were actually sending their children to school in Hawaiian. They recounted how terrible this was, and how these children could not speak English, were such academic failures, etc. They nearly fell out of their chairs when Bill told them that Keli'i attended one of those schools and that she spoke only Hawaiian with Bill, Kauanoe, and her brother.

Hulilau's peer group was a group of surfers from Hilo High. One day he parked his car across from the beach, facing the wrong direction. When the policeman—a Hawaiian—came to ticket his car, Hulilau intentionally answered his questions in Hawaiian—a language the officer did not speak. Hulilau was arrested for resisting the officer.

A number of community activists wanted to use Hulilau's arrest "for speaking Hawaiian" to defy "the system." We did not see this as the right venue or approach to move Hawaiian language use forward, and we enlisted the help of a family friend who was a lawyer. The lawyer convinced the judge to let Hulilau off after he expressed regret for taunting the Hawaiian officer. This was the best outcome possible, especially for a boy whose own mother's brother was a policeman.

After high school Keliʻi went directly to college at Loyola Marymount University, where she earned a B.A. in political science. Today she is the Hawaiian culture and language expert for the Hawaiʻi State Tourism Authority, a position that allows her to provide direction relative to the revitalization of Hawaiian culture and language throughout the state. Hulilau took a trip to Tahiti after high school and then enrolled at UH-Hilo, earning a B.S. in agriculture and a B.A. in Hawaiian studies. He established his own construction and landscaping company—Nā Hana ʻĀina. He uses Hawaiian on the job, hiring many of his friends, some of whom were from other schools but got a working knowledge of Hawaiian simply from socializing with him and other Nāwahī boys. Both young people participate in the spread of the social use of Hawaiian, which is supporting its expansion into other fields, including television. Hulilau also serves on the statewide board of the ʻAha Pūnana Leo.

While our own family of Hawaiian speakers is still just the four of us, a number of the graduates of Nāwahī have had children and have enrolled them in Nāwahī. Some of them have also spoken Hawaiian with their children from birth, joining with the increasing numbers of graduates of our college program who are doing the same thing. In the 2009-10 school year, 33 percent of the children from the Pūnana Leo through grade 12 at Nāwahī had one or more parents speaking only Hawaiian with them from birth. Hawaiian is also increasingly the language of interpersonal interaction among Nāwahī students on the playground and outside school, especially among the younger age groups, where first-language speakers are predominant. This is a major change from the beginnings of the program, when English was much more predominant among children.

Hawaiian has definitely grown stronger, yet we still have no neighborhood or community where Hawaiian is the language of the street. That will come someday. We continue to make advances in our efforts and open new *honua*, which is what we call places where Hawaiian is dominant. Through those *honua*, we continue to reclaim long abandoned *paepae*—old stone foundations of the Hawaiian people—to build new Hawaiian-speaking *hale*, or homes.

He Makamae Nā Pōhaku Paepae, He Mana—House Foundation Stones Are Precious, They Contain a Spiritual Power

Many young indigenous people beyond Hawai'i are seeking to learn and strengthen their ancestral languages today. They may be contemplating, as we once contemplated, establishing indigenous-language-speaking homes inhabited by indigenous-language-speaking children.

Throughout the indigenous world there must be many old home sites marked by stones, be they rectangular platforms as in Hawai'i, or ovals, circles, or squares—some multistoried on cliffs, others partially dug into the ground. Near those old home sites there must remain—also long neglected like those house stones—precious words, distinctive ways of expressing thoughts, meaning-filled stories, powerful songs. May those indigenous language foundations be reclaimed. May they be built upon again. May the world once again ring with the beautiful sounds of children speaking our many distinctive and precious indigenous languages. May they ring in homes of many and diverse kinds. *E ola nā hale 'ōlelo 'ōiwi o kākou!*—Let there be life for those indigenous-language homes for our families to inhabit!

He Mau Mana'o No Ka Hānai 'Ia 'Ana
na Keli'ihoalani Nāwāhine'elua Kamanā Wilson

Ua hānai 'ia māua 'o ko'u kaikunāne, 'o Hulilau, ma ka 'olelo Hawai'i wale nō ma ko mākou home ma Ka'ūmana ma ka mokupuni 'o Hawai'i. Ua komo pū māua i ke kula 'ōlelo Hawai'i mai ka Pūnana Leo a hiki aku i ka puka 'ana ma ka papa 'umikūmālua ma ke Kula 'O Nāwahīokalani-'ōpu'u. I ka puka ana o'u mai ke kula ki'eki'e, holo akula wau i ka 'āina haole ma Kaleponi e komo ai i ke kulanui 'ōlelo haole 'o Loyola Marymount kahi i pa'a ai ia'u ka mēkia Kālai'āina me ka maina pālua ma ka Mō'aukala a me ke Kālaimana'o. Ua komo ko'u kaikunāne i ke Kulanui O Hawai'i Ma Hilo a puka akula me ka mēkia pālua ma ka Mahi'ai a me ka Ha'awina Hawai'i. I kēia wā, 'o wau ka Lunaho'okele Kuleana Mo'omeheu no ke Ke'ena Maka'ala 'Oihana Ho'omāka'ika'i no ka Moku'āina 'O Hawai'i. He pā'oihana kūkulu hale nō ho'i kā ko'u kaikunāne e kālele ana ma ke kūkulu me ke kuana'ike Hawai'i.

Ua 'ike māua i ko māua wā 'ōpiopio no ka 'oko'a o ka hānai 'ia 'ana o māua mai ko nā keiki 'ē a'e. Hānai 'ia ma ka honua 'ōlelo Hawai'i wale nō, ma ka hale a ma ke kula pū kekahi. 'Akahi a 'ike 'ia i kēia wā 'ānō, ma hope ho'i o nā makahiki lō'ihi, ka loa'a pū o nā 'ohana i like

me ko māua. Ua pi'i ka nui o nā 'ohana 'ōlelo Hawai'i mai ko māua wā
'ōpiopio a he hō'ailona kēlā o ka holomua o ke aukahi 'ōlelo Hawai'i
a no ka mea ke pa'a ka 'ōlelo Hawai'i 'o ia ka 'ōlelo o ka home, ola ka
'ōlelo makuahine. Ola nō ma kahi e pa'a mau ai ka mauli Hawai'i mai
ka wa kahiko, ma ka 'ohana nō ho'i. Me kēia e holomua mau ai kā
mākou hana ma Hawai'i nei, a ma nā ke'ehina li'ili'i e lanakila ai. Pēlā
ka mana'o o māua 'o Hulilau e ho'oholomua hou aku ai i kēia hana a ka
'ohana, ma ka hānai 'ana ho'i i kā māua mau keiki o kēia mua aku ma
ia 'ano ho'okahi.

Thoughts on Our Upbringing
Keli'ihoalani Nāwāhine'elua Kamanā Wilson

My brother, Hulilau, and I were raised speaking only Hawaiian in our
home in Ka'ūmana on the island of Hawai'i. We also attended Hawaiian-
language medium schools, from the Pūnana Leo Preschool through
graduating from Nāwahīokalani'ōpu'u School in the twelfth grade. After
graduation I decided to venture out to California. I attended an English
medium college at Loyola Marymount University, where I graduated
with a major in political science and a double minor in history and philosophy. My brother attended the University of Hawai'i at Hilo, where
he graduated with a double major in agriculture and Hawaiian studies.
Today I serve as the director of cultural affairs for the State of Hawai'i
Tourism Authority, while my brother runs his own construction business specializing in building with a Native Hawaiian perspective.

We were well aware, growing up, of the difference between our
upbringing and that of our peers. We were raised in a Hawaiian-
language world, completely immersed in the home and in school. We
are now beginning to notice, after many years, that there are families
similar to ours existing today. The number of families speaking Hawaiian in the home has grown and this is an encouraging sign that the
Hawaiian language revitalization movement continues to move in a positive direction. When Hawaiian is the language of the home, our mother
tongue lives on. As we know, when it exists in the family, the very core
unit from the time of our ancestors, it lives and is carried through the
generations. This is how we will assure that our language lives on, and
Hulilau and I plan to contribute to this as we have our own families in
the future and raise our children in the same way.

8: Anishinaabemowin

LANGUAGE, FAMILY, AND COMMUNITY

Margaret Noori

*Mii o'ow gidinwewininaan. Mii ow minwewebagaasing miinawaa
sa go gaye minweweyaandagaasing. Mii ow memadweyaashkaagin
zaaga'iganiin miinawaa sa go gaye bineshiinyag nagamotaadiwaad
megwayaak. Mii ow enitaagoziwaad ma'iinganag waawoonowaad,
naawewidamowaad. Mii ow gidinwewininaan wendinigeyang
bimaadiziwin, gikenindizoyang anishinaabewiyang,
gidinwewininaan gechitwaawendaagwak gaa-ina'oonigooyang
gimanidoominaan.*

This is our language (yours and mine). It is the pleasant
sound of the leaves blowing in the wind and the whisper of
the wind in the pines. It is the sound of the waves lapping
the shores of the lakes and the birds singing to one another
in the forest. This is the sound of the wolves howling to one
another, sounding in the distance. This is our language, from
whence we obtain life, which enables us to know who we
are as Indian people, our language, this sacred gift bestowed
upon us by our creator.

—adapted by Waagosh (Anton Treuer) from the words of
Maajiigwaneyaash (Gordon Jourdain)

Ode'iminan—Heart Berries

Say *"ode'imin"* to my daughters and they will think immediately of the little red heart-shaped fruit, a friend from the lodge with that name, the legend of love adrift, and women's ceremonies. This is not because a language class taught them the word *"ode'imnan"* in Anishinaabemowin literally means "heart berries" and is used to represent the fruit "strawberries." This is also not because at home we say and write the phrases *ode'imnan n'gii giishpinaadoonan miijimidawegamigong* (we buy them at the grocery store), *ode'imnan mijinaanan endaayaang* (we eat them at home), *Fionna aapchigwa ode'imnan bishigendaanan* (Fionna really likes them), or *Shannon ode'imnan gaawiin bishigendsiinanan* (Shannon doesn't like them). They know the word because it is a name called out while playing along the lakeshore and whispered during a feast. They have pulled tiny wild berries from beneath the leaves just like the long-ago *aadisookwe* (story woman) who found them and was reminded of her true love. They have washed them and carried them to the fire circle in a wooden bowl beneath the full moon. They will remember the word *"ode'imin"* as a taste, a time, a place and a person because families working to save languages do not exist in solitude and children do not grow and learn in isolation. I may have experience as a teacher. I may have spent hours singing, reading, and speaking in the language, but the true transfer from one generation to the next occurs when students become daughters, nieces, grandchildren, best friends, and young women on their own choosing to use, or not use, a fragile ancient language.

The American Indian Movement of the 1970s cleared space for reclamation of indigenous languages in the United States and Canada. The Native Languages Act of 1991 mandated that attention be paid to the problem of dying or, in many cases, already extinct languages. Language programs and publications began to appear and many received funding, but there is still much debate about what really works, and most languages continue to decline. One point on which everyone agrees is that a language must be used at home to truly survive as part of a community. Some questions related to that truth remain to be explored. What is home? Who is family? What tools and topics work best? How can a language that takes hold in the safety of a home, much like the children themselves, venture out into the wider world and be welcomed and find support and acceptance? There is a need for both orality and literacy beyond the walls of comfort and shelter. Parents and children working hard to save endangered languages need to hear the words of their people in culturally supportive classrooms, at friendly local businesses, around the drum, and in the digital space created by computers and cell phones. Anishinaabemowin has reached a point where it is not possible to raise a monolingual child. A decline in speakers, combined with the arrested development of the vocabulary during the last century, has led to the use of English in even the most committed and proficient households. The question is, how can we support the existing efforts of families working together to revitalize the language? As Leanne Hinton reminded us in her overview of language revitalization, "successful language revitalization programs have a number of key characteristics, among them persistence, sustainability, and honesty with oneself."[1] The following essay addresses the ways we can extend the definition of family, focus our discussions on culturally relevant subjects, incorporate language into our most important ceremonies, find help in external communities, and use the new tools technology provides to be persistent with our language efforts.

Ingitizimag—Family

Along with "*ode'imin,*" another word my children have lived is "*nikane.*" This is one of those larger-than-the-dictionary words used differently by different speakers. Anishinaabe children in the Great Lakes area hear it is as the refrain used in the lodge, while the rattles are settling at the end of a prayer, when friends and relatives dance out of the circle back into the world. In ceremonial settings it is the one word to know if you know no other. Elders offer a variety of translations for "*nikane,*" some pointing to the verb "*nigane,*" which means "to lead," but most leading back to the word for "cousin," or "relative." Just as this is considered a highly significant word, the concept of family is critical when discussing the process of restoring an endangered language in a family setting. The term "family" needs to be intimate enough to include those who gave a child life and broaden to include all those who provide love, safety, and nourishment—all the aunties, uncles, friends, and other good grown-ups who become part-parents and pseudo-siblings over the years. Family is made, and family is chosen, and families change. Family includes single-parent households, multigenerational households, foster homes, and homes in transition. Everyone in a community working to save language, not just the equation of two parents and one or more children, should believe they can learn and use the language. When children understand their language to be a part of who they are, then all those

Margaret Noori with daughters Fionna and Shannon. Photograph courtesy of Margaret Noori

who support and protect those children should be part of the effort to preserve and practice the language.

Statistics show that American Indian and Alaskan Native children have the highest death rate of any group of young people, the highest percentage of teens not in school, the highest percentage of children living in families where no parent has year-round employment, and the second highest percentage of children in poverty.[2] It is clear that language revitalization can easily be marginalized by these pressing social inequalities. Yet despite problems, poverty, and different models of parenting, most native homes are loving homes. And some of them are places where destroying boundaries between the majority language and a heritage language is important daily work. Consider the example of my own home and the home of my friend Amy McCoy. We are both full-time teachers of Anishinaabemowin. I teach college students at the University of Michigan. Amy teaches at a Bay Mills Ojibwe Tribal High School. We both have two children and run our households alone. I am always amazed at the similarities when I visit her. Mountainous linguistic data is stored carefully in stacks along the edges of nearly every room. Toys, clothes, and backpacks overwhelm the living space. Walls, refrigerators, doors, and mirrors have been taken over by verb charts, vocabulary lists, and kid art with Anishinaabemowin subtitles. Kids are not surprised by out-of-town elders who won't speak English, and bedtime often includes one of the growing number of bilingual or Anishinaabemowin-only picture books. Amy's kids are featured in two of the books we read, *Odaminodaa Iskigamiziganing* and *Ozhiitaadaa Dab-waa-izhaayang Waadoododaading.*[3] The language is audibly and physically a true part of the household.

What can be improved is the way the children and visitors view the language. When the learning is continual and includes everyone who crosses the threshold, the children can pick up the passion for the language and move from being students of something sacred to also being teachers of a practical skill. Every kid who visits needs to learn and use a little Anishinaabemowin. We don't hesitate to teach nonnative friends the language, and we don't save Anishinaabemowin for when people leave. We welcome everyone into the family. Adults are encouraged to use Anishinaabemowin if they know it, and asked to try saying a few words if they don't. This practice of counting friends as family and allowing the community to define connections can be extraordinarily empowering for kids. It is important to keep the habits of language use close to the heart, but it is also important to bring everyone who is part of the family circle into the project. Otherwise the language becomes a barrier between the home and the "real world," and using the language becomes a burden that divides relatives and friends.

This also teaches us to go out and find the language in the family beyond the four walls where we sleep. Children often find older relatives or community members who have more time than their parents and who may remember the language or even be interested in practicing and learning it themselves. Jim Northrup is an example of a speaker who uses the language with his grandchildren and many of the other children in his large extended family. Sometimes he is simply practicing numbers with a grandson on the way to the school. At other times, he is championing and organizing the first, and then second annual language camp held on the Kiwenz Campgrounds. In the passage below from Jim's book *Anishinaabe Syndicated: A View from the Rez,* he tells the story of snaring rabbits, first in Anishinaabemowin, then in English[4]:

Enda-ninawind megweyaakong wiiji gwiiwizens biigiigaazo
gizikanend. Wayeshkwad gisinaa. Wendaniikaadad! Michaa
gisinaa. Ninawind okosidoo biizik aanish inange. Imaa goonikaa.
Noozishe ginoozi minose megwayaakong nano-bizogeshin apape.
Niinawind babimose wendad. Nidaamisaaband ginandagikend

ginitaa bimose zhaabaayi'ii zazaagaa miinawaa goonong megwekob.
Ni mikwend nibabimose aazhawayii'ii eshkaa nimishoomis
inawemaagan izhichigaade miikana niminochige. Ni mino giziigad
izhichigaade miikana ninoozhishe.

Just being in the woods with the little boy brought back memories. First, of course, was the cold. It was ten below zero with
a wind chill of fifty below. We were layered up for the cold,
so no problem. Then there was the snow. My grandson is tall
enough now to walk in the woods without tripping all the time.
It makes it easier. I could see he was learning how to walk
through the brush and snow. I remembered walking behind as
grandpa or some older relative broke trail for me. I felt good to
be breaking trail for my grandson.

Although the story is one of winter trails and wind chill, the real trail
Jim is breaking is one that shows a young speaker how to bring the
language back by walking with his family—following and defining the
trail.

Another positive example of families extending toward the language
is the process of a young adult bringing the language home. I have had
this happen at least once or twice every year as I teach in the university setting. A student who did not have the opportunity to learn as a
child uses the adult skills of literacy and linguistics to gain proficiency
in the classroom and then leaps beyond the page into the lives of loved
ones. Christy Bieber completed Anishinaabemowin courses and went on
to create an interactive lesson about the *tiginaagan* (cradleboard).[5] She
worked with Howard Kimewon and me to write and record phrases to
be used by Judy Pamp and other members of the Saginaw Chippewa
Tribe at the 15th Annual Family Language and Culture Camp hosted
by the Little River Band of Odawa. Her project bridged dialects and
communities and brought several families together, including my children, Judy's foster sons, and Christy's mom, who like Christy is a member of the Sault Tribe of Chippewa. The phrases and her voice can be
heard on the *Noongwa e-Anishinaabemjig* website and are now part of
the second-year curriculum on campus.[6] Her work became a model for
connections between the university and families. We realized that a
vision of connections between academia and native communities is just
a vision. To make it reality, real people and projects came together as

friends and family. The subsequent year, Elise McGowan and Michelle Saboo completed projects that were also presented at a conference and then posted on the website. Elise and her mother worked to train their puppy in Anishinaabemowin and Michelle taught her younger sisters to make corn husk dolls and translated *Zhaawskwa Waawanon miinawaa Gookosh Wiiyaas* (*Green Eggs and Ham*) by Dr. Seuss. These students also taught us it is never too late to foster the language in a home. Change is constant. None of these young women had mothers who were able to learn the language. Their daughters brought it back to them. None of these young women were able to take the language as a course in high school, but they found it at a large public university. Their sisters and nieces in northern Michigan are now attending high schools that offer Anishinaabemowin. As one era of the language ends, another is beginning.

Dibaajimowinid—What to Talk About

In this new era of creating bilingual speakers whose central support has its roots in a broadly defined family, it is important to think carefully about the steps taken to reach proficiency. Children and adults know the aim of language learning is to understand and use the language, but too often their only model for educational success and evaluation is the one offered by the dominant majority. Parents and children alike have a tendency to strive for perfection, create hierarchies of skill, and fixate on the vast distance between the present mortality and the future vibrance they desire for the language. This can be devastating for revitalization. When a language that should be a source of sovereign pride becomes a tool for measuring inadequacy and a source of emotional stress, children and adults will tune out and stop trying. In an immersion setting with little time for reflection, students are often faced with either understanding and knowing how to respond—or not having a clue what to say. In my experience, students of all ages need to be encouraged in immersion environments to play and make mistakes; and in the bilingual classroom students should use both languages to ask questions about what they are hearing and trying to say.

In their book *Supporting Indigenous Children's Development*, Jessica Ball and Alan Pence explain how they worked with the Meadow Lake Tribe in Canada to find new ways to think about the ways native students learn today.[7] This was not an ethnographic adventure in recreating the ways they might have once learned in close-knit oral communities prior to colonization. This was an effort to look at the ways children whose languages are endangered, and whose culture has long been marginalized, might think about their language and identity. The Generative Curriculum Model they developed is based on this partnership and leads to very effective learning. Their discussion of the collapse of objective knowledge and the subsequent shift away from various European theories is not one that most language teachers have time to explore. But at the core of their model is the belief that "the terms 'expert' and 'professional' must be problematized and their modernist roots exposed and reconstructed in collaboration with those impacted by experts' practice—children, families and communities." In short, learning a language should not mimic the dominant model, but should instead be generated by the needs of the learners.

For instance, I can insist that my kids know and use the term Kchimookimankiinag (Land of the Long Knives) for America, but my bilingual children need to be given space to talk about the history of that term and why they would prefer not to say it to their American friends. I have never learned terms for "racism," "politically correct," or "socially conscious" in Anishinaabemowin. We can speak of the ideals of *minaadendamowin* (respect) and *dibaadendizowin* (humility), but to truly counteract and deconstruct this basic term rooted in political violence and misunderstanding, we need to ask the speakers of the future what terms and ideas they need to learn. What words are needed to make sense of this place and time? Making space for these and other discussions about the process and practice of learning is important. So often, parents and children are simply told to use and learn the language as much as possible. I strongly recommend that even informal groups and families make time to talk about what is happening in a constructive and, as Ball and Pence would suggest, generative way. Simply asking learners, "What else do you need to know?" can result in a partnership of learning that leads to two-way engagement. Even the littlest learners have ideas about what works and what doesn't, or ideas for stories they'd like to tell and words they'd like to learn. One recent example in our home was a shape game created by my daughters because I had simply never taken time to teach them geometric words. We cooked, we cleaned, we got ready for school, we came home and stayed quite busy, much of which we could, if pressed, describe in

Anishinaabemowin, but we had never taken time to learn one of the concepts that belonged only to the realm of school. The outcome was a wonderful lesson in etymology and description as we worked with Howard Kimewon and Francis Fox, realizing that, of course, the words *"giiwaajiwaayaa"* (oval) and *"giiwaajikaakadeyaa"* (rectangle) are literally composed of a morpheme for "elongated" added to the words for "circle" and "square."

How and what is taught is inevitably connected to formal learning in school. In the best of all worlds, education specialists would create curriculum capable of bridging the gap between home and classroom, but so often, the task of building literacy and writing and distributing materials falls to the teachers in schools who carve out time from teaching to write and record as much as possible. Many communities are working to compensate first-language speakers for their work creating curriculum, and some lessons have been learned about how to build successful models of cooperation.

One of the first areas to consider, after agreeing on the place and value of literacy, is orthography. In many communities much of the learning is still oral, and that is fine, but in places where writing has been used effectively, basic agreement on conventions has been hugely helpful. The two dominant forms of orthography used to write in Anishinaabemowin are syllabics and the Fiero double vowel system. Both have taken hold and there is regional agreement in the north to use syllabics while in the south most teachers use the double vowel system. This has resulted in more publications to support learning. Although it is true that a first language is acquired prior to literacy and structural knowledge is not needed to begin speaking, I have found that one of the best ways to support bilingual speakers is to strive for equality in format and function. This does not mean texts need translations, nor does it mean that English and Anishinaabemowin should be considered the same. It does, however, mean there is value in leaving a visible trace of the language in a world dominated by English. Students and teachers both gain knowledge of the language and learn ways of working together by recording and transcribing an elder's story, working with an artist to depict a verb, or taking photos to be part of a book about the sugar camp. I have often been asked to defend my heavy use of writing in instruction, to which I respond, "When my daughter asked me how to spell *g'zaagi'in* (I love you) was when I felt I had to focus on spelling." Additionally, I have tried to listen to the students and speakers of the future who frequently tell me they learn more quickly and can form their own sentences sooner when they can see on the page the way our complex language is constructed.

One successful elementary program that incorporates literacy is the Wikwemikong Heritage Organization (WHO). Located on the Wikwemikong Unceded Indian Reserve on Manitoulin Island in northern Ontario, Canada, WHO represents the "unique and holistic Anishinaabe perspective of the Ojibwe, Odawa, and Potawatomi people." Their objectives, stated below, blend language and culture:

1. To maintain and provide opportunities to sustain the Anishinaabe language.
2. To improve artistic opportunities for Anishinaabeg who are emerging and the accomplished artists in professional attainment.
3. To engage in collaborative efforts with other cultural and historical based initiatives.
4. To promote and research the original Anishinaabe philosophy and belief systems

Together an incredibly talented group of storytellers, teachers, actors, and artists form the Anishinaabemowin Curriculum Development Project Committee. Their publications range from illustrated picture books to DVDs and theater productions. Some of their resources are used at both the elementary and college level in Michigan because the cultural content is relevant for all age levels. To cite only a few examples, at the University of Michigan we have used the *Wenaaboozhoo* book and audio CD published entirely in Anishnaabemowin without any translation.[8] We have also used *Aanhsokaanhensan: Short Stories for Each Season*[9] and *Wikwemikong Odenang miinwaa Nokaming D'nakiiwanhsan Mikziibiing geyii: Kitchi mewzha Anishinaabe Bimaadziwin* (*Wikwemikong Village and Surrounding Area: Our History*).[10] Both of the latter books include translations on each page and language-learning activities at the back of the book. Most importantly, they have been created by and for Anishinaabe people. The historical perspective is ancient. When the narrator asks, "*Gwiya na giikendan minik nso biboon Anishinaabeg gaa bi igo danokiiwaad?*" (Does anyone know how long the Anishinaabeg have lived here?), the answer is not based on primary documents searchable in current libraries of the world. The answer is "*midaatchingshimdaaswaak nso biboon*" (ten thousand years) because that is what the

storytellers say. And interestingly, research conducted recently at the
University of Michigan proves that indeed, remnants of caribou runs
under Lake Huron indicate that those storytellers have been right all
along.[11]

Highly relevant lessons are critical for success in language
revitalization. Although we may wish to avoid the issues, when asked,
a class of high school students' at Bay Mills wanted to translate a song
about sanitariums and death. Not one to shy away from any request
that would lead to her students' use of the language, their teacher,
Amy McCoy, sent the English lyrics to the teaching team in Ann Arbor.
Together, Howard Kimewon, Alphonse Pitawankwat, and I translated
the song "Welcome Home" written by the heavy metal band Metallica
in 1986. At first, we merely wanted to challenge a kid who had yet to
connect with the language, but as we worked through the lyrics we
found phrases with chilling connections to the problems faced by native
youth today. In a world where the Indian "vanished" at the start of
the century, where poverty and suicide are common and the education
system still excludes the worldview of indigenous people in the present,
the following lines ring too true: *biindigeg maampii gii boontaasegoba
ga zhwebgeba* (welcome to where time stands still); *gaawiin wiika
aanjinaagozisii pane gwa mooshkineaapkizi* (the moon is full, never seems
to change); *gibaakwaaigaazoyaanh mii maampii maanda waakaaiganing*
(they keep me locked up in this cage); and *nd'zegiz wii geyabi
bimaadiziyaanh* (I fear living on). And when Howard and Alphonse, two
residential school survivors, came to the line "the natives are getting
restless now" it was a priceless lesson to realize the only possible
translation is "*Anishinaabeg bgooshkaajizheyaawag.*" Anishinaabemowin
has no means of framing indigenous people as "the other." Such terms
as "Indians," "natives," "indigenous," and "aboriginal" are necessarily
self-referential, which turns a phrase intended to invoke fear upside
down. What might "the natives are restless" mean to a teen who has
been kicked out of public school and is not planning to go to college,
perhaps not even to graduate from high school?

In and around these difficult moments, where the past confronts the
future, we work to save a people, an identity, a sense that the moon
never changes, and a language that can describe all that has happened
and will happen.

Manidooke miinwaa Jingtamok—Ceremony and Celebration

On a less somber note, there are an increasing number of ceremonies that are starting to include Anishinaabemowin again. The chain of cultural practice was frayed but not broken. With the American Indian Religious Freedom Act of 1978, communities began practicing traditions more openly, although it was not until the 1994 amendments that all aspects of religious practice were finally considered legal. Exercising these rights, many of the families want the language to be woven into the fabric of the family in a permanent way. Naming ceremonies are once again conducted in part or in full in Anishinaabemowin and there is a trend for names to be more complex and verb-based. Many forty-year-olds named in the 1980s have simple animal or weather names, while names given today often have multiple morphemes and describe an event or talent. This doesn't always hold true and there is certainly no difference in quality, but from a linguistic standpoint it is worth noting that complexity is returning. At one time names were Baginagiizhig (Hole in the Day), Nakwegiizhig (Noonday), Siginak (Blackbird), or Chibineshi (Great Bird). Now, even when the name is a single animal, it is likely to be more specific, for instance Dindisii (Blue Jay) instead of just Bineshi (Bird). And two young girls were recently named Nitanimikwe (Good Dancer) and Nitamazinbiigekwe (Fine Writer), which sounds much more like Jane Johnston Schoolcraft's name from the 1800s, Obabaamwewegiizhigokwe, (Sound of Movement through the Sky).

Song is often a part of naming and other ceremonies and, like the names themselves, has increased in complexity. There have always been a number of "big drums," the all-male groups that sing at powwows, with native names and lyrics. It is interesting to note that a quick scan of the drum group list on powwows.com (where all powwow planners network and organize) shows that most groups with names in indigenous languages are from the northern Great Lakes area, the High Plains, or the Southwest. This corroborates the rate of language loss and pace of colonization on the coasts of this continent. In a recent essay for the literary magazine *Black Magnolias,* I discussed the way Anishinaabe songs have begun to use a more complex poetic structure through use of the Anishinaabemowin.[12] Students are working with teachers to revive not only the vocabulary, but also the indigenous patterns of sound and meaning. In some cases, entire metaphors are changed to move away from a structure based on nouns in favor of one based on verbs and relationships.

A good example of how this works to revitalize comprehension occurred recently when the women's hand drum group in Ann Arbor was asked to perform their version of the American Indian Movement song. The lyrics include the line "We must speak Anishinaabemowin if we wish to live well." What became obvious quickly is that a decision needs to be made about the audience each time the song is sung. If the audience is predominantly nonnative, the line should be *"aabdeg Anishinaabemoyaang ji-minobimaadiziyaang."* If the audience is predominantly native, the line should be *"aabdeg Anishinaabemoying ji-minobimaadiziying."* There is no difference in the English translation, but in Anishinaabemowin the difference is the *"ying"* and *"yang"* of an inclusive or exclusive reference. When the singers want to tell an audience they view as family or community to use the language along with them, they conjugate the line to reflect that sense of "we" as "all of us here." When the singers want to tell an audience they do not expect to speak Anishinaabe that the language is their connection to health and well-being, they conjugate the line to mean "us" as in "just those of us singing, not those of you listening." Recently, when the song was sung at a local restaurant a few of the singers noted that they thought of the staff as part of the community and only the guests as outsiders. When I was asked to sing the same song at a funeral on Walpole Island during the summer of 2009, I knew that the inclusive form included all those listening above and below and in every direction. Understanding these points of difference and rendering them recognizable is an important part of revitalization. We need to acknowledge and practice the language of celebration and sorrow as we learn a language, so that when a family or community experiences its greatest joy and deepest sadness, the words and sounds are familiar, not foreign.

Naadamajig Oodenang—Community Helpers

Another way to support families saving languages is to problematize the notion of what is foreign. When communities that once were foreign see indigenous traditions as American, the result is a more productive diversity, along with more support for the language. Native families often have to explain the value of their language which now sounds "foreign" in America. Yet so many states, counties, and towns have

Back row, left to right: Howard Kimewon (Margaret Noori's teaching partner); Shayla Pawlicki (age 4) and her mom, Jasmine Pawlicki, "who lived with us last year and had many 'Anishnaabe-only' meals"; Margaret Noori and daughters Shannon/ Nitaamazinbiigekwe (14) and Fionna/Nitaamiimikwesens (9). Front row: on the left is Marsha and in the middle is Diindisi McGowan, a friend and former student. Photograph courtesy of Margaret Noori

native names. In the case of Anishinaabemowin, several words have been accepted as proper English: "toboggan," "moccasin," "moose," "totem," etc. The name of the state of Michigan and one of the Great Lakes comes from the term "inland sea" (*m'chigaaming*), but it also sounds very much like the name of the University of Michigan's mascot, a "wolverine" (*miishkaan*). I have yet to meet a Michigan sports fan or alumnus not delighted by this fact. Several nonnative friends who teach science say they offer students an example of how language impacts understanding by referencing the concept of Chigaaming, a single name for the entire water system known in English by five proper nouns: Huron, Ontario, Michigan, Erie, and Superior.

When nonnative communities begin to understand and share the significance of native languages, the task of revitalization suddenly has many more supporters. We live in a world of exchange and rapid change. If we expect our language to continue in sovereign space, it needs to become connected to the other worlds in which we work and play. Certainly, our languages belong first and foremost in the homes and community centers of native nations, but when they are acknowledged and appreciated beyond these walls, the walls begin to disappear.

One recent example of support in Anishinaabe country was the Pangea Theater production of a play by Heid Erdrich which features Anishinaabe dialogue and songs. *Curiosities: A Play in Two Centuries* is based on the life of Maungwudaus, who traveled with the artist George Catlin in Europe in the nineteenth century. In 1848 Maungwudaus self-published his observations of Europe in a book titled *An Account of the Chippewa Indians Who Have Been Traveling among the Whites in the United States, England, Ireland, Scotland, France and Belgium.* While the majority of the play is in English, several songs are sung in Ojibwe, and at one point the main character translates for his wife and fellow travelers the proclamations of their British host. Yet when their host says, "You will find that settled and industrious habits are preferable to a roaming and uncertain kind of life," Maungwudaus says, *"Gii kido gego nametwaakeg,"* which translates more directly as "He wants us to live in one place forever." For the native playwright, cast members and their families, use of the language and a new view of the 1800s were a refreshing change from the old Hiawatha pageants in which Anishinaabe culture was written by men who had never lived in the woods.

Another example of native and nonnative communities supporting language use is the current work done by Noongwa e-Anishinaabemjig and Zingerman's Community of Businesses in Ann Arbor. An unusually progressive and creative business, Zingerman's states in their Guiding Principles that their chosen responsibility is to "strengthen the health, social, educational, and cultural fabric of this community." What is amazing is that they really do. For the past several years in fall, their Native Harvest dinner has honored the tradition of a fall feast in a way that is indigenous to the area. They encourage Anishinaabe cooks to return to healthy and organic old ways of hunting, harvesting, and preparing food, and they give native and nonnative members of the broad urban community a reason to use Anishinaabemowin. In preparation for last year's dinner, the chef, Alex Young, and one of the company's founders, Ari Weinzweig, visited Bkejwanong Reserve to practice cleaning, breading, and frying fish Anishinaabe-style. The entire trip was documented and became an interactive lesson online. For this year's dinner, Howard Kimewon harvested his own crop of corn, ground it in a traditional *botaagan,* and then went to work alongside Alex to make ash-cured hominy soup. Again, the entire process was recorded, and many old words were put back in use, as duck meat ran with clear juices (*zhishiibwiiyaasmideabo*) and bacon (*gokosh wiiyaas*) was added to really wild wild rice (*manoomin*). In addition to Howard's contribution, Zingerman's invited Anishinaabe author basket maker, and traditional ricer Jim Northrup to share stories about the rice he harvests, parches, winnows, and cleans each year. Every guest at the restaurant went home with copies of two of his poems in Anishinaabemowin, and staff wore shirts that said they serve "*aapchigwa minopogwad Chi-mookimanakiing miijim*" (really good American food). Their contribution to the community may appear to be focused on one event per year, but in truth, their commitment is year-round. My daughters and I can visit the Zingerman's Roadhouse any day of the year and be greeted with "*aanii*" (hello), and when we order *maakademaashkiikiiabo* (coffee) or *bakwezhigan* (bread), the staff understands. This kind of subtle, consistent support has a profound and lasting effect on the children, who are proud to share what they know with adults outside their immediate family. Connecting communities in this way gives positive energy to both enterprises, the language revitalization group and the diverse Zingerman's staff. I would strongly encourage language revitalization leaders in other areas to consider casting a wider net when looking for support. Sometimes help is found when and where you least expect it.

Oshkiwiigwaasbiigewinan—New Bark to Write On

The last subject of this essay is simultaneously the easiest and most difficult to adequately address. Using new technology can be as simple as recruiting your six-year-old to help log on to the Internet or as complex as finding a good information architect and web designer who knows Anishinaabemowin. The myriad manifestations of electronic learning and networking are so much a part of life now that not leveraging them to save languages is nothing short of foolish. And yet, as anyone who has ever engaged in social networking knows, much foolishness has been unleashed in the arena of technology. Before there was Facebook, "speech communities" were discussed by linguists as "those people who communicate with one another or are connected to one another by chains of speakers who communicate with one another."[13] Now that we work on a wireless Web connected by servers and clouds, the speed between those connections is much shorter and the distance between them much greater. The sociolinguistic implications are nearly mind-numbing, but perhaps the linguists of early days had the same thoughts when Gutenberg got going in the 1450s, just a few decades before Columbus set sail. Politics and possibility have always influenced languages.

Anishinaabemowin is the heritage language of over two hundred reserves and reservations in Canada and the United States. In many of these communities elders work with teachers and students to keep the language alive. The potential for debate over differences has proven to be as seemingly infinite as some of the verb declensions. But the potential for finding commonality and creating a venue for contemporary use is equally great. In fact, these are the three main reasons to engage technology: to understand the language and its speakers more fully, to create and share data, and to continue moving forward.

The University of Michigan website *Noongwa e-Anishinaabemjig* went live in June of 2007. Since that time it has had over thirty-five thousand visitors. A very political discussion of the repatriation of human remains has had the most visits, followed by a page supporting University of Michigan sports and the story of the Zingerman's fish dinner. All of these stories were presented as language lessons accessible to anyone, with enough notes for beginners to enjoy them, but enough complexity for fluent speakers to find them satisfying as well. Because the site is linked to a Facebook page, 2,964 images of fans offer a visual record of who cares about the language. The site also uses Twitter to announce new posting and places video clips on YouTube. In short, anything your average teen is doing to stay connected, we are trying to do too. We have never done a survey to see if more women than men use the site, or to find the age of the average user. Judging from the Facebook profiles, gender distribution is even. Fans are mostly in Ontario, Michigan, Wisconsin, and Minnesota. And the average age is over twenty-five, but much younger than the average age of our last generation of first speakers, whose ages are fifty-five and up. The site has interactive lessons, many with digital audio and flash cards, but students and teachers have to move to the Facebook page to enter their own comments.

We used to worry about the clash of dialects and spelling we saw on the page, but we then realized that any use was better than none, and we have archived every comment posted. This means we not only have a record of changes in the orthography and grammar of individuals, but we also have a record of the range of dialects readers are able to understand. The postings offer real-time verification that more words are universal than unique and that even across Ojibwe, Odawa, and Potawatomi communities, people can understand one another. Based on observations on the site and at various language conferences that include a similar range of speakers, the primary predictor of success in communication is the level of fluency. This should of course come as no surprise, but for many years, funding and curriculum decisions have been made by listeners and learners who, while serious and eager, were not proficient speakers. Their skill level caused them to identify more words they did not know than cognates and similarities in grammar. Highly proficient speakers move with ease in and out of conversations that cross numerous dialect lines. In some cases, they pause to clarify, or offer their own contrasting terms, but in every case that we have recorded, fluent speakers of Anishinaabemowin are able to understand Ojibwe, Odawa, and Potawatomi.

Certainly there are accents, idioms, and colloquial terms that are very regional. In fact on most reservations there are words used by only one generation, gender, or family. This is true as well for English. Our belief is that if these nuances are to be preserved, students have to become proficient enough to work around them and recognize them as options, not barriers. I certainly want to always hear Barb, Martina, Bev, Pat, and Gertie say "*aaniindinaa*" when I walk into their kitchens, but I soon realized these sisters had their own way of turning that word that not even their husbands and children could duplicate. To find the time, Howard asks, "*Wenesh epichaak?*" while his own sister Marjorie asks, "*Wenesh nsa dibaganek?*" And further west, Jim Northrup asks, "*Aaniin endaso dibaaganeg?*" Sometimes, when Jim is sassy, he asks, "*Aanish minik tick tick?*" which is literally "How many ticks (on the clock)." My girls, by now, recognize all of these common variations and I have seen several of these varying interrogatives, patterns of dropped vowels, and creative recombinations on the site. If technology can help prepare my family and students for the diversity they'll inevitably encounter at the next gathering, powwow, or language conference, then it is worth the investment in time.

Besides rendering the structure and variation visible, technology allows linguistic data to be preserved. The sheer amount of vocabulary that can be exchanged and later accessed is immense. Early uses of technology were more formal and required programmers to spend years or months gathering and then inputting words and phrases. Now, Stacie Sheldon, our web designer, and I have a system for collecting what linguists would call metadata and data quite efficiently. Often before I am done texting or emailing her the transcription of an interview or conversation, she has taken pictures and recorded the names and biographies of contributors. While some of our work has been complex, many of the lessons are simply a matter of gathering what students want to see and hear in order to learn and practice. In my opinion, the most powerful lessons are those that can be easily completed. Students can become contributors and all the fluent speakers who connect with our community are invited to share stories and conversation. This allows students to hear a wide range of speakers and often hear conversation, something that can be lacking in a classroom of learners with only one proficient instructor.

The final asset is publication and dissemination. Since we began using the site in 2007, we have been able to post and share (with permission, of course) the contributions of over fifty-eight individuals, and this number is always growing. While it is sad to know that a few of these speakers have walked on and others are no longer able to speak clearly, it is satisfying to know that we have saved their contributions to revitalization. The words that mean the most to us are of course "learned by heart," but the heart has incredible capacity, and what I am convinced one year I'll never remember I find myself using in casual conversation the following year. By saving the work of our elders and making space for the work of our students we create an online community that challenges all of us to keep learning. There was a time when I had read every word in my first year Ojibwe notebook a hundred times and I had nowhere to go for more until class began again the next week, next camp, or next semester. Now, as I post poems that some elders must think as strange as Shakespeare might consider e e cummings, I at least know that I come close more often than I miss and that they mostly understand. When one of us decides to write a roundance or translate some blues, hip hop, or hymns, we can share it with friends immediately so that they can learn and laugh at home with their families, or take the songs out into their communities to share as evidence that we are still here and still singing.

As with many of the topics discussed so far, this is only one viewpoint, skewed perhaps by the perspective of an urban, second-language learner trying to teach and parent in tangled times. In my opinion, teachers need to listen and learn from students, and follow them to the places where they learn and play, which is deep in the woods of technology today.

Noongwa nd'nisdotaanmi—What We Know Today

I remember reading Leanne Hinton's poem "To the Lonely Hearts Language Club" in the early 1990s. It spoke so eloquently of the struggle against time and silence, and the need to connect the work of linguists to the stories of elders. It ended with a "ceremony of resurrection" which seemed so serious and extreme to me at the time, a young doctoral student with no children and too much hope.[14] I attended language tables, even wrote a poem, "*Anishinaabemowin Dopwin, N' Bazigeminaa,* to the Language Table, Our Sweetheart," speaking about the table where we studied as if it were alive, because it brought us together, made us a family of learners.[15] The poem was right, "all our prayers and dreams gather there," but what I didn't know then was that some dreams are bad and some prayers are desperate. Now, when young students and teachers ask me what they need to start learning the language at home, or start a language table in their community, I know what they want is help with curriculum; they want to know where to find speakers and stories and words to put on the page and into their own hearts. What I tell them is, "Mind the silence." There is silence that can help and silence that can hurt. Take time between the sounds and struggle to gauge which kind of silence is present.

Jon Reyhner, a leader in the stabilization of indigenous languages, has written, "There are many ways that people can argue about how languages should be revitalized. Any of these arguments can damage language revitalization efforts."[16] Ultimately, saving a language that is endangered as a result of racism is in fact a battle with racism itself. Families and communities can come together or disassemble as a result of making a commitment to face and change racism. Not everyone can see past it, or break its invisible bonds. Some groups or individuals internalize the anger and paranoia of racism to the point that it becomes their way of life, and just as the world has tried to tear native language and culture apart, they begin to tear those around them down with negative comments, silencing attitudes, and needless comparison or gossip. Although revitalization is already an interdisciplinary combination of ethnography, educational theory, linguistics, literature, and history, successful families and communities find ways to be healthy as they work to revitalize a language. They find elders willing to cooperate, social workers and psychologists to help with planning and negotiation. Build a fire of positive energy that cannot be quenched. Because there will be days when personal lives don't stop at the door, when tears of frustration erupt, when self-doubt creeps in and hope tries to escape. Be ready for this. In a very recent exchange over email, an elder in our community wrote, "I love you all." Who writes "I love you all" on a listserve? In our community it was Sandy Momper. This is something only the bravest and most sincere keepers of our fires will do. They are perhaps the one ingredient without which we simply cannot succeed, so find your sparks of energy, feed them, love them back, and keep them close.

Mii sa I'iw—Conclusion

This essay began with a quote from Gordan Jourdain which spoke of Anishinaabemowin as something shared between people, families, and communities. He describes it as the sound first of the water and trees, then the animals who share the land. In his description it is at first distant, but then becomes the giver of life. The circle he draws around language is beautiful, complex, and reflective of an Anishinaabe way of thinking. In the original language the morpheme for language itself, "*enwewe,*" flows through the passage as parts and pieces are added to more clearly define its relationship to the people. He concludes by saying, "*Mii ow gidinwewininaan wendinigeyang bimaadiziwin, gikenindizoyang anishinaabewiyang, gidinwewininaan gechitwaawendaagwak gaa-ina'oonigooyang gimanidoominaan*" (This is our language, from whence we obtain life, which enables us to know who we are as Indian people, our language, this sacred gift bestowed upon us by our creator). And thus he explains why individuals who wish to understand the ways in which they connect with all their relations would pursue and protect a language that reflects their identity. He reminds us it is a gift, one that once learned cannot be stolen, ruined, or returned, but the trick lies in the task of accepting that gift. *Nd'bagosendam naadamawinegwa nsostawegwa, noongwa e-Anishinaabemjig—wiinwaa eta gikendasowaad aanii waa ezhiwebag waabang.* I hope that I have helped readers understand those who are speaking Anishinaabemowin today—only they know what the future holds.

Notes

1. Leanne Hinton and Ken Hale, eds., *The Green Book of Language Revitalization in Practice* (San Diego: Academic Press, 2001).
2. Annie E. Casey Foundation, *2010 Kids Count Data Book: State Profiles of Child Well-Being* (Baltimore: Annie E. Casey Foundation, 2010). Available at http://datacenter. kidscount.org/DataBook/2010/OnlineBooks/2010DataBook.pdf.
3. Miskwaanakwadookwe (Amy) McCoy and Maajigwaneyaash Jourdain, *Odaminodaa Iskigamiziganing!* (Hayward, WI: Waadookodaading Enokiijig, 2008), and Miskwaanakwadookwe (Amy) McCoy and Maajigwaneyaash Jourdain, *Ozhiitaadaa Dabwaa-izhaayang Waadoododaading!* Hayward, WI: Waadookodaading Enokiijig, 2008).
4. Jim Northrup, *Anishinaabe Syndicated: A View from the Rez* (St. Paul: Minnesota Historical Society Press, 2010).
5. Christy Bieber, "Tiginaagan," *Noongwa e-Anishinaabemjig,* http://www.umich. edu/~ojibwe/community/tiginaagan.html, 2008.
6. The *Noongwa-e Anishinaabemjig* website is at http://www.umich.edu/~ojibwe/.
7. Jessica Ball and Alan Pence, *Supporting Indigenous Children's Development: Community University Partnerships* (Vancouver: Univ. of British Columbia Press, 2006).
8. Wikwemikong Heritage Organization (WHO), *Wenaaboozhoo* (Wikwemikong, Ontario: Wikwemikong Heritage Organization, 2007).
9. WHO, *Aanhsokaanhensan: Short Stories for Each Season* (Wikwemikong, Ontario: Wikwemikong Heritage Organization, 2007).
10. WHO, *Wikwemikong Odenang miinwaa Nokaming D'nakiiwanhsan Mikziibiing geyii: Kitchi mewzha Anishinaabe Bimaadziwin* (*Wikwemikong Village and Surrounding Area: Our History*) (Wikwemikong, Ontario: Wikwemikong Heritage Organization, 2006).
11. John O'Shea and Guy A. Meadows, "Evidence for Early Hunters beneath the Great Lakes," *PNAS* 106, no. 25.
12. Margaret Noori, "*Ezhi-Anishinaabebiige Noongwa:* Tradition in Contemporary Anishinaabe Texts," *Black Magnolias,* special 2011 issue (Winter 2010-11).
13. George W. Grace, "Regularity of Change in What?" in *The Comparative Method Reviewed: Regularity and Irregularity in Language Change,* ed. Mark Durie and Malcolm D. Ross (New York: Oxford Univ. Press, 1996), 157–179.
14. Leanne Hinton, *Flutes of Fire: Essays on California Indian Languages* (Berkeley: Heyday, 1994).
15. Margaret Noori, "Anishinaabemowin Dopwin, N' Bazigeminaa, to the Language Table, Our Sweetheart," in the chapter "Wooden Heart, Dopwin, Language Table" by Heid Erdrich, in *Sovereign Bones: New Native American Writing,* ed. Eric Gansworth (New York: Nation Books, 2007).
16. Jon Allen Reyhner, *Education and Language Restoration* (Philadephia: Chelsea House, 2006).

Additional References

Brian Edward Brown, *Religion, Law, and the Land: Native Americans and the Judicial Interpretations of Sacred Land* (Westport, CT: Greenwood Press, 1999).
N. Bruce Duthu, *American Indians and the Law* (New York: Penguin, 2008).

Samina Hadi-Tabassum, *Language, Space and Power: A Critical Look at Bilingual Education* (Toronto: Multilingual Matters, 2006).

Mari C. Jones and Ishtla Singh, *Exploring Language Change* (New York: Routledge, 2005).

Adrian Kelly, *Compulsory Irish: Language and Education in Ireland 1870s–1970s* (Dublin: Irish Academic Press, 2002).

Marie-Noelle Lamy and Regine Hampel, *Online Communication in Language Learning and Teaching* (New York: Palgrave Macmillan, 2007).

Steven McDonough, *Applied Linguistics in Language Education* (New York: Oxford Univ. Press, 2002).

Robert Miles, *Racism* (London: Routledge, 1989).

Noongwa e-Anishinaabemjig, "Name Zaagiganing Huron Chizhaazhagwa: Under Lake Huron Long Ago," http://www.umich.edu/~ojibwe/lessons/semester-three/huron/ (2011).

Paul Prucha, *The Great Father: The United States Government and the American Indians,* vol. 2 (Lincoln: Univ. of Nebraska Press, 1984).

Arnulfo G. Ramirez, *Creating Contexts for Second Language Acquisition: Theory and Methods* (New York: Longman Publishers, 1995).

Christopher Vacsey, *Handbook of American Indian Religious Freedom* (New York: Crossroad Press, 1991).

9: Irish

BELFAST'S NEO-GAELTACHT

Aodán Mac Póilin

In 1975, myself and my wife, Áine Andrews, decided to build a house
in a small Irish-speaking community in our hometown of Belfast, Northern Ireland. Both of us had learned Irish as a second language, and both
of us had connections with the language through our families. Áine's
father and two of her mother's brothers had learned Irish to a high standard. My father's father had learned Irish in the 1890s and, although
he never learned to speak it fluently, briefly taught it at night classes (a
not unknown phenomenon in the early years of the language revival).
The woman he married had been raised in an area in the west of Ireland from which the language had just been lost. Both her parents were
native speakers, and her grandmother had only broken English, but my
grandmother could not speak Irish. My father never fulfilled his lifetime
ambition of becoming a fluent speaker, but my mother had attended
an Irish medium school in the south of Ireland. Her own father was a
native speaker, but her family discovered this only recently, more than
half a century after his death. Over four generations, every generation
in my family had either a native or a revivalist speaker who did not
pass the language on, through the family, to the next generation. This is
how languages die.

We wanted to break this pattern; in fact, to reverse it. We knew of
families in Belfast who, with varying degrees of success, had brought up
families with Irish, and we knew of other families who had tried, but
failed, to do so. To be honest, we were not convinced that we would

have the strength of character to succeed ourselves. But there was an alternative. A group of married couples, most of them a decade or more older than us, had already set up a community of Irish speakers, and we knew some of them. By joining this community, we would not have to face the difficulties of trying to bring up children in isolation, and we would also be able to benefit from their experience. The community also had land available, and, having built their own houses, had the know-how to guide us in building our new home. To put it another way, they had already done most of the hard work. What was daunting was not knowing how the community worked: was it like a commune, or a kibbutz, or was it just a group of people who had chosen to live in close proximity? It was also daunting to discover that while Áine and I could talk about literature and history and politics in Irish, our new house was going to be full of everyday objects like plugs and sockets and doorknobs and skirting boards for which we did not have the terms, and none of our language courses had taught us how to speak to babies.

We still live in the community, and we brought up our daughter, Aoife, with Irish as her first language. She survived the experience without any major trauma beyond a mild period of teenage rebellion when she would speak to us only in English—how else could you rebel against parents who are language activists?—unless she wanted something, which gave us a bit of leverage. She never really turned against the language, as we had seen in some other families. This was as much as we had dared to hope for—we decided early on not to pressurise her into becoming a language activist. This may have been a clever move, for, in fact, Aoife also lives in the community, teaches in an Irish medium school, and is bringing up her two sons with Irish as their first language.

Involvement in the community enabled us to succeed far beyond our expectations. Not only did we pass the language on to the next generation, but we enabled our daughter to pass it on to our grandchildren. The community enabled us to succeed, as a family, to live a significant part of our lives in a language that could have died out completely sometime over the last century. Whether the example of the community indicates a new direction for the Irish language movement is a more difficult question to answer.

In this chapter I will be giving an account of the community in which I live. Much of this account is secondhand, for when the first meeting about the community took place I was twelve years of age, and when the first houses were being built I was still at school. Although I have lived here for thirty-five years, and have spent most of those years actively involved in the language movement, I will try to be as objective as I possibly can. My community is a social experiment that may or may not transfer to other societies. If this account is to be of any use to anybody considering a similar venture, it must be seen, firstly, within its particular social (and political) context, and secondly, it has to be treated as an experiment, and its strengths and weaknesses analysed as coldly and clearly as possible.

The cluster of houses we live in is on the outskirts of the city, and is known to our English-speaking neighbours as "the Irish houses." It had its origins in 1961 when a group of families came together to develop a community in which their children would be brought up speaking Irish as their first language. The first houses were completed in 1969. In the early years the community, revealingly, described itself as a *cóilíneacht*—a colony—and called itself *Pobal Feirste*, *"pobal"* meaning "community" and *"feirste"* deriving from the Irish language version of the name Belfast. It is usually referred to as the Shaw's Road *Gaeltacht*. In this chapter, I will be using both *Pobal Feirste* and the term *Gaeltacht.*

The word *Gaeltacht*, which originally meant something like "Gaeldom," has now become what could be described as a geo-linguistic term. It usually refers to those scattered areas—mainly in the west of Ireland—where the thread of linguistic continuity has never been broken, where the language has been passed on from one generation to the next for thousands of years. These survival language communities, all situated in rural settings, are quite small and increasingly fragile: probably fewer than thirty thousand people in the historic Gaeltacht use the language on a daily basis. (In the mid-nineteenth century there were more than three million native speakers of Irish.) The geographic sense of the term was actually a borrowing from Scottish Gaelic, a close relation of Irish. The Scottish Gaelic term *Gàidhealtachd*, however, refers to the geographical entity of the Highlands of Scotland, once Gaelic-speaking, but where the language survives now only in isolated pockets: paradoxically, it does not apply to the Western Isles, where the language is strongest.

However, if we accept that a Gaeltacht is a geographical entity in which Irish Gaelic is the language of a significant proportion of its inhabitants, then the two acres in Shaw's Road is undoubtedly a

Gaeltacht. However, it is significantly different to the historic Gael-tachts in that it was created, deliberately, by learners of the language, and is situated in Belfast, an urban setting which has been overwhelmingly English-speaking for more than four hundred years.

There are not many neo-Gaeltachts in Ireland. Twentieth-century Ireland has had a remarkable record in developing an unusual pattern of language maintenance, a pattern of intergenerational transmission that involves generation after generation transmitting Irish to the following generation as a second language, mainly through the education system.[1] To date, this process has been remarkably successful, if knowledge of the language is your yardstick. Census returns in the Republic of Ireland (where Irish is designated as the first official language) show that perhaps one and a half million people—the vast majority of them learners—have at least a reasonable competence in the language. Only a small minority of these people use Irish to any significant degree in their daily lives. Where the society has failed, spectacularly, is in promoting intergenerational transmission within the family. While there are a number of isolated families who raise their children with Irish as their first language, the society has failed even more spectacularly to create new, organic language communities outside the historic Gaeltacht areas.

There have been other attempts to establish neo-Gaeltachts. In the 1930s the Irish government gave farms in the rich lands in the east of the country to groups of native speakers of Irish from the beautiful, if unproductive, western Gaeltacht areas. The most successful of these was Rathcarn, forty miles from Dublin.

These state-sponsored efforts to transplant traditional Gaeltacht communities to anglicised parts of Ireland were an exclusively rural phenomenon, but there have also been Irish-speaking communities in Irish cities in the past. We know that the language had a considerable presence in most of the major cities in Ireland during the eighteenth and nineteenth centuries. This is not surprising, as more than half the population of Ireland in 1800 spoke Irish. Even Belfast, in the anglicised, industrialised northeast, had clusters of Irish speakers in the nineteenth century. However, except possibly for the Claddagh district in Galway City, which survived into the twentieth century, these could be described primarily as secondary language communities, consisting primarily of incomers from Irish-speaking areas. These linguistic communities tended not to renew themselves, and generally lasted no more than one or two generations unless they were revitalised by new waves of Irish-speaking incomers. Inevitably, they declined with the decline of the language in the historic Gaeltacht.

The Shaw's Road Gaeltacht was not the first attempt to create an urban neo-Gaeltacht, although it is by far the largest and is generally acknowledged to have been the most successful. As early as 1924, shortly after the establishment of the new independent state in the south of Ireland, a housing society was formed in Dublin whose purpose was "to establish and maintain a community of Irish speakers" in the capital city.[2] By 1927 the group had been leased two acres of land in the northern outskirts of the city by Dublin Corporation. The following year they had built ten houses. This could have formed the nucleus of a significant linguistic community, as there were a further twenty-nine acres on the site which could have been developed as a significant urban Gaeltacht. Unfortunately, the group did not have sufficient funds to build the necessary access road into the development. Although one of the central aims of the new state was the revival of the Irish language, the authorities gave it no support, even though the group had been under the impression that the entire site "would be utilized solely for the erection by the Nua-Ghaedhaltacht [Neo-Gaeltacht] Society of houses for occupation by Irish speakers."[3] The remainder of the site was developed by other rather better organised housing societies, who built 250 additional houses. Little else is now known of the experiment, but the community, soon enveloped in an English-speaking environment, did not survive, and all that remains of this attempt is that the estate is known as *Páirc na Gaeltachta*—Gaeltacht Park.

The failure of the Dublin scheme was partly due to a lack of understanding by the authorities of the dynamics of language revitalisation. This is not surprising; the new independent government of the southern Irish state had, in the 1920s, no precedents for their attempt to restore a language that had been in retreat for hundreds of years and that was now the native language of only a narrow segment of the population. The main focus of the state-sponsored language revival at that time was, firstly, increasing knowledge of the language through the education system (Irish was made a compulsory subject), and secondly, using the language, along with English, in the state system. It appears to have been assumed that widespread knowledge of the language would automatically be followed by widespread use. We have learned, to our cost, that it is by no means as simple as that, and that a much more sophisticated approach, involving the development of linguistic communities, and, in particular, intergenerational transmission through the family, is the most effective way of maintaining a threatened language.

It is possible that there were other factors which militated against the development of the Dublin community. The pioneering sociolinguist Colm Ó hUallacháin told me in 1974 that his father had been invited to join this community in the 1920s. Although the elder Mr Ó hUallacháin and his wife were then raising their family with Irish, his response was that it was bad enough to meet Irish language activists at conferences and meetings and festivals without having to live beside them. Such a response—while a surprising one from a committed language revivalist—is not unique in the Irish context. When schemes such as this are proposed, which happens every so often, a common reaction is for people to respond that they would be happy to live in such a community, but not if X is going to live there. The identity of X varies from time to time and from place to place, but the man in question—it is always a man—belongs to a recognisable type; he is prominent in the language movement, has a strong, prickly personality, and is noted for his dedication to the language, but is suspected by other language activists to be slightly unbalanced and to suffer from either a Napoleonic or a messianic complex. In spite of this, in various parts of Ireland, small groups of Irish-speaking families have chosen to live in close proximity. Except for one small group outside Cork City, they tend to do so quietly and without drawing attention to themselves. One of their reasons for doing so is to avoid the possibility of living within an ass's roar of X.

Little is known of the Dublin experiment, which leaves behind it a number of unanswered questions: How long did it survive as a linguistic community? What impact, if any, did it have on the wider community? What language did the children speak among themselves? What kind of education did they have?

While the experiment itself seems to have been forgotten, the ideal behind it never was. The theme of an urban Gaeltacht emerged again in the second half of the century. During the sixties, for example, the writer Máirtín Ó Cadhain argued for the creation of city communities which would have all the characteristics of modernity—at least what passed for modernity in Ireland in the sixties:

> You could have in the Galltacht [English-speaking areas]...real
> Gaelic communities, juvenile delinquency, Beatles, shebeens

[illegal drinking dens] and all. There must be one big community in Dublin. It is a challenge. Are we worthy to take it up? If
we had flourishing communities such as I say throughout Ireland, and specially in the big urban areas, the Gaeltacht itself—
the historical Gaeltacht—would no longer be anything except
one other Irish-speaking community.[4]

Ó Cadhain, an important literary figure as well as a language activist,
was one of those people around whom an entire folklore has gathered.
Among the many anecdotes about him is that he himself was invited to
join an Irish language community in Dublin, but when he discovered
that a certain individual (X) was also intending to become a member,
he refused. The community never got off the ground. There is a whole
list of possible contenders for the identity of X.

Pobal Feirste, the Shaw's Road Gaeltacht

The establishment of Pobal Feirste, like other twentieth-century
attempts to build new Irish-speaking urban communities, was a conscious act of language revival. In a circular written in the early sixties,
the proposed new community was contextualised as a kind of vanguard
to a radical re-Gaelicisation of Ireland, one that would involve the linguistic reconquest of Ireland by the historic Gaeltacht: "We believed
that if the real Gaeltacht [*an Ghaeltacht cheart*] was to expand, Irish
speakers in the Galltacht [English-speaking areas] had to strengthen
themselves as a unit so that the preparatory work could be done to
facilitate that expansion."[5] This model of language revival envisaged
a reversal of the centuries-long process by which Ireland had originally been anglicised, where nodes of anglicisation gradually expanded
to embrace the entire island except for remote, isolated communities.
While the historic Gaeltacht already provided such potential nodes of
expansion, this approach did not involve the expansion of the historic
Gaeltacht field by stony field, but the establishment of linguistic nodes
in the major centres of population. By 1982 it was realised that establishing language communities in anglophone areas was central to the
language movement: "Unless Irish-speaking communities are founded
in the Galltacht [English-speaking areas], Irish will not survive, never
mind be revived."[6] They also argued that a community had a better chance of having an impact on the state system than individuals or
scattered families: "Without such a community we cannot demand our

rights as citizens: for local authorities or government cannot provide for people who are scattered among those who have other requirements."[7]

As well as reviving Irish in the broader society, the community also aimed to revive the language within the family structure—what came to be known as intergenerational transmission. One additional reason for coming together as a community was to make that task easier. On 14 November 1965, the *Sunday Press* newspaper published an article about the community's plans, including their intention of setting up an Irish medium school:

> At the moment there are thirty-six Irish-speaking families in Belfast but the school would be open to anyone who wants to send their children along....The idea for the school and houses originated four years ago. At that time there were only seven Irish-speaking families in the city, and most of us had just got married. We came to the conclusion that one of the difficulties of bringing up a family through Irish was that we lived in different parts of the city. The idea of living together in one community emerged.[8]

Around 1973, the community issued a bilingual pamphlet which gives an insight into the early history of the project and the community's view of itself:

> A group of newly-married couples were bringing their children up with Irish in Belfast in the early sixties. Most of them knew each other and they had opportunities to share their ideas and experiences.
>
> They also could learn from the experiences of the generations which had gone before them, a half-dozen or so Belfast families who had been Irish-speaking for twenty-some years....The young couples decided, in order that their children would not be raised in isolation, as had happened to other Irish-speaking families in Belfast and Dublin and in other parts of the country, that it would be a logical, natural step to live beside each other.
>
> At one stage there were nineteen families who favoured this idea, but for all that, when a piece of land had been bought on Shaw's Road on the edge of Andersonstown there were only five

families remaining. During 1968/9, with borrowed money, the land was bought and five houses built. Two years later, another three families came forward and built houses on the site.[9]

At the time of writing (September 2011), there are twenty-two houses in the community, with a third generation growing up, most of them grandchildren of the generation which founded Pobal Feirste. There is not space here to deal in detail with the history of the community, but, as it would never have existed without the extraordinary achievements of its founders, it may be useful to provide some analysis of the founding generation—those who built their homes between 1969 and 1975—and of the society from which they came.

There were ten families in this group, and nine houses (one family left to go to the Donegal Gaeltacht around 1974). The houses were built in three stages. The first group of five families moved into their houses in the spring of 1969, a few short months before the community tensions within Northern Ireland erupted into civic violence, followed by a thirty-year low-intensity war that saw the deaths of more than three thousand people. Three more homes were built within the next couple of years, and then a single house was built in the mid-seventies. All adult members of the community had learned Irish as a second language. They were all Catholics, were all from Belfast, and most of them lived in West Belfast. (For those not familiar with the Irish situation, the island, originally a colony of England, was absorbed into the United Kingdom of Great Britain and Ireland in 1800. Most of the country broke away in 1921-22, but Northern Ireland, an area with a Protestant majority and a significant, disaffected Catholic minority, remained in the United Kingdom.) West Belfast is a rather atypical society, which I have tried to describe in an earlier publication:

> After partition, consistent hostility from successive unionist governments in Northern Ireland towards its Catholic minority, which in Belfast sometimes took the form of orchestrated pogroms, drove that community back in on itself. The extraordinarily cohesive society that developed as a reaction to institutionalised discrimination was to have a major effect on the development of the language....Two factors were at work here; ideological nationalism, sharpened by the compulsion to resist

a hostile state, and the communalist dynamic of the Catholic community. Catholic communalism was itself reinforced on an institutional basis by segregated education and on a social basis by the fact that much of Belfast is divided into exclusively Catholic and Protestant areas. Some of these ghettoes are the size of a small city: the main Catholic area in West Belfast currently has a population larger than that of Derry [i.e., more than 100,000 people].

The survival of Irish in the city was tenuous enough for a long time, but the unusual if unappetising social structure of Belfast actually worked to the advantage of the language movement…. The socio-linguistic and political circumstances in which Irish has survived in Belfast are distinctive; a small organic Irish-speaking community within an urban network of language learners within a large disaffected Catholic/nationalist minority with a high birth-rate in a Protestant/unionist city in an unstable Protestant/ unionist state within a Catholic/nationalist island.[10]

Because of this unusual situation, the Irish language in West Belfast has what a sociologist might call a high level of emblematic cultural capital; it is often referred to as "our language" by people who do not speak it. Some of the status of the language rubs off on speakers of the language—as a kind of lay priesthood they can be accorded the respect due to those who live the dream, but sometimes mixed with a certain level of ambivalence involving negative memories of particular teachers or natural suspicion of the zealot. However, it should be added that Pobal Feirste relied to a very large extent on the goodwill of the broader community, and that its school, which will be discussed below, would never have survived without the active support and generosity of the people of West Belfast.

The traits of cohesion and group loyalty described above as Catholic communalism are even more pronounced among Irish speakers, and the founders of Pobal Feirste belonged to an even tighter social grouping, a factor which may have contributed to the success of the project. All ten couples were associated with a club called Cumann Chluain Ard, an organisation noted for its radicalism on language issues. Indeed, many of them had first met there. Not only did they belong to the same social circle, they largely belonged to the same generation—most having been born in the period between the mid-thirties and the mid-forties. Many of them were related—in fact, seven of the families had a brother or a sister in the group, and there was one group of three siblings.

Most of them also had a similar socioeconomic background. Gabrielle Maguire in her book *Our Own Language: An Irish Initiative* notes that "The founder members of the Shaw's Road Community were mainly working class people," a statement which reflects the community's self-image.[11] This is a reasonably accurate statement, and, in the early days, would be supported by any socioeconomic breakdown of the jobs held by the menfolk. Only one man would be classed among the professional middle class; typical job descriptions would be carpenter, bus driver, mechanic, sheet-metal worker.

However, it was rather more complicated than that. Interest in and commitment to educational achievement were relatively high within the group (this was a common characteristic within working-class Catholic Belfast, where education was commonly seen as the main path to economic advancement). There was also a tendency for the womenfolk to have higher levels of academic achievement than the men: two of them were qualified teachers and another had a university degree. Many of them, both men and women, sought academic qualifications after they had come to live on Shaw's Road. Three men and three women studied for university degrees as adults, and some went on to get postgraduate qualifications. Their work profile also changed, and not only for those who had pursued higher education. A socioeconomic profile of the first generation in the 1990s would have placed more than half the parents firmly in the professional or business middle class: teachers, an accountant, a translator, newspaper editors, managers, a lecturer in a third level college.

This indicates that the founders of Pobal Feirste were an unusual group of people. They were, in fact, both social and economic entrepreneurs. Not only did they manage to create a small estate of houses with few resources, and not only did they create a minority language community within a linguistic community that speaks English, the most overwhelmingly powerful language in the western world, but a high proportion of them showed ability, through either business or education, to advance their own economic circumstances. This small group of people also managed to have a major impact on the society around them, as we shall see.

The next generation: Shaw's Road children with friends. Photograph by Fiontánn Ó Mealláin, courtesy of Aodán Mac Póilin

Perhaps the greatest challenge facing the families in the early years was in creating a linguistic environment in which the children spoke Irish as a matter of course. They had no exemplars to follow, and this issue was a cause of great concern. Some of the families already had young children, and had experience of bringing up children in Irish in isolation. Because of this, they were highly aware of just how powerful the general linguistic environment can be, and were aware that, while Irish would be the language of the home and of communication between the parents and between parents and children, there was a good chance that English would become the default language of communication between the children on the street. Even if they could manage to create a linguistic bubble in which Irish was the dominant social language, there would be no lack of English in the wider society, from relatives, from English speakers in the wider neighbourhood, from friends, in shops, on the television—everywhere, perhaps, except in the two acres of land belonging to Pobal Feirste. It was also understood that in social situations in which bilinguals are in contact with monoglots, the language of the monoglots will tend to dominate even when the monoglots are in a minority. It was also understood that children are not ideologues, that they will understand the real social dynamic around them, respond instinctively to that environment, and will automatically adjust to the linguistic patterns around them. It was assumed that it would take only a couple of English-speaking children in frequent contact with the Shaw's Road children to have a significant impact on the children's language patterns.

In this respect, the situation of the houses was particularly fortunate. When the first houses were built, Shaw's Road was situated on the edge of the city—a rather ragged edge, as the city was expanding well beyond Shaw's Road, but this expansion was uneven, leaving large tracts of undeveloped greenfield sites. Behind and below the houses were large fields. Above them were a row of houses, rural labourer's cottages from an earlier era, inhabited by older people who had no children living with them. Facing the houses was a large, well-established estate of hundreds of homes and thousands of children, but between Pobal Feirste and this estate was a busy main road. In the early years there were enough young children among the various families to form a cohesive social group. While they were small, and too young to cross the road by themselves, there was an opportunity to develop Pobal Feirste as a small linguistic island, and the parents took advantage of this temporary isolation. They organized events among the children to strengthen the linguistic environment, to create a sense of cohesion, and to develop Irish as the default language among them. Children from a number of other Irish-speaking families in Belfast were included in these activities.

More research is required on the dynamics of language use within communities in which bilingual speakers of a fragile minority language are in contact with monoglot speakers of a powerful one. In the absence of such, we depend largely on personal experience and anecdotal evidence. The following account is based primarily on my own experience when myself and my wife came to live on Shaw's Road in 1976. By this time, as I have noted, most of the most difficult work had already been done by the pioneering generation.

Patterns of language use among the children were already well established when we joined. There were about thirty children, mostly below ten years of age, and they formed a coherent group, with rather less stratification by age than would be found across the road. Irish was the language they used among themselves, although all children were

fully fluent in English by the time they were four or five. If monoglot English-speaking children from the estate across the road joined
them, as they occasionally did, they spoke English to them, and sometimes among themselves while these children were present, but invari-
ably switched back to Irish when the English speakers were not present.
When our own daughter was born in 1977, the children in Pobal Feirste
spoke only Irish to her. For us the most valuable and most amazing feature of the Shaw's Road Gaeltacht was that it enabled us to bring up
our daughter in a linguistic environment which, while it had been created by an act of will, and could be criticised by detractors as an artificial creation, was, for her, completely natural. The great achievement of
the founders of Pobal Feirste was to prove that a small group of determined people could create such an environment. (It should perhaps be
added that this environment was reinforced by the Irish speakers in our
own immediate families.)

No community remains static, and there have been major changes to
the language environment surrounding the next generation of children.
However, before we discuss these changes, I would like to turn to the
issue of education, as it is in this area that the wider world was most
likely to impact on patterns of language use. Indeed it was in this area
that Pobal Feirste was to have its most significant impact on the wider
society.

As has been noted above, the community was already planning for
an Irish medium school in 1965. They had identified education as a
key issue, one that could change the community's linguistic dynamic
completely. Education in Northern Ireland was an exclusively English
medium system, so a couple of bilingual children in a class of monoglot English speakers, or a handful of bilingual children scattered over a
number of classes, would inevitably speak English with their peers. This
itself would not be a problem, but there was a distinct danger that they
would also begin to speak English among themselves. English medium
education could, and almost certainly would, affect the children's use of
Irish as a default language among themselves.

By 1971, two children in the community had reached school age and
had already begun to attend English medium schools. However, in that
year there was a concentration of children at or approaching school
age; seven children in the community itself and two from other Irish-
speaking families. The community decided to set up their own school.
Two years previously, hundreds of families had been burned out of

their homes in Belfast, and many of them had been provided with temporary accommodation in prefabricated chalets. As the families were rehoused, these chalets were beginning to become available, so the community bought one, dismantled it, and then re-erected it on the site behind the houses—over a weekend, according to the folklore. The school opened on 1 September 1971.

Their first teacher was a native speaker from the Donegal Gaeltacht who had recently retired, the second was a young Belfast woman who had been raised as an Irish speaker, and then the classes were taught for a number of years by qualified teachers from within the community itself. Until 1979, all but one of the children were from Irish-speaking families, and numbers gradually rose from the original nine children to just over thirty.

There were two further developments, in 1978. A number of children had reached secondary school age, which itself introduced another challenge. Their parents set up a secondary school for the five or so older pupils. Heroically, they managed to keep it going for two years, but the challenge of trying to involve a range of specialist teachers—all teaching on a voluntary basis—for such a small number of children proved too much and the school ceased to operate. Two of the families continued to provide Irish medium education for their children by enrolling them in a school in Dublin, one hundred miles away. Their fathers each spent half a week in Dublin looking after the children after school.

The second development was to have a more lasting impact. Although the community was concerned to maintain the language as a living presence, which involves a certain level of protection of its linguistic ethos, Pobal Feirste never saw itself as an isolated linguistic bubble defending itself against a flood of English, but as part of a language movement which aimed at both the survival and, more importantly, the revival of Irish as a community language. It was not envisaged as a ghetto, but as a seedbed to enable the language community to grow.

One way of achieving this was to open Irish medium education to children from English-speaking families. This had already been done, with some success, in the Republic of Ireland. In recent years, however, a more scientific approach had been taken to early-years immersion education, particularly in Canada and Wales. My wife, Áine, who was a primary school teacher working in the English medium sector, had made a particular study of the literature on the subject, and offered to set up an immersion preschool as a feeder to the primary school.

Uptake was slow at first; immersion education was new to Northern Ire-. land, and people were understandably wary. Seven children took part in the first session, and of these four went on to the primary school. The subsequent growth was astonishing. Thirteen children joined the following year, all of whom went on to the primary school, followed by twenty-five, then forty, and then fifty. By this final year, children were being turned away and other groups were beginning to set up their own Irish medium preschools, and not just in Belfast. An Irish medium primary school stream was set up in Derry City, seventy odd miles to the northwest, in 1983 and eventually developed into a free-standing school. In 1987 a second school was founded in Belfast and another school in Newry, forty miles to the south. There are now more than four thousand children in Northern Ireland who receive their education through the medium of Irish, at preschool, primary, and secondary levels.

This was a considerable achievement from a tiny beginning with nine children in a secondhand hut in a muddy field. At the time, the school was illegal. When the group wrote to the Ministry of Education to outline what they proposed to do, they received a reply in November 1965, citing paragraph (c) of Section 66(1) of the Education Act, and saying:

> [I]t is the Ministry's view that instruction given entirely through the medium of Gaelic would not constitute "...efficient and suitable instruction..." for the children of an independent school. A complaint would then be served by the Ministry.... [I]f the proprietors do not remove the deficiency complained of within a specified time the Ministry then formally strikes the school off the register. It is an offence against the law to conduct an unregistered school.[12]

When you have decoded the message here, you realize that the letter says that the parents would be prosecuted. The parents dealt with this problem by ignoring the education authorities. This may have been easier in the early 1970s than previously or subsequently. When the school was set up, Northern Ireland was in turmoil, hundreds of people were being killed every year, and the authorities had more on their minds than a small illegal school. In 1972 the Northern Ireland Parliament was prorogued, and we were being governed directly by the London government. London did not know or care much about the Irish language, but they were by no means as hostile to it as the unionist government had been. Even so, the authorities were not keen to include Irish medium schools in the education system. The implications were significant; to endorse an Irish medium school would be to endorse the legitimacy of Irish medium education. Once they began to administer a bilingual rather than a monolingual system, they would inevitably come under pressure to begin funding Irish medium schools. This they had no intention of doing, and they dragged their heels for years.

When Áine and I joined the community, the issue of the school dominated everything; endless meetings, endless fund-raising activities. We had no children at the time, and I made a personal vow that I would not allow Irish medium education to take over my life. It is a mistake to miss a meeting, however, and at one monthly meeting in 1977 I was volunteered in my absence to take over the correspondence with the education authorities. Irish medium education then took over my life for the next seven years. The school was finally recognised as an independent (nonfunded) school in 1979—an important strategic breakthrough which established the legitimacy of Irish medium education, although it did not make the fund-raising any easier. It was finally grant-aided in 1984, thirteen years after its foundation. The campaign for recognition of the school opened the doors for the development of the entire Irish medium sector.

Even today, education in Northern Ireland tends to be divided on sectarian lines, but in the 1970s, almost all Catholic children went to Catholic schools, and Protestant children attended schools in the state sector. The community, although offered status as a Catholic school, refused, even though such a status would have made it much easier to achieve state funding. This was primarily for two reasons; the first was that the parents would lose control of the school if if was part of the Catholic sector, and they were not persuaded that the Church would maintain the school's linguistic ethos. The second was a matter of ideological conviction, and was by no means pragmatic; a significant proportion of the parents believed that in spite of intense sectarian tensions, and although the school was situated right in the middle of a Catholic ghetto, the first Irish medium school in Northern Ireland should remain open, in principle, to people of all and no religions. A newspaper interview with one of the parents in 1973 makes this clear:

> Mrs O Monachain said the school was not directing its attention
> to only the Catholic side of the community. "The Irish language
> is not the property of Catholics," she said. "The founder of the
> Gaelic League was a Protestant, and in fact there are many
> Protestants in Belfast who are fluent in Irish."[13]

Protestant uptake was highly unlikely at that time; the previous year
nearly five hundred people had been killed in the civil disturbances,
which had a strong sectarian element. This spirit of inclusiveness has
survived within the sector. A significant proportion of Irish medium
education is conducted in streams within the Catholic sector, but most
of the pupils attend schools which are outside the Catholic system, even
though the vast majority of their pupils, even today, come from a Catholic background.

The funnelling of the community's energies into the school did, however, take its attention away from some of its other concerns. In the
early days of our involvement, the meetings at which issues relating to
the community were discussed were conducted in Irish. The influx of a
large number of new families changed the dynamic completely. Instead
of relatively informal meetings among a small number of closely knit
families, attendance expanded to the point where more than one hundred families were entitled to attend, and the meetings were conducted
in English. For a long time the monthly meetings were open to all parents and all major decisions were decided in an open forum. This was
so unwieldy that eventually a more streamlined forum was necessary
for the school. Once funding from the public purse was made available,
the school began to be run by a statutory board of governors in which
the community has no input by right. Although the community still has
a legal entity, regular meetings ceased entirely, and it comes together
now only at rare intervals. This involved a considerable loss of the kind
of social cohesion which had marked the community at the time of our
original involvement, and we now tend to meet our neighbours only on
a casual basis in the street or over a garden fence.

To some extent, this was inevitable. The extremely high level of
interaction which we encountered in the early years was partly due
to the fact that the school was in a permanent state of crisis, a crisis
that lasted for thirteen years. It is not surprising that people would be

A secondhand hut in a muddy field: the Belfast Irish medium school in 1980. Photograph courtesy of Aodán Mac Póilin

delighted to pass responsibility for the school on to other people, and the enormous, sustained effort had left many people exhausted.

A relative decline in community cohesion—indeed in community coherence—may have been unavoidable, but the actual decline was surprising. To some extent, it may have been due to a tension between two of the community's primary aims, between the wish to develop a sustainable language community in a sea of English, and the wish to expand the use of Irish in the wider community, which meant involving English speakers directly in running the school. The second of these took precedence. I should perhaps add at this point that I was surprised at the time that the transition from Irish to English was accomplished with so little debate, and so early. It actually took place early in 1978, a few months after the establishment of the bilingual preschool. At that time the preschool—with only a handful of parents—had a separate committee, whose business was conducted in English. Because of some overlap in fund-raising activities, a proposal was made by one of the school's founders that the two committees should be amalgamated. In my memory, I was the only person to question this proposal, which was passed within a quarter of an hour. In hindsight, this decision, which involved monoglot English speakers directly in the running of the school, which their children were not even attending at this stage, was of tremendous importance in giving them a stake in the school, and in maintaining their commitment—many of them made an enormous contribution to its success, and this success has been a vital element in fuelling a vibrant language movement in Northern Ireland. The decision also persuaded them that the Irish speakers genuinely welcomed their input, and were not acting as an arrogant elite. However, it is also possible that the community, as a language community, may have lost some of its own dynamism from this decision.

I have spoken above about the campaign to have Irish medium education recognised. By the time I took over the correspondence (along with my brother-in-law), the authorities no longer felt able to argue that Irish was an unsuitable medium of instruction and had fallen back on the argument that, because of its small numbers, the school was not economically viable. This stand, which looked safe enough when first formulated, was taken over by events. To our own surprise, demand for Irish medium education became so strong that the school began to expand at an astonishing rate. This presented us with another dilemma. While children in an immersion setting are learning the other language, they build up relationships in the language they know best—in our case, in English. In the first few years of the immersion programme, only a small number of children from English-speaking backgrounds were absorbed into the school, and in classes in which they were in a minority, they adapted to the pattern which was already established and spoke Irish to the other children. The expansion of the school was so rapid that it became impossible to control the linguistic dynamic—some classes had only one or two native speakers of Irish among up to thirty children, and the language of informal communication between the children often shifted to English. This in its turn sometimes affected the language of informal communication between children brought up with Irish as their first language.

I had already known about this possibility through my family. My mother, like all her brothers and sisters, was educated entirely through the medium of Irish in the 1920s and 1930s. But she was the only one of ten siblings who made an effort to use the language after leaving school. Language immersion education is the most efficient way of passing knowledge of the language to the next generation. On its own, however, it does not guarantee a new generation of active speakers. We identified this issue early on, and tried to establish after-school activities, but the burden of fund-raising was so great that our energies became dispersed. It was obvious that too rapid an expansion could weaken the linguistic ethos of the school. On the other hand, without rapid expansion, the school would never qualify for government funding and would, in fact, collapse under the weight of a moderate success. It was decided to go for expansion. That dilemma between building an active language community, on the one hand, and increasing the number of speakers on the other (two strategic issues), as well as the financial necessity to achieve numerical viability in a short period (a purely pragmatic issue) have bedeviled the movement for Irish medium education ever since.

I would like to turn now to the expansion of the community from the original nine houses described above. The expansion came in three phases. Our own home and that of my wife's brother were built in 1975-76. To some extent, our two families fall between the original group and those who followed, but for the purposes of this analysis will be lumped with the newer arrivals. It is worth noting that all four individuals had third level education before they joined the community. After a long delay, five new houses were built during the 1990s, two of which had a relatively rapid turnover of owners, some families staying for only a few years. Many of the new families also had a connection with Cumann Chluain Ard, and two families included children from Pobal Feirste's first generation. The final phase was developed when the school was transferred from the Pobal Feirste site to adjoining land, freeing up land for a further six houses. These sites were offered first to children from the original, five of whom took up the offer. The sixth was offered to the cousin of one of the children. As a result, the network of blood relationships was extended even further. Eighteen of the twenty-two families now living in the community have family ties with at least one other family; one group comprises five related families, and there are two groups of four.

The socioeconomic profile of the new arrivals was different to that of the original group. More often than not, they are professionals working in the public sector, mainly in education. Of the twenty-nine adults involved (including those who have since moved on), nineteen have at least a university degree, and most of these have postgraduate qualifications, including a handful with master's degrees and four with doctorates.

The linguistic dynamic has also changed. Of the families who began to live in the community over the last twenty years, in only a minority of cases could both partners speak Irish fluently. This means that in these families there are at least two languages of habitual communication. In fact the situation is even more complex. One of the two families from 1975-76 used both Welsh and Irish at home; among the newer families are two in which Irish, English, and, respectively, Spanish and Portuguese are used.

To some extent, while such bi- and multi-lingualism might tend to weaken the linguistic dynamic among the families, this is offset by the fact that most of the very young children have grandparents—not to mention grand-uncles and grant-aunts—who also live in the community. However, the linguistic dynamic has also been influenced by another, possibly more significant factor. Twenty or so years ago a large estate of more than one hundred houses was built as an extension of the original access road. Although the estate attracted a small number of families where one or both parents spoke Irish, most of the children in this development speak only English. These children, naturally, play with the children of Pobal Feirste. As a result, whatever language or languages are used the homes of the Pobal Feirste children, their default language on the street tends to be English.

The current language patterns within the community vary enormously from family to family. In a few cases the children appear to prefer to use English within the home. In most cases they tend to associate a particular language with particular people, and to switch easily between their languages (although there is usually a short period, when the children are very young, when one language—usually Irish—predominates).

This is a rather sketchy overview of a complex subject, and I have not touched at all on a number of issues, including the development of a specifically urban demotic which is very different to that of the Irish of the historic Gaeltacht. Nor have I dealt with those who grew up on Shaw's Road and are now adults but live elsewhere—whether they have passed the language on to their own children, or even if they are still active speakers of Irish. As regards those issues with which I have dealt, there is no doubt that Pobal Feirste had an enormous influence on the language movement in Northern Ireland, but whether or not the linguistic dynamic created by Pobal Feirste in the seventies can survive into the future, or whether or not it can survive its founders as a linguistic community in any meaningful sense of the word, is something that none of us can know at this time. Nor do we know whether or not it could provide a model for others to follow.

For me, on a personal level, while it has involved a lifestyle that has often had its difficulties, participation in this community, and spitting in the eye of a seemingly irreversible trend of language decline, have been among the most rewarding things I have ever been involved in, both personally and as a language activist. When our daughter and her husband decided to raise their family in the Shaw's Road Gaeltacht I asked her why she chose to do so. She replied, only half-jokingly, that it would be handy to have babysitters on her doorstep. But she also said that as an adult she had felt it to be a great privilege to have had the opportunity to be brought up in a bilingual community, and that she wanted to pass on that privilege to her own children. For Áine and myself this brought us another, totally unforeseen, piece of good fortune—daily contact with our grandchildren, who are now, in September 2011, approaching their sixth and third birthdays.

Notes

1. Joshua Fishman, *Reversing Language Shift* (Clevedon, Eng.: Multilingual Matters, 1991), 144.
2. Ruth McManus, *Dublin, 1910–1940: Shaping the City and Suburbs* (Dublin: Four Courts Press, 2002), 274.
3. Ibid., 275.
4. Máirtín Ó Cadhain, *Mr Hill, Mr Tara* (Dublin: Aistí Éireannacha, 1964), 5.
5. Gabrielle Maguire, *Our Own Language: An Irish Initiative* (Clevedon, Eng.: Multilingual Matters, 1990), 72.
6. Seán Mac Aindreasa, "Bunscoil Ghaelach Bhéal Feirste" (publicity leaflet, 1982 version).
7. Maguire, *Our Own Language*, 71–72.
8. Ibid., 72.
9. Mac Aindreasa, "Bunscoil Ghaelach Bhéal Feirste," 1973 version.
10. Aodán Mac Póilin, "Irish Language Writing in Belfast after 1900," in *The Cities of Belfast*, ed. Nicholas Allen agus Aaron Kelly (Dublin, Four Courts Press, 2003).
11. Maguire, *Our Own Language*, 71.
12. Ibid., 78.
13. Belfast *Sunday News*, "These Belfast Kids Speak No English," 23 April 1973.

Part IV

VARIATIONS ON A THEME

10: Kypriaka

MAKING CHOICES: ENRICHING LIFE

Aigli Pittaka, Brian Bielenberg, and Aliosha Bielenberg Pittaka

What sets worlds in motion is the interplay of differences, their attractions and repulsions. Life is plurality, death is uniformity. By suppressing differences and peculiarities, by eliminating different civilizations and cultures, progress weakens life and favors death, impoverishes and mutilates us. Every view of the world that becomes extinct, every culture that disappears, diminishes a possibility of life.

—Octavio Paz

Introduction

It was a Sunday night, some three years after the decision. As we prepared for bed, our son's voice resonated through the hallway. He was talking in his sleep...in two languages! When we mentioned it to him excitedly at breakfast the next morning, his reaction was nothing more than a shoulder shrug and "So what? Doesn't everybody?"

Aliosha, Aigli, and Brian. Photograph courtesy of the Bielenberg
Pittaka family

So what? Doesn't everybody? Perhaps for him it is nothing, but for us the
issue has impacted our lives consciously and subconsciously ever since
the day we first learned that we would be parents. It was an issue that
had arisen strongly some years earlier as we pondered an apparently
ideal offer sitting on the table in front of us, the details of a job offer
from a well-known university in California. Why couldn't we simply do
what everyone expected us to do and accept the position?

In this chapter we will detail some of our experiences of *attempting* to raise our son as a balanced multilingual/multicultural child. We
use the word "attempting" because we have found that it is very difficult to maintain an equal balance between two languages, particularly
when one language is English and the other is a heritage dialect used
only by a small population. We will share the ups and downs of making
a lesser-used language the language of the home in an English-speaking
society, discuss the deeper meaning of what a particular ethnic identity
means, and explain the reasons that led us to do what many would consider irrational in order to insure that our son developed deep senses
of identity and belongingness to both of his worlds. Overall, we aim to

highlight the benefits of making the choice for a heritage language—benefits for the child, for the parents, for the extended family, and perhaps most importantly, for society as a whole.

Setting the Stage

For over a decade I (Brian) had been an advocate of language and cultural maintenance for various groups of people. As a family, we had been putting theory into practice in our own lives as well. Our child had been growing bilingual from birth. His first words were in Kypriaka (a dialect of Greek spoken in Cyprus), forty-nine of his first fifty words were Kypriaka, and at age four his two languages, Kypriaka and English, were well balanced. However, by age six daily attendance at English medium schools in California and the United Arab Emirates had begun to lead his English past his Kypriaka. Still, with visits to Cyprus and the use of the heritage language in the home, he continued to communicate in Kypriaka and evidence an understanding of what it means to be Cypriot. We were aware that there would be times when one language took precedence over the other in our child's life, times when he might refuse the minority heritage language, preferring to "fit in" with the majority. For the most part, though, we felt we were being successful at raising a balanced bilingual/bicultural child. Yet the school years, and the English dominance that go with them, were just beginning. Now it was time to *really* put our theory into practice. As our son grew, each day at English medium school seemed to be drowning out the lesser-used home language. We heard him speaking more and more English to his mother, whose native language is Kypriaka. Home was no longer his dominant source of language input. His recollections of his school day would begin in Kypriaka, but soon transition into English as he became frustrated at the need to continually search for vocabulary he had never experienced in Kypriaka. Summer visits to Cyprus enabled us to continue his language and cultural development at close to age-appropriate levels, but would summer visits continue to be enough? We had already begun to notice that it took increasingly longer periods of time for him to communicate with Cypriot family in the ways expected of a child his age. In other words, he was falling further and further behind in his Kypriaka every time we were away from the language community, and he was becoming ever more uncomfortable with using the language. English, on the other hand, was everywhere.

Accepting the job offer would enable me to work with linguistic and cultural minority children and their families, to show that raising a child with a lesser-used language is possible. We could draw on our experiences of having our son grow with two languages in a society dominated by English in order to serve as a model for others. But as we helped other families, and encouraged them to create contexts which support heritage language use and development, we would have taken our son further away from the very support networks that would enable him to be Cypriot and speak the Cypriot language, Kypriaka. Where would he get Cypriot input if we lived in California? American culture and communities could be found around the world; how much Cypriot culture and community could be found in California? Could I honestly continue to promote language maintenance and the necessary sacrifices as I watched half of my son's identity dissolve, so that only surface aspects remained? We had to think deeply not only about the language, but about what else would be lost if we chose to live in the US. In essence, we were asking ourselves what it *really* means to speak an endangered heritage language.

Kypriaka: A Fading Dialect

Kypriaka is a dialect that is, in its deepest forms, unintelligible to speakers of Standard Modern Greek (SMG). The *Ethnologue* lists a total of 689,000 speakers of Greek in Cyprus, but this number is deceptive, hiding a very real shift away from Kypriaka. The dialect ranges along a continuum from heavy (*vareta*) to light (*elafria*) to high-class Kypriaka. *Vareta Kypriaka* (Βαρετά Κυπριακά) is the variety of the language spoken by the grandparent generation and older, with young people associating it with poor, uneducated village people, though many young males do adapt it as an identity marker. It is different enough from SMG that some scholars have argued that it is a separate language. *Elafria Kypriaka* (Ελαφριά Κυπριακά) is currently the most commonly used form of the dialect. It is spoken both by the parental generation and today's youth. It is the language that is used in the home and among friends in most areas of the country. The one geographic exception evident to most scholars and speakers is Nicosia, the cosmopolitan capital of Cyprus, where people are said to speak "high-class" Kypriaka. This variety most closely approximates SMG, and is the language spoken by and identified with residents of Nicosia. Many young Cypriots view the dialect as a key aspect of their identity and a connection to their roots. At the same time, however, they hold negative attitudes towards it. The school system essentially views it as a deficit the children bring with them to school, something that can and should be fixed over time. The fact that it is primarily oral leads most Cypriots to feel that it is not a real language. Being a small dialect, Kypriaka is not taught or used in schools anywhere in the world. At present, an overall shift away from the language of the island toward something that much more closely resembles SMG is strongly evident.

I (Aigli) was born and raised in Cyprus and learned to speak Kypriaka in the home. While in school I learned how to speak, read, and write Standard Modern Greek. Thus I grew up speaking Kypriaka and SMG, but never learned how to read or write Kypriaka, only Greek. I later attended university in Greece and graduate school in the US, and now fluidly move among Kypriaka, SMG, and English on a daily basis.

In contrast with this rich linguistic background of my wife, I (Brian) grew up in a predominately monolingual midwestern town in the US. Like many US families, my parents were monolingual English speakers despite the fact that some of my grandparents had started school in the US with very little to no English. I studied German in high school and university and learned French while a Peace Corps volunteer in Africa. After getting married, I began to learn Kypriaka, mostly through oral interaction with my wife and in-laws. The language I have learned is the language of the house and of the περβόλι (orchard). To date I have achieved a level of basic fluency, though as my son likes to point out, with "several pronunciation errors." Still, my Kypriaka allows for daily, casual interactions in the language.

English, English Everywhere

So our son is speaking English. "What's the problem?" many people asked. "With English he will have so many more opportunities in life. He can go anywhere, he can do anything. He can always learn Greek later on." When our child was four, we chose to leave the US and move to the United Arab Emirates. The choice, we thought, would allow us to pur-sue our careers while at the same time being close enough to Cyprus for regular visits and the necessary linguistic and cultural input. Living in the UAE, we had the added benefit of being part of a community that was made up of many families similar to ours; cross-cultural couples of different language backgrounds striving to raise their children bilingually, what Una Cunningham-Andersson and Staffan Andersson call "mixed language families."[1] It would be, we hoped, a built-in support network and source of ideas for how to make it work. Yet the feelings and practices of many families we encountered, mixed-language couples and Arab speakers alike, were that English is what is most important, and if it means only a rudimentary knowledge of the heritage language, then so be it. In the homes of most of the people that we looked to for support and ideas, English dominated among the children and parents whenever one of the parents was a native speaker of English. So what? So what if small local dialects and lesser-used languages are lost, when so much else is gained through solid acquisition of English? But can culture, identity, and a sense of belongingness be maintained without the language?

Making Kypriaka Part of the Home

When I (Aigli) married a person from a different culture and background, English, our common language, inevitably became the language of the home, particularly since we were living in the US. However, when our child was born, even while he was still in my belly, in fact, we began speaking to him in Kypriaka. It was something that emerged as a natural act, nothing that we talked and rationalized about. The decision, at least initially, was unconscious. My husband had been open to learning my native language orally through personal interaction with my family, and this was, at first, sufficient for his interactions with our newborn child. We sought to make the use of Kypriaka in our home as natural as possible. This process was further supported by having my mother live with us for extended periods of time during the first years of our son's life. She helped with child-rearing and provided additional Kypriaka input, both directly to our son and indirectly through increased adult use of, and interaction in, the language in the home. Beyond providing input for our child, these actions supported what for me were deep emotions connected to the language. Using my mother tongue at home while living in a foreign country enabled me to validate to myself that I still existed as the same human being that I (used to) understand myself to be.

Our child was born in the US and raised there during his first four years of life. Despite the apparent simplicity of using the heritage language in the home, we faced numerous challenges during those first

Aliosha learning about "eggcracking," a Greek Cypriot Easter tradition, with his grandparents. Photo by A. Pittaka

years, challenges that continue today. The first and foremost was how to maintain two mother tongues. We focused on providing Kypriaka input in the home as English was everywhere outside of the home. The second, but equally important, challenge was how to socialize our child into two native cultures. In our case it was geographically and financially unfeasible to spend extended time in both Cyprus and the US. There was no Cypriot community in the area of California where we were living, and thus the home remained the sole input of Kypriaka and what it means to be Cypriot. We became ever more focused on insuring that we addressed our young child only in Kypriaka, practicing traditional Cypriot activities, and eating Cypriot meals. Even so, we still faced uncertainties that were brought on by broader societal views, from the looks of disapproval in the grocery store when we would use Kypriaka to the uncertainty evidenced by family as to how to interact linguistically with our son as he began to speak. Even educators spoke against our practice. When our son was only two years old, his teacher told us that he would do better in day care if we spoke more English to him at home. We soon realized that we were actually thinking to change our linguistic practice because of the uninformed comment of this educator. We were, after all, new parents and he had years of experience. Fortunately, we were strong enough in our beliefs to go back to the teacher and explain how beneficial it is for a child to grow with two languages.

As our son grew, we continued to live away from Cyprus. Bedtime came to be an important language socialization activity, and it is here where the two languages began to assume their own roles in the home. For both parents it was exciting to sing the songs that we had learned while growing up, and to read or tell stories steeped in familiar cultural traditions and beliefs, developing with our child a shared understanding of the world. Many of the bedtime stories in Kypriaka were spontaneous, as we knew of only two storybooks that had been written in Kypriaka. Creating our own stories became a necessary habit. Soon we had a nighttime ritual. First it was Papa's time to read English books and sing in English. Next came Mama's time to make up stories in Kypriaka, with our son's contributions increasing over time. Oral stories are good stories, we found; not everything has to come from a book. Kypriaka is, after all, an oral language.

English Encroachment

It sounds straightforward to say that we spoke an endangered heritage dialect with our child in the home. The reality is that the day-to-day routines of life while living in English-speaking environments often meant that to stay in the language required conscious effort, and at times became quite exhausting. Over time we found ourselves increasingly using English at home. For me (Brian), it was a matter of reaching a point where I did not have the vocabulary needed for answering the ever expanding range of questions asked by a growing child. Slowly we found ourselves transitioning from using primarily Kypriaka in the home into a "one parent—one language family," with each of us using our native language with our son, at least in theory. In practice, our language became a regular mix of Kypriaka and English, with code-switching being the norm. As our child's English became stronger through formal schooling, it became ever more difficult to stay fully in Kypriaka. We would become frustrated, not knowing whether our son was ignoring us because he didn't understand a request in Kypriaka, or because he was simply playing deaf to avoid the task. The issue was similar when it came time for discipline, as I (Aigli) would often find myself explaining in both Kypriaka and English to make sure that he understood his action and its consequences.

Our son has been a very conscientious learner of both mother tongues. As he grew he accepted without complaint the afternoon home-schooled Kypriaka lessons that we felt were necessary to support his language and identity, though in his memory these attempts "were rather futile." During holidays from school I (Aigli) would take further opportunity to do more language lessons while the other children were playing outside. There were times when I felt guilty for doing so and yet deep inside I knew that it was the right thing to do. During the early preschool years it was mainly oral language transmission, but during his primary years our efforts were geared towards helping our son develop Greek literacy and numeracy as well, as preparation for the possibility that he might one day go to school in Cyprus. Even with all of this effort, though, something seemed to be missing. There were no longer any environments where only the heritage language was being used in our family. We had no local community or groups that were committed to speaking to each other, to our children, and to each other's children in Kypriaka. As in many of the mixed-language families we knew, English was becoming a comfort zone, and perhaps it was time for us to become uncomfortable, through both examination and alteration of our own practices. To outsiders our family appeared multilingual, but as we have shared above, the story is much more complex. And the job offer was on the table.

Growing Bilingual

Several years ago I (Brian) was asked to summarize the literature on the cognitive advantages of bilingualism.[2] In my summary I included a description of how bilinguals are able to analyze language as an abstract system earlier than monolinguals, that bilinguals have greater metalinguistic skills that can be useful for learning how to read, and that they use more academic oral language in schools. I finished my summary with the statement, "I certainly would not be raising my son bilingually if I did not believe them," referring to the findings of the researchers. While cognitive benefits and improved school performance are important goals, I now realize how naive and narrow-minded that statement was. In fact, I would now place the cognitive benefits of bilingualism at the bottom of my list for why we are raising our son with more than one language, though they no doubt make us feel more comfortable in what we are doing. The cultural, social, and identity issues behind speaking a heritage language are far more important, even more so when use of that heritage language is on the decline.

As we went through the process of deciding whether to accept the job offer, we sought the advice of friends and colleagues. We were aware of some potential difficulties we would face in the US, and wanted to know the thoughts of others. Naturally, they made very sound arguments for how they felt we would be able to continue the bicultural, bilingual, biliterate development of our child, highlighting the existence of Greek festivals, Greek language lessons, and the Greek Orthodox Church in the region. While reflecting on their comments, however, we realized that we were seeking something much different for our child than what was being suggested. It became apparent to us that if we focused on the suggested Greek language lessons, dance, and food, to live in the US would require us to accept Kypriaka being dissolved into Greek, and the Cypriot traditions giving way to the more widely accepted Greek stereotypes seen at the annual Greek festivals. Yes, our child could continue to learn to speak Kypriaka/Greek in the US, and yes he could learn some Greek dances, but these would only scratch the surface of the reasons why Kypriaka is so important to us. Speaking a heritage language means more than being able to form correct sentences and phrases or use isolated vocabulary—often this is all that is learned in community- and church-sponsored language classes and schools. More importantly it means being able to communicate effectively and intimately across generations, with cousins, friends, parents, and grandparents, to feel comfortable in both worlds, to understand the nuances of how the language is used and the feelings that accompany certain sounds and expressions. Acquisition of these abilities, we realized, requires language immersion in the community.

Joining the Community
Growing with only one of your mother tongues and knowing only one culture intimately is like viewing the world with only one eye. Language is culture and intimacy; it is a means of belonging. It is a tool with which to perceive the world and simultaneously express it. When a

child's parents are part of two different worlds, their child should learn both languages in order to be able to understand both worlds, not just linguistically, but also emotionally, socially, and *intuitively*. This is even more important when one of the heritage languages is endangered. Speaking only one language or growing in only one culture would mean that the person who is born of two different worlds is being denied something very important. If that is a parent's choice, we can respect it and accept it, but we don't share such a view. We wish for our child to be a fully bilingual, biliterate, and bicultural child. To raise a child with a bicultural background as monocultural would, we feel, hinder that child from fully participating in all the worlds to which she or he belongs. To raise a child without his or her endangered heritage language or dialect impacts not only the child and the family, but the community and society as well. As fewer and fewer people speak the language and know the cultural aspects inherent within the language, a whole way of viewing the world slowly disappears. Would we ever consider cutting half of the roots of a tree? No. A tree needs sturdy and deep roots to grow strong and healthy, and providing a child the opportunity to establish a full set of roots ultimately leads to a healthy tree and thus a healthy ecosystem.

Making the Choice
It became obvious to us that by remaining in the US we would be sabotaging our own efforts and above all those of our child to continue to grow with his two heritage languages and identities, his full set of roots. Access to the deeper aspects of Cypriotness was simply not there. We wanted to enable our child to fully immerse himself in the language that had until then been limited to our interactions in the home. It was time for us to join the community of Kypriaka speakers, and this would mean fully immersing ourselves in Cypriot society, including entering the public school system. The playground would provide a source of language input that had up to now been missing, extended input from peers. We needed to build on our efforts to date for our son to become fully competent in what it means to be a Cypriot. The "one step forward and one step backward" was frustrating for us as parents but most of all for our son, as a learner. We wanted him to learn the language in its natural environment, in its full cultural context. It would be a learning with the heart.

Cutting *Vasilopita,* a traditional Cypriot cake, to welcome in the New Year. Photo by B. Bielenberg

Thus, we decided to decline the job offer and move to Cyprus. We were fortunate in that a community of Kypriaka speakers still exists. For other endangered languages, such a community must be formed with like-minded families. Even so, a new set of challenges awaited us. Doubts concerning the wisdom of our decision rose up early as our son experienced bumps with family and school, often misunderstanding the comments made by his grandparents or other children, which led him, initially, to withdraw. In his own words:

> I (Aliosha) guess that you can imagine my difficulty becoming comfortable in the mostly Kypriaka environment I was coming into. I remember one night in particular, the eve of my first day in "Greek school," I think, when I started stomping around the room, half-shouting half-crying, "NO! NO!"

His vocabulary, or as he puts it, his "library" of Kypriaka was a mess, with a limited "stock" of "books," words and phrases scattered everywhere. It took too long to find the appropriate ones, so it was easier to just remain quiet. Beyond language deficiencies, he also recalls "lacking one of the most important things":

Knowledge of "their" culture. For instance, because in those days I had a tendency to "crack" my fingers, a classmate asked if I was trying to furtively give her "the finger."[3] I had no idea what she meant, and after many such episodes I gradually became even more separated socially. Another thing I noticed later on, when I knew the language well enough to get along, was that many common (mostly Kypriaka) words remained unknown, thus preventing me from understanding many jokes, as well as much breaktime banter.

With time, though, that passed, and now both his Kypriaka and English "libraries" are well stocked and organized. In his words, "I can now state that my Kypriaka library is in good shape, continually adding ever more items." Equally important, he has been able to live the local rhythms of life, to celebrate the local public holidays and to participate in the social practices. These cultural interactions have provided multiple contexts to know the language with full senses, and to express feelings, sounds, images, smells, tastes, and experiences in more than one language.

Conclusion

American society, unfortunately, has been subjected to the myth that it is best to raise a child monolingually. This leads many families, like those we knew in the Emirates and many others in the US, to dive willingly, or be swept into, the river of English language and the ways associated with the American and British mainstream societies. We use the term "mainstream" intentionally at this point in order to draw attention to its metaphoric implications. A mainstream washes away soil from the banks and absorbs tributaries, mixing and diluting until the newly added soil and water are indistinguishable from the water in the mainstream.

In a similar way we saw the English language assimilating mixed-language families, our own included, dissolving values, languages, and ways of living. We sought to enable our child to be strong in all of his identities, to be comfortable and feel belongingness to both the community associated with English and that associated with Kypriaka. For us it was the social, cultural, and identity issues that eventually led us to place our child's heritage language and cultural development ahead of our career choices. In so doing we had to deeply think about the concept of learning a heritage language within the cultural milieu where it is used. Maintenance of a heritage language is more, much more, than going to Saturday classes and putting together grammatically correct sentences; it is feeling the living language to such a degree that a child has become one with the language and all that is shared through it. Annual festivals, language classes, and summer holidays as a visitor support the process but are insufficient. What is required is to become a contributing, sharing member of the linguistic community.

As our child grows he has come to love rolling words around in his mouth, using them in creative and imaginative ways, and he now does this with both languages. We hope that our son will continue to be proud of his bicultural background. We hope that he will raise his children bilingually and that in time multilingualism will become the norm in places like the US. We hope that our son will appreciate that his parents put him through the challenges and rewards of changing cultures, readjusting to totally different educational systems, and rebuilding networks of friends from scratch. At present, he views our actions from a rather neutral perspective, though one that indicates that we may have made the best decision:

> I (Aliosha) think that it was an okay decision on my parents' side to come to Cyprus, because otherwise I would have learned the language as a foreigner, never actually grasping the "culture." However, I sometimes wonder what I have missed out on, not fully experiencing my "other" culture.

No doubt the time will come, perhaps sooner than we expect, when we will need to return to the US. Through our experiences, it is clear to us that learning two mother tongues has benefit despite the pains and sacrifices it requires by the whole family. Recently I (Brian) was asked if I regret our decision. Taking a short-term perspective, I answered, "I do wonder what might have been." But as we reflect on the past four years, I am led to a different thought:

> Many years from now, when I see my son reciting poetry in both languages, moving comfortably in and out of different

cultural settings, being seamlessly accepted as a member of the community, whether in Cyprus, the US, or even elsewhere, then I will know that we have made the right decision.

When we hear our son expressing himself comfortably in both words and worlds, even in his sleep, when he looks at us with that same *"So what"* expression, we know that we have contributed our drop into the ocean of people that celebrate multilingualism, multiliteracy and multiculturalism. We know that our child is one of many who can dream rich, pluricultural dreams, enriching possibilities of life. We know that we have made the right choices.

Notes

1. Una Cunningham-Andersson and Staffan Andersson, *Growing Up with Two Languages* (2d ed.) (New York: Routledge, 2004).
2. Leanne Hinton and Ken Hale, eds., *The Green Book of Language Revitalization in Practice* (San Diego: Academic Press, 2001).
3. "Giving the finger" in Cyprus differs from the extended middle finger of the US. In Cyprus, "the finger" is given by curling the middle finger back towards the open palm.

11: Warlpiri

ABOUT DAD

Ezra Hale

In 1998 I joined my father, Ken Hale, and some of his colleagues at a dinner in his honor in Tucson, Arizona. Dad had just received an honorary degree from the University of Arizona for his work in linguistics. My father was a polyglot, a speaker of many languages, of which he taught me three: English (my native language); French, to get me through a year in Belgium; and Warlpiri, because it was his favorite. Warlpiri is an aboriginal language with around three thousand speakers in central Australia. Dad spoke Warlpiri with my twin brother, Caleb, and me almost exclusively from the day we were born until the day he died.

Late in his life, dad had a virus in his vocal chords that affected his ability to communicate; sometimes the words came out in a whisper. His doctors and friends tried all sorts of remedies for his ailment— botox injections, a microphone and portable speaker. Some worked better than others. When I was at the London School of Economics in 1990 Dad visited and his friend and colleague David McKnight, who was then a professor there, took us out to lunch. David was hard of hearing and used an ear horn. They spoke in Damin, an Australian ceremonial language of which they were the two last remaining speakers. The extreme irony of the situation was not lost on the three of us. Dad strained to speak, and David strained to hear a language which was—but for the two of them—lost to the world.

Ken Hale and Ezra Hale in Lexington, Massachusetts, 2001. Photograph by Sally Hale, courtesy of Ezra Hale

On this night in 1998 in Tucson, we gathered at a relative's house for coffee and conversation. The warm smell of the desert wafted through the room. We had just been out for a big Tex Mex dinner. As I leaned towards my father along with everyone else, straining to hear him, I accidentally squeezed out a squeaky little fart. Oops.

Everyone looked a little embarrassed. Thinking quickly, I covered my gaffe with a sidelong glance at a dog that was conveniently lying under my chair. The awkward moment passed and everyone went back to whatever topic was at hand.

A few minutes later, though, I turned to my dad and said in Warlpiri, *"Purdanyangunpa kujarna kuna puurr-manu? Maliki lawa, ngulajurnaju kuja kuna puurr-manu."* In English it means "Did you hear how I just farted? It wasn't the dog, it was me who farted!"

Dad just smiled and said simply, *"Yawai,"* meaning "yes."

When Caleb and I were kids, this was typical of our communication with Dad in Warlpiri. It had a joke, a bodily function, and an animal. It was the kind of humor six- to twelve-year-olds could get their hands around. Dad shared his love of Warlpiri with us and we returned the favor by sharing our love of bathroom humor with him.

Ken Hale with Lindsay Roughsey, Mornington Island, Australia, 1967. Photograph by Sally Hale, courtesy of Ezra Hale

My dad spent several years in Australia before Caleb and I were born. He learned several native languages while he was there but none more than Warlpiri. We never went to Australia with him, much to my regret, and I have, as of this writing, never been. Caleb and I grew up understanding Warlpiri, as he spoke it, in the same way that we understood English. As I learned other languages, French and Spanish, I noticed that my understanding of them was very different from my understanding of Warlpiri.

With French and Spanish I always do some sort of mental translation in the back of my head. Warlpiri was not like this. It was more like English, like a first language that one just understands without any translation. There is no need to translate, and nothing to translate to. Of course in later years, when I had the good fortune to meet actual native speakers or even other speakers of Warlpiri, I found their speaking almost unintelligible. This was startling to me and I think it speaks to the weakness in a single person's conveyance of a language. Dad shared Warlpiri with us, but to be honest, he gave us a somewhat limited window into the language. We learned it through his voice alone. We never heard any other voicing of the language that might have given us a more complete understanding. This is why I consider my understanding and even speaking of Warlpiri to be an anomaly. This is why I can't say that I am a true speaker.

In fact for most of my life, but for the bathroom humor I didn't really speak Warlpiri back to my father. He would speak to us in Warlpiri and we would respond in English. When I was in my twenties I suddenly decided to start speaking. I can't really say why I did this. I just felt like I was ready. I had to go back over the grammar with my dad to understand why I said the things that I said. It was only then that I came to understand the actual grammar of Warlpiri.

Dad loved Warlpiri; he often said that it was his favorite language. He liked how the words of a sentence could be rearranged and strung together into a single long utterance. Some of his favorite turns of phrase were *Yulkami karnangku* (I love you) and *Kapurnangku pinyi* (I'm going to hit you). Both phrases really meant the same thing: "I love you." He had some great phrases in English, too: "Piss on you!" and "Go piss up a rope!" You can see where my love of bathroom humor came from.

I think Dad also liked the bond that Warlpiri created between us. Warlpiri was something that, in our community, we shared exclusively.

When Dad was dying of cancer, I moved back to Lexington to be with him. We had planned to go to Australia together, but the cancer got in the way. I built a fire pit out in our backyard where we could sit around and speak Warlpiri together. I figured that if I couldn't go to Australia with him, perhaps I could bring a little bit of the outback home.

Some of my fondest memories of speaking Warlpiri with my dad come from that time. We sat around the fire and talked about the trees and the animals, the fire, the natural world around us. We also spoke in English, and that was also special. We spoke about his youth, growing up in Arizona, the hunting and trapping that he did as a boy. One night as we sat next to the fire, a parking car spooked a passel of wildlife in a nearby woodland. In the pitch dark, the earth seemed to come alive as dozens of opossums swarmed around us and melted once again into the woods.

I loved my dad very much and I wanted to be as close as possible to him. I thought that Warlpiri was the key, that it would bring us even closer together than we already were. But upon reflection I don't really think it mattered what language we spoke. It was more about spending the time together, speaking together.

In the days before my father died I spent time caring for him in hospice at our house in Lexington. One night when we were helping him go to the bathroom, my brother Caleb and I sat next to him on either

Ken Hale with twin sons Ezra and Caleb. Photograph by Sally Hale, courtesy of Ezra Hale

side. He reached out and put a hand on each of our heads. "Your names are very important and I want to make sure you know how to pronounce them," he said. "Kayilipi and Yijira." Caleb and Ezra. We repeated them with him.

Today there is a new Kenneth Hale in the world. My son Kenny was born on July 30, 2008, seven years after my father passed away. When Kenny first started potty training I sat with him and was reminded of that time. "Poopy!" he said. I smiled at him and repeated it, "poopy," and we laughed.

Part V

FAMILY LANGUAGE-LEARNING PROGRAMS

12: Kawaiisu

THE KAWAIISU LANGUAGE AT HOME PROGRAM

Laura Grant and Julie Turner
Kawaiisu Language and Cultural Center

Sixty years later, Betty Girado Hernandez stands on the massive granite slab dotted with shallow holes where she and her mother and her grandmother placed acorns they had gathered and ground them into meal to prepare mush for their family. These days her family buys groceries with the paycheck she earns as a medical technician. She prepares instrument trays for surgeons who may replace a hip joint with a high-tech titanium ball and socket. She has a broad smile that comes easily as she tells a story about using flattened cardboard boxes to sled down the grassy hill above the mortar rock with her brother and sister. She seems to have navigated this huge leap in lifestyle well, taking life as it comes, with a great deal of humor. She is a woman who leads her family. No one could have predicted she, her older brother, younger sister, and one other relative would be the last native speakers of Kawaiisu.

The Kawaiisu People
The Kawaiisu are the indigenous people of Kern County, California. Their traditional lands are in the Kern River Valley, south to Tehachapi,

and include the Tehachapi Mountains and part of the Mojave Desert. They have lived in the foothills of the Sierra, from the grasslands studded with oaks to the piney highlands, for thousands of years. In 2008 archaeologists from California State University, Bakersfield, took DNA samples from the sixteen-hundred-year-old skeleton of a young girl found north of Tehachapi. Her DNA matches that of the last male speaker of Kawaiisu, Betty's older brother, Luther Girado.

In the past 150 years, like the majority of California Indian people, the Kawaiisu have experienced federal and state policies for assimilation, population loss from various diseases, and wars that came with the waves of immigrants; as a result, only a handful of their people know the Kawaiisu language and cultural practices. After the US government attempted to relocate the tribe in the late 1800s, traditions such as dress, music and songs, and knowledge of sacred sites were largely lost; only the language, some traditional stories, and survival skills remained. The Kawaiisu managed to remain in traditional homelands, however, and adapted to ranching, logging, and farming lifestyles. The Girado family is proud of their reputation as horsemen and working cowboys, a tradition that is carried on today by Betty's great-niece Loreen Park.

The Kawaiisu have no reservation. The California state government allotted land to them in the 1880s, but only one family lives there now, because the property has no paved roads, running water, power, or any other kind of infrastructure to support modern households. Over two hundred Kawaiisu adults are enrolled with the Kern Valley Indian Communities Council as tribal members. Of these enrolled Kawaiisu adults and their families, 10 percent live in the area of Tehachapi and the Walker Basin, another 60 percent live in and around Bakersfield, and 30 percent live in other states. Though they have an unbroken chain of speakers of their language and DNA evidence that proves their long-standing presence on the land, the Kawaiisu are not a federally recognized tribe.

Kawaiisu Language Revitalization

Four native speakers of Kawaiisu remain. Three of them are siblings: Luther Girado, 70, in Walker Basin; Betty Hernandez, 66, in Palm Springs; and Lucille Girado Hicks, 64, in Montclair, California. The other speaker, Pauline Gallegos, is a cousin to the Girado siblings. She is in her nineties and lives in Texas. Luther, Betty, and Lucille teach their language and have been the driving force for Kawaiisu language revitalization in their community along with Luther's eldest daughter, Julie Turner. Julie has a sweeping vision for the future of Kawaiisu:

> I would love to see a full-time language class offered to all ages, taught in our schools that have Kawaiisu children, families speaking in their homes, a cultural center for the community to come and see and hear that there are real, live, Indian people living and thriving in our communities, that we are not just a spot on a language map. I want to see my nieces and nephew speaking and teaching their children. I just don't want to see them lose out on the great experience that I am having right now with my dad, learning everything that I can from him to share with the world. I want my dad and aunties remembered for all of the hard work we are doing for future generations.

Rafael and Gladys Girado raised their children in a small wood-frame house just outside the tiny town of Lorraine in the Walker Basin. Luther and Lucille were born in the 1940s at home. Luther and Lucille tease Betty because she is a "hospital baby," born in Bakersfield. The family made a living working on the local cattle ranches. Gladys and her husband's mother, Marie, drew water for the household from the creek in buckets and praised Luther for being able to sprint back to the house with two full buckets while they had to take two stops on the way back up the hill to catch their breath. Luther, especially, learned how to hunt and use plants for food and medicine as he assisted his grandparents, parents, and aunt and uncles in gathering and preparing them. Gladys was very different from the many Native American women of her generation who suppressed the native language in their children in hopes that they would have an easier time growing up in a world where English was now the dominant language. The Girado children grew up in a community of other Kawaiisu people and were surrounded by the language, called Nuwa. Rafael had a personal goal to make sure all of his children could speak the Nuwa language. (He himself spoke five languages.) Gladys backed him up. She encouraged her children to speak their language and told others not to make fun of them when they tried.

The Girados felt strongly about a mainstream education for their children too, so the kids went off to the Caliente school, carrying their tortillas and beans in lard-can lunch buckets. All of them recall being teased about speaking their language so that they kept it to themselves. Luther became proficient with his fists. Betty in particular had a hard time learning both a new language and her schoolwork. She remembers her mother trying to help her with numbers in English by counting out spoons, fork, and knives. Gladys, who lived until 1986, almost never spoke English.

In 2002 Lucille and Luther held monthly language classes combined with potluck meals. These were open to community members, native and nonnative alike. When asked why, at that time, she finally decided to teach, Lucille replied, "The younger generation was interested and kept after me, 'Teach me, teach me!' I crossed that barrier and went against the closed ways of the elders to teach only those within their households or clans. For years I had the same attitude because I was brought up that way."

Julie remembers:

> When my dad, aunties, and grandma got together they always spoke Nuwa. I can remember my grandma Gladys coming to see us up in the mountains where we lived. Her English was so bad that she would speak Nuwa most of the time. We understood some of what she said, but she talked so fast that it was hard to keep up. She would teach me and my sister Joy some words, but I couldn't tell what they were. My Auntie Lucille always was great about teaching me new words. I was always mesmerized. I just loved to hear them talk. Now I feel that it's my job to preserve our language and share it with anyone that wants to learn. I wish that I was a little more persistent with my family to teach me. I always feel now that I am running out of time.

In August 2003 the Kawaiisu group gained the support of the Nüümü Yadoha program run by the Owens Valley Career Development Center of the Paiute Shoshone Indians in Bishop, California. This program trains native language advocates to teach and learn California languages, focusing on language immersion methods, and to document their languages using digital media. In 2003 the program was new and, as the director, I (Laura) was seeking to support existing language revitalization efforts in Inyo, Kern, Tulare, Kings, and Fresno counties. I first met Lucille at one of her classes, an open-air event in the pine forest of Tehachapi. I especially remember her dynamic presentation, her voice carrying through the trees, and some special guests: a group of Chemehuevi elders from Arizona. From 2003 to 2006, the Kawaiisu submitted yearly plans for community-based language activities to the Nüümü Yadoha Program.

The Kawaiisu advocates eagerly participated in several training opportunities, including the Master-Apprentice Language Learning Program. Offered by the Advocates for Indigenous California Language Survival (AICLS) since 1993, this program pairs a fluent speaker of the language (the master), usually an elder, and a younger member of the tribe committed to learning the language (the apprentice). Luther participates in this program as a master speaker and has "graduated" two apprentices, his partner, Christine Corcoran, and his daughter, Julie Turner. In January 2009 he started with a new apprentice, Loreen Park, his granddaughter.

The master-apprentice program trains people to learn a language in much the same way that children learn their first language—through hearing it in real-life situations in which the context makes it clear what is being said. Instead of sitting around a table or in a classroom, the team uses their language in real-life activities such as cooking, discussing the weather, washing clothes, going to the store, or practicing traditional skills. The master-apprentice team attempts to speak only in their native language without lapsing into English. The ultimate goal is for the apprentice to in turn become a teacher, especially one who can teach children.

By 2006 the Kawaiisu language advocates had outgrown the Nüümü Yadoha program and formed the Kawaiisu Language and Cultural Center, a tax-exempt, nonprofit organization, so that they could broaden the scope and depth of their activities. They created a mission statement with long-term goals for Kawaiisu language and cultural preservation and revitalization. By that time Laura and Julie had become close friends and Laura had recognized that the talents and dedication that Julie and her family brought to the program made Kawaiisu language revitalization a real possibility.

The Language at Home Program

Julie and Laura urged Betty to join the master-apprentice program because, living in Palm Springs, she was separated from the Kawaiisu community in Kern County and was unable to participate in the growing number of diverse projects there. Betty wanted to teach her entire family, however, and that did not fit into the criteria of the master-apprentice program. The program limits participation to two-person adult teams. How could the AICLS Master-Apprentice Language Learning Program be modified to promote language acquisition in multigenerational family groups at home? The number and age spread of the many learners in a home-based program could greatly multiply challenges already faced by one-on-one adult teams.

In 2008 Leanne Hinton and Laura submitted a funding proposal to the Sociological Initiative Foundation so that this question could be addressed through a pilot training program, Language at Home. It began as a collaborative project between AICLS, the Kawaiisu Language and Cultural Center, and Betty's extended family. By training family groups, they hoped, more people would have an opportunity to learn from rare native fluent speakers, and the base number of speakers of endangered languages would increase. Though Betty knew about Luther's efforts in the master-apprentice program, she had never received any training herself, so that made her the perfect candidate to test the effectiveness of a new training program. Betty volunteered to participate with the following members of her family who either live in the same apartment complex or in nearby Palm Springs:

Richard Hernandez, 40: Betty's son
Merlene Knight, 42: Betty's daughter
Oscar, 23; Kayla, 19; Jeremy, 17: Merlene's adult children
Avin, 13: Richard's son
Raina, 3: Oscar's daughter
Connor, 3, and Sophira, 1: Kayla's children
Oma and Robin: Raina's grandparents on her mother's side

We began in July 2008 and meant to continue for about three years. To start, Leanne observed Betty's family in Palm Springs and, along with Julie and Laura, gave them an introduction to immersion. Leanne and Betty recorded "survival phrases," simple questions that would allow the family to ask Betty questions in Kawaiisu as they began to learn the language. Julie gave several demonstrations of teaching using the communication-based instruction model. Laura videotaped Betty teaching Julie and Leanne, in Kawaiisu, how to make tortillas—until the smoke from the hot pan set off the smoke alarm in Betty's small apartment, ending the initial orientation.

Over the next two months we passed a draft of the family language plan back and forth. A family language plan frames the actions of the family and their mentors during their participation in Language at Home. The Hernandez Family Language Plan included broad goals stated by the family at the start of the program and defined milestones for language acquisition for the coming year. The family agreed on topics that represented useful, communicative language for everyday situations. We wanted the plan to be brief and easy to read so it could serve as a communication device between the diverse participants.

We didn't set time limits for accomplishing milestones. In the first year of the pilot program we simply wanted to observe the pace of the family's language acquisition. As you can see below, the time it took Betty's family to complete each milestone was noted. As we move into the future, we envision that we will draft new plans with more milestones. Here is the completed plan for the first year.

Hernandez Family Language Plan

Families in the Language Revitalization at Home Program may participate in the program for up to three years (or 36 milestones). Year 1 has six milestones. (The first part of this document included ten numbered guidelines that Leanne drafted after spending the day with the family and talking to Betty about what she had in mind and ways to get started.)

1. Betty, the only fluent speaker in the group, will teach the language to her family.
2. The adults want to learn Kawaiisu, and want the young children to learn it as well.
3. The extended family as a whole will meet twice weekly on Thursday and Saturday and spend much of the day together. The family will try to arrive on time, practice immersion sets for at least one hour, and try to focus on the Kawaiisu language for as long as possible.

4. Part of the day should be devoted to Kawaiisu language play with the children.
5. Adults will continue with language practice when the children go off to do other things.
6. The main focus of language learning will be on usable phrases that the family can use with each other every day.
7. The group will try to do "immersion sets" where they will stay in the language as much as possible. Julie and Laura will train Betty and her family to use the principles of immersion, repetition, and variation that we went over in the July meeting.
8. At least once a month, recordings will be made of the phrases and words being learned, and CD copies will be made for distribution to the households.
9. During the rest of the week, family members will try to use the phrases they have learned with each other, and will listen to and practice with the CDs.
10. Julie, Laura, and Leanne will provide monthly mentoring, by phone or mail or in person.

Each month, Betty, Julie, and Laura will create at least two immersion-style teaching activities for adults and two for children using the topic selected for milestones. Each month Julie and Laura will demonstrate the activities so that Betty and her adult learners can learn to teach using immersion sets. Each activity will have built-in comprehension checks. Each month Betty will record a new audio CD that will be distributed to family members for practice in listening and speaking.

Here are the milestones for Year 1 that Betty, Merlene, Julie, and Laura agreed on after meeting on August 15, 2008, with completion dates added later.

- Milestone 1 (completed July 2008): Initial visit and orientation.
- Milestone 2 (completed September 9, 2008): The family and the mentors will work together to complete the written family language plan and set monthly goals for the first six months.
- Milestone 3 (completed October 4, 2008): Create and learn at least four teaching activities and one new audio CD for greetings and good-byes, "survival" questions for asking for Kawaiisu

Julie (left) and Betty, first day. Photograph courtesy of Laura Grant

words and sentences from Betty, and serving, eating, and preparing food together.

- Milestone 4 (completed December 13, 2008): Create and learn at least four teaching activities and one new audio CD for asking for numbers of things, and more language for eating and preparing food together.
- Milestone 5 (completed February 21, 2009): Create and learn at least four teaching activities and one new audio CD for activities around the swimming pool, learning language for clothes, and helping the children to dress. Order the Marantz recording set and train team members in its use.
- Milestone 6 (completed August 3, 2009): Create and learn at least four teaching activities and one new audio CD for scheduling events such as childcare, going to work, and shopping, and transportation for the day.

Mentoring Language at Home Families

We started mentoring the family using a three-person team that we called the "development team." That sounds a little formal but we were conscious of the research component of our proposal to our funding organization, the Sociological Initiative Foundation. In the AICLS master-apprentice program, one person serves as a mentor. The Language at Home mentors are Luther and Julie, who had "graduated" from the master-apprentice program, and Laura, their mentor, who had guided several teams through the AICLS program. Luther and Julie are board members of the Kawaiisu Language and Cultural Center. Julie also serves as the regional coordinator of AICLS master-apprentice teams in Central and Southern California. Using Kawaiisu mentors provides Betty's family with believable role models for immersion-style learning and creates a relationship for ongoing support into the future. Laura provides extensive planning and implementation experience. She created a structure for training and site visits using the framework of the Hernandez Family Language Plan. Plans for immersion-style teaching activities were derived from the milestones. The diverse talents of the mentors created a support team that increased the likelihood of the family's success.

In August 2008, Luther, Julie, and Laura began meeting monthly for training with the Hernandez family so that Betty could teach at home using the same immersion-style language acquisition techniques

The Hernandez family. Photograph courtesy of Laura Grant

as master-apprentice teams. In the first year, the family became comfortable with the principles of language immersion, learning language
through activities, and using lots of repetition. In the first year, we videotaped four assessments of the family's conversational proficiency.

Luther was invaluable. He talked to Betty in their language and
helped her improve her speaking ability, which had grown a bit rusty
through lack of use. He helped us all by providing words and phrases
for immersion sets. Special little memories came floating up, like the
song Betty remembered that a mother uses while tending a baby. We all
trained Betty's family to stay immersed and not to speak English while
she was teaching. Julie and Laura provided Betty with activities for the
diverse ages of the learners, especially activities for young children. We
made recordings and created audio CDs for her family. We visited each
month to demonstrate language immersion and help her with "dress
rehearsals" of planned immersion sets. These mentor activities were
included in the family language plan.

For master-apprentice teams, visits by the mentor are encouraged but
not required. Mentoring may occur mostly over the phone. Teams may
choose to receive training only at the required group trainings twice a
year. Mentors can, but are not required to provide examples and demonstrations of immersion sets and teaching activities. For the Language
at Home program, we feel that it is critical for mentors to understand
and commit to the training component. Among master-apprentice teams,
the demands of the program, combined with the challenges of daily life,
often cause teams to drop out. With the challenges facing Betty as she
committed to teach an extended family, we felt a high level of support
should be guaranteed.

Creating Goals for Language at Home Families

Broad goals, the milestones of the family language plan, were further
divided into smaller goals so that the family had definite bite-sized tar-
gets to achieve. For example, the goal for Milestone 4 (Create and learn
at least four teaching activities and make one new audio CD for asking
for numbers of things, and more language for eating and preparing food
together) was broken down into smaller pieces, much like the lessons
in a unit plan are when designing curriculum. Betty and her daughter
Merlene determined the smaller "bites" with significant guidance from
Julie and Laura. For future families who may participate in Language at

Home, this is a skill that can first be provided by the development team with the expectation that, after training, it will be done by the adult members of the family.

Smaller Goals of Milestone 4
Betty and Merlene thought about the daily mealtime routines of their family and outlined these smaller Kawaiisu language acquisition goals.

- Count 1 through 10.
- Use numbers 1 through 10, as in "I want three eggs," "Bring me four cups."
- Use the survival phrases "What am I doing?" and "What are you doing?" to elicit information from Betty or another speaker.
- Set the table as instructed in Kawaiisu using plates, cups, forks, knives, and spoons.
- Respond to requests to identify and bring different foods, drinks, dishes, and utensils.
- Ask for and serve drinks: water, tea, iced tea, coffee, and milk.
- Ask for and serve food: eggs, bread, beans, meat, salad, tortillas, cookies, salt, pepper, jalapeños, cheese, tomato, lettuce.
- Be able to ask and respond to the question "What are you making?" This is in regards to what someone is preparing in the kitchen. Learners will be able to give at least eight replies.
- Tell the children to eat and drink a variety of things.

Examples of Language Acquisition Activities
Julie and Laura then created immersion sets meant to last about an hour, based on the communication-based instruction model, to reinforce the target language of each smaller goal. We left typed copies with Betty after we had demonstrated them during one of our monthly visits. We also collected all the "props" required to present the activities and left those with Betty. Here is an example that would have come near the end of the milestone. (Because Kawaiisu does not have a writing system, the Kawaiisu-speaking parts are represented by italics.)

Put dishes that you will ask the learners to bring to the table into a container. (Use paper and plastic dishes.)

1. First direct the learners to bring you items. For example, *"Bring me a fork. Bring me two cups. Bring me three spoons. Bring me a knife and two spoons."* If learners hesitate, assist them by picking out the correct items and saying the phrase again as you do this. When a learner has brought you the correct items, tell him or her to put the items back. *"That's good. Put them back in the container."* Model the actions rather than explaining in English. When everyone seems confident with this, go on to the next activity.

2. Next, ask learners to put items on the table as if you were setting the table for a large meal. Show them what you want them to do until they are correctly putting the things you request on the table. For example: *"Put four cups on the table. Put five spoons on the table. Put eight forks on the table. Put seven plates here. Put five plates and five cups here. Put salt on the table."*

   When learners act confused, help them by picking out the correct items and repeating your request as you do this. When you see they can easily follow these types of directions, ask everyone to sit. Pass out small pads of paper and pencils for the next activity.

3. In this activity, the learners themselves will direct other learners to draw pictures of things based on the cards picked from two decks. One deck will have pictures of table settings and foods they have learned so far, and the other will have the numbers 1 through 10. Demonstrate first in the following way.

   Pick one number card and one picture card. Do not show them to the learners. For example, you may pick the number "4" and a picture of a spoon. You will say, *"Draw four spoons."* Draw four spoons quickly and then show the drawing to the learners. Pick two more cards and say the next phrase. Then say, *"Now you do it."* Time the learners for a minute and then say, *"Stop."* Have them show their drawings. When they are successfully drawing your requests, it will be their turn to try saying the phrases in Kawaiisu. Next have a learner take your place with the cards. Hand over the decks and say, *"Now you do it."* Be sure to start with the learners who are the most confident in speaking, so the less confident ones have a chance to listen more. If a person can't say the phrase, say it first and then have him or her repeat after you. Give learners a chance to say it on their own, but don't let them become uncomfortable. Model the language and be consistent: do not give a variety of ways to say the same thing. Give lots of praise. When everyone is doing well with this activity, demonstrate the next level of difficulty. Pick two number cards and two pictures. Create phrases like *"Give me two eggs and four plates."* Again ask learners to draw cards and say their own phrases until they can speak confidently. End the lesson by saying, *"That's all!"*

For independent practice, have learners listen to tracks 1 through 6 on the "Serving Food CD." (Julie and I recorded and copied CDs for the family.) Ask them to practice directing other people, especially the children, in setting the table each day.

Measuring Progress for Language at Home Families

Milestones were considered finished when Betty and the family successfully demonstrated some of the activities that showed they could use the target language. Laura videotaped these assessments. We then sent the assessments on DVD to the family so that they could see their own progress, and because the children dearly loved to see themselves on television!

The family language plan can be shared among the adults of the group and periodically discussed by the mentors and family together. This helps the family stay focused. The two-person master-apprentice teams are not required to create formal plans of this type, though they are strongly encouraged to set goals. (See the accompanying table for a thorough comparison of the Master-Apprentice Language Learning and Language at Home programs.) Julie, especially, felt very strongly that goals would be crucial in creating a clear path for the family to follow. As a former apprentice and a current coordinator for master-apprentice teams, she had watched new masters and apprentices become scattered in their efforts for many months after the initial orientation because they were overwhelmed by the scope of learning and teaching a language. Betty faced a huge challenge in teaching so many people of diverse ages. She also had a full-time job and was the primary bread-winner for the family. We felt it was the responsibility of the Language at Home development team to support her in forming goals, creating

Laura Grant filming during an assessment. Photograph courtesy of Laura Grant

activities, and providing teaching materials so that the Language at Home program would not overwhelm her.

Some Challenges

Like most people setting goals that are dear to them, the Hernandez family found their ambitions quickly tested. As experienced mentors, Julie, Luther, and Laura knew not to squash their enthusiasm but to be present in time to gently correct the course of action and emphasize the successes. Adaptations can be folded into the family language plan.

Betty found it difficult to bring all family members together for learning sessions each Thursday and Saturday as originally specified in the family language plan. She adapted by coaching them in groups and individually as their work schedules allowed, instead of requiring that everyone attend learning sessions together. Because she worked three days a week and had the other days free, she could teach Kayla, Connor, and Sophira at their home on Wednesday evenings; Raina's grandparents and anyone else who could attend at the grandparents' home on Thursdays; and on Saturdays she taught the rest of the family, typically Merlene, Jeremy, Raina, Avin, and often Kayla and Connor. Her

Learning Kawaiisu for daily life. Photograph courtesy of Laura Grant

apartment became too crowded and chaotic when more than four people gathered for teaching, so this solution worked for that issue as well.

Some family members continued in the program and others dropped out. This is likely in any language-learning effort, though with Betty's family, even those who didn't attend much were still very supportive of her. Betty's view is that everyone should be encouraged to participate at whatever level they would like, and that no one should be criticized. Everyone has a place in the process.

Immersion-style teaching and learning are foreign to most Americans. The Hernandez family tended to model their learning time together on their experiences in American public schools. Learning sessions often turned into discussions in English about Kawaiisu rather than practice at speaking Kawaiisu. There was a lot of note taking. Now, during monthly visits, we may do a private "dress rehearsal" with Betty to be sure she practices the immersion-style teaching activities and comprehension checks. To a fluent speaker, the amount of repetition required for a second language to embed itself in a new learner must seem excessive and certainly sound ridiculous. We watched Betty present activities to the family and reminded them to hold questions in English until she was done teaching. We emphasized that questions in Kawaiisu are allowed and encouraged so that immersion time is extended.

We revised the frequency of our videotaped assessments to once every four to six weeks instead of quarterly. This put a little pressure on the group to practice their immersion activities. This particular group enjoyed being in front of a camera and seeing themselves on television, so this solution works well for them.

We found it very challenging, as mentors, to prepare materials and travel to coach the pilot family each month, but we also feel that it is important to continue this coaching schedule so that we can address problems quickly before they deflect the family from their plan. We concluded that in the future when we pair mentors with families we will have to be sure they are aware of the extent of the commitment.

Some Results

By participating in the Language at Home pilot program, the Hernandez family, who had no previous training in teaching and learning language, acquired language much quicker than the majority of our master-apprentice teams. Betty and Merlene attended the group training for master-apprentice teams in November of 2008, when they had been in the Language at Home program for four months. During the training exercises they performed as well and with the same degree of confidence as master-apprentice team members who had been in the program for two years. During their second videotaped assessment, in December of 2008, the family group also displayed skills far beyond those of most master-apprentice teams during their second assessment. This can be attributed to initial goal setting in the Hernandez Family Language Plan, the intensive monthly coaching at the family's home, and the constant interaction of family members in the language, even when they are not with Betty. Adults practiced almost daily with the young children. Children welcome interactive play with language. Not only can the Language at Home program reach more learners, those learners progress more quickly.

It is significant that the family has found a common cause that has deep meaning for them all. Everyone knows intellectually that it is important to keep the language alive for the next generation, but they work at it because they love doing things together and especially because they love "Granny" (Betty). Health, money, and scheduling

distractions come up daily. It is important that family members in a
Language at Home program like each other and naturally enjoy spending time together, because it is very challenging to learn new skills
and a language, and this is what will carry them through. It is equally
important, for the same reasons, for mentors to be paired with a family
they enjoy.

Potential funders are often critical when people involved in a language program start out working among their own families. One big
reason that some California languages have survived into this century,
however, is that individual families have believed that is important and
have passed their languages from one generation to the next. Regardless
of funders' regulations against nepotism, this motivation has worked
and should be retained as a strategy for indigenous language survival.

There is no doubt that there is a trend here in California towards
families, rather than isolated individuals, practicing language revitalization. The family-driven movement is often powered by graduates of
the master-apprentice program, who see this as the next logical step.
Awareness of language revitalization has been raised by workshops and
conferences nationwide. Families are aware that there is an opportunity
for training and they are eager to have it. The research process supported by the Sociological Initiative Foundation has informed us how
this can be done.

In October of 2008 Julie and Laura took Betty on a tour of the old
home place in Lorraine. Of course the huge granite grinding rock abides
in its spot on the hillside. Incredibly, the screen of brush that Rafael
had built for Gladys so that she might have privacy when she prayed
was still there. The little wooden house had been demolished and most
of it burned or carted away. There were a few twigs left, however, from
the old nest to add to a new nest. We found the old metal mailbox,
slightly squashed, and Betty carried it back to her present home in Palm
Springs.

We took a few dents in our Language at Home family too. Betty was
diagnosed with a brain aneurysm and her doctor ordered no work, no
stress, and no travel. Julie's family suffered through the onset of the
recession and a mortgage crisis and put everything on hold until that
was over. Merlene and her kids moved off to Texas for a few months.
Now everyone has converged again and is in good health. We have
our jumping-off spot from the family language plan of Year 1 and the

Hernandez family is ready for more language work. That whole cycle of life events, though unplanned, tested our work together. The language and the skills were not lost. The perfect time to start language revitalization at home may present itself again and again.

Comparison of Programs

Some Criteria for Those Applying to the Program

Master-Apprentice Program	Language at Home Program
The master speaker is fluent in the language.	Same.
The language learner lives close to the speaker.	Same.
Not applicable	There is an existing support network such as a tribal language and/or cultural program to support the family's language revitalization activities after they have completed the program.

Comparison of How the Programs Operate

Master-Apprentice Program	Language at Home Program
One master speaker.	At least one master speaker. There may be more.
One adult apprentice.	Several language learners of diverse ages. The emphasis is on including families and children.
One mentor.	A development team. The number is not set. This depends on the needs of the family.
Initial training and videotaped assessment, usually at a group training workshop for several teams.	Initial training is combined with an observation in the home of the family.

Participation is measured in hours and tracked by weekly self-evaluation reports and monthly invoices. There is no initial formal goal setting although setting goals is emphasized at training workshops.	Participation is measured by completion of milestones that are determined by the family in their family language plan.
Teams receive training at two group sessions each year. Mentors may coordinate training for their teams at any time but site visits are not required.	The family receives training once a month. Site visits are expected. Families may attend group training with master-apprentice teams but this is not required.
Teams receive training in immersion-based language acquisition between two adults.	Families receive training in immersion-based language acquisition with emphasis on activities to suit the various ages of participants.
Teams can receive equipment and training for making recordings on CDs.	Same.
Teams are evaluated on conversational proficiency through a video-taped assessment about every six months and through a mentor report each quarter.	Families are evaluated on conversational proficiency through a videotaped assessment. This completes each milestone. Mentors submit reports but the interval has not yet been established.
Stipends may be received by masters and apprentices each month for hours worked. Mentors receive stipends each quarter after submitting a report.	Master speakers and mentors receive stipends at the completion of each milestone.
Duration of training program: 900 hours.	Duration of training program: 36 milestones.

13: Scottish Gaelic

Taic/CNSA and Scottish Gaelic

Finlay M. Macleod

The Birth of CNS

In 1982, after many years of creeping decline, there came together on the Island of Skye a handful of dedicated people determined to save the Gaelic language and culture. Thus the organisation Comhairle Nan Sgoiltean Araich (CNSA), now known as Taic, was born, with the following four goals:

- To help revive and promote the Gaelic language and culture
- To provide children with Gaelic medium preschool education
- To collect, collate, and create for the Taic/CNSA groups the very best Gaelic medium education package found anywhere.
- To collect, develop, and create a stimulating and innovative range of language courses, materials, and resources for adults/ parents with young children for use mainly in the home.

Over the last thirty years, we have striven to bring Scottish Gaelic into people's lives, their homes, and their communities. Through research and experience, our programs have developed over the years with the goal of bringing parents, other adults, and children to Gaelic fluency with the capability of bringing the language back into their daily lives.

Total Immersion Plus (TIP) Explained

TIP, or to give it its full name, Total Immersion Plus methodologies, is our operating system of language acquisition. It has a number of very different features from those found in most other Gaelic language-learning packages.

For example, all TIP-based courses insist that the only language to be used by both tutor and students in the learning environment is the one to be acquired—in our case, Scottish Gaelic. We have found that strict adherence to this rule is absolutely essential; any deviation negatively affects the students' progress, and if breaches are allowed to continue unchecked, they will undermine the language's credibility in the students' eyes.

There are certain fundamental language-learning components employed by TIP via action and activity. What we are not concerned with in the initial phase is any focus on grammar, reading, writing, translation, and books. Again, within TIP methodology, there is the expectation that students will be speaking the Gaelic language, however haltingly, within the first session of any course.

The thrust of TIP is that one acquires Gaelic by way of the imaginative use of themes, tasks, strategies, nonverbal communication, and intensive repetition. Another vitally important aspect of TIP is that each theme, once begun, is not then abandoned until it is completed in its entirety, whatever its duration. This is essential practice for students, as it helps them make sense of each theme and its accompanying language. It has even more relevance insomuch as it aids students in trying out Gaelic at home. Also in support of homework, students are advised to acquire a recording device to use during course sessions so that they can then play back and employ the material at their own convenience.

Another important factor of all TIP philosophy is the use of a wide range of everyday equipment, items, objects, tools, materials, and furniture relevant to the particular course theme. The value of this is that through handling, seeing, making, doing, using, plus role play and discussion of the various items, students see not only a real and evident connection between item and word, but also an ability to transport the theme to their own personal environment and make use of it there.

A particularly effective feature of TIP strategies is that they employ intensive and substantial amounts of repetition. And admittedly, students in the initial stage of a TIP-centered course often find such ploys intimidating, if not irritating. However, given just a little longer time and patience, students quickly revise this view and come to realise the real value of repetition. Indeed, almost every student that has ever partaken of a TIP-based course has come to regard repetition as a lifeline.

It is worth mentioning two further important points. One is that contrary to long-held beliefs that children learn more quickly than adults, in actual fact, if TIP language acquisition methodologies appropriate to an adult are used, adults will unquestionably learn Gaelic faster. The second point is, TIP methodologies were originally developed as a consequence of observing in action Gaelic preschool language-learning methods.

In conclusion, it is good to report that such is the popularity and value of TIP as a language acquisition tool that its fame has spread far and wide. For example, Nova Scotia, Canada, has a flourishing Gaelic language-learning program based on TIP methodologies.

The Family Language Plan
In 1985, Taic/CNSA began work on the Family Language Plan, which would take seven years to complete. The following five handbooks were the products. (See Appendix for further details.)

- Family Language Action Plan
- Family Language Plan (Omnibus Edition)
- Family Language Plan (Neither Parent Gaelic Speaking)
- The Officer's Handbook
- The Gaelic Tracker

We were convinced that if parents wanted their children to grow up fluent both in Gaelic and English, it would be essential for them to plan strategically for the implementation and use of Gaelic, both in the home and the wider world. Ground rules governing language use must be laid down and then always adhered to when using the two languages. This is essential in order for children to feel secure and therefore confident in knowing that the language they are using at any time is the right one It is important that parents using the Family Language Plan maintain a strong thread of consistency throughout the language strategies they use with the child. Consistency is one of the most important factors in determining whether the child will grow up speaking Gaelic or not. The best time for putting the Family Language Plan into practice is before the child is born or as soon as possible after the birth. The timing is crucial, for it can be difficult to change the language spoken to a child, once a pattern is established.

It is our intention that wherever possible, children have the opportunity to learn Gaelic as a first language in homes where one or both parents are fluent Gaelic speakers. In homes where neither parent is a Gaelic speaker, we want to assist both the children and the adults in learning to speak the language. Having a customised family language plan is an important step toward the ultimate goal of having a family which is not only conversationally fluent in Gaelic, but also uses it continuously. A family language plan is a road map for parents who wish to create a Gaelic environment and regime within their own home. Understanding the plan will undoubtedly alleviate much of the frustration and many of the problems experienced by parents in pursuit of a long-term Gaelic-speaking family. Success in this endeavour will do much to set up a strong intergenerational transmission structure.

Tutors, or field workers, work with each family to guide them in the development and implementation of their own personal family language plan. Field workers also help the families review and evaluate the plan during the process, and update and amend the material with them as needed. The field workers also highlight and thus raise consciousness about issues, myths, misunderstandings, problems, and situations surrounding family language planning. It is important that everyone involved in the work realise that they have a role to play not only within a particular family but also in helping ever more children and parents to become fluent in Gaelic. Explaining that role and how to go about it is equally important. Helping more households and the wider community to become fluent and use the language is something that should be in the minds of everyone. With these elements all working together in harmony, then and only then will Gaelic realise its rightful place in Scotland's future.

An important precursor to putting a family language plan into practice is an introductory meeting which, for simplicity's sake, has been divided up into a number of parts. It is possible for a family language plan meeting to be held in a variety of venues, such as a community centre, a school, or a family home. Follow-up meetings are also very important. At the meetings, parents plan their own language-learning process as needed and plan ways they can enhance the Gaelic-language environment for their children. The following are some of the points they must consider in their language plan:

1. Recognize their own learning needs and plan for their own language learning as needed. Their family language strategy must differ depending on various factors. Perhaps the most important factor is the level of fluency of the parents. The three main variants are: a home where both parents are Gaelic speakers; a home where one parent is a fluent Gaelic speaker; and a home where neither parent speaks any Gaelic whatsoever. Each of these three home situations calls for a different set of strategies.
2. Make a list of people who might be useful to their goals, such as Gaelic-speaking neighbors, relatives, other Gaelic-speaking families, professionals, such as doctors, dentists, and storekeepers, who speak Gaelic, and other people the family would come in contact with.
3. Plan how to approach and guide people to get them to speak in Gaelic to their family.
4. Become aware of and take advantage of available Gaelic language resources, such as Gaelic medium schools, special interest clubs, events, TV and radio programs, etc.
5. Parents are asked to track their language use (Gaelic vs. English) using a "language tracker" and also to keep a journal.
6. Set their start date for beginning to speak entirely in Gaelic (if fluent) or to use as much Gaelic as possible if they are still just learning.
7. Parents also sign a "Gaelic-only" declaration, as an aid for taking their commitment seriously.

We learned many lessons from Taic's Family Language Plan program. After the initial implementation of the program, we have seen that the family language plan is the most effective and efficient language acquisition guidance tool for parents to use when embarking on the objective of having their whole family as a Gaelic-speaking unit. Besides this very important task, it also plays a major role in raising consciousness among those families who would like to be Gaelic-speaking.

It is very difficult to measure exactly how much effect the Family Language Plan program has had in bringing more people into the Gaelic-speaking network. Suffice to say that Taic/CNSA headquarters and field staff regularly receive requests from all sorts of people who wish to gain a Gaelic fluency, whether it be for themselves or as a family group. We have also seen that since family language plans have become the norm, there is now an evident strengthening of family language bonding, which in today's world can only be a force for good.

We also learned that we need a range of very different preschool groups, especially for children younger than three. One example would be full-time playgroups for two-year-olds (thirty hours per week). Another would be a structured all-day parent-and-child group that embraces wholeheartedly Total Immersion Plus strategies, which are highly effective in bringing the pre-three age group to a Gaelic fluency in the shortest time and by way of user-friendly techniques.

While there is Gaelic medium communication in Scotland, one issue that came to light quite unexpectedly is that the language of the school does not transfer well to the home. Language acquired in schools was perfectly fine for the school domain. And we all originally thought it would serve the language acquisition requirement very well. However, it became increasingly evident that when it came to the home, the wider community, and interacting with one's child, the language was found to be wanting. Thus intergenerational transmission was neither alive nor active.

Because of this gap between the language learned at school and the language needed for the home, we recognized the need for two new courses, namely: the Gaelic in the Home Course and the Altram Course. Both of these are directed primarily at those who went through Gaelic medium education but had no experience of Gaelic in their home environment either as babies or young children, although anyone wishing to acquire Gaelic fluency can undertake one or both of these courses.

Research has indicated that a great many learners of Gaelic have little or no experience of the language of affection in Gaelic. We believe that this aspect of interaction between parent and child is of vital importance. Not only does such language—endearment terms and other kinds of language of affection—create bonds between the child and parent, but it also creates a bond with the language that the affection is expressed in. We currently have two handbooks covering this topic, but it has become increasingly obvious that there is a real need for several more handbooks, DVDs, etc.

We are now in the preparatory stage of a second phase of the Family Language Plan, where it is our intention to take this concept to a much wider audience, both here in Scotland and beyond.

Gaelic in the Home Course

While family language plans were becoming part of the everyday Gaelic acquisition guidelines for families, they also began revealing a need for a more varied vocabulary in order to meet the day-to-day Gaelic language requirements of a family. As mentioned earlier, it came to light that the Gaelic that children acquired while at school, which we all thought would serve life outside the school equally well, did in fact fall very short. Thus was born the Gaelic in the Home Course, providing a comprehensive level of Gaelic that a family would use in their daily lives. The course is centered around a home setting with all that entails. There is also a venturing out into the wider community regarding visiting and other social activities, shopping, and seeing doctors, dentists, friends, etc. equipped with Gaelic that will allow one to progress smoothly and effectively through conversations in these situations. Families also learn how to talk about home maintenance, household budgeting, cleaning, dining, cooking, clothes, social activities, and other home-centered topics.

Some forty Gaelic in the Home courses were set up that served around four hundred students over a five-year period. The client groups are made up of expectant parents, couples considering parenthood, parents of newborns or older children, grandparents, and other relatives, and those who simply wish to acquire Gaelic fluency for the home setting. The ideal is that a course runs continuously for six, seven, eight, or nine weeks and for between twenty and forty hours each week. If executed in an unbroken two-hundred-hour block and set in a conducive environment, a Gaelic in the Home course can bring a non-Gaelic-speaking adult to a conversational Gaelic fluency speedily.

Every day we are given evidence of the growing popularity of the Gaelic in the Home course methods and their importance in the acquiring of a Gaelic fluency. One particularly good point being made is that this learning tool is in no way in competition with formal school language teaching; indeed, it is the natural precursor to school-based language learning. Moreover, without the first step, language transmitted from parent to child, there will certainly not be any intergenerational transmission taking place.

Gaelic in the Home and Altram courses are particularly harmonious, as they employ a similar format, share many themes and TIP strategies, and work through comparable parameters. Thus they can ideally be run as partner courses without too much adjustment.

The Altram Course

Almost from the moment we began working on the Gaelic in the Home course, a need surfaced in regard to a range of specific Gaelic language courses relevant to those considering parenthood, expectant parents, and parents with babies or very young children (to five years). This age range is then divided into four groups: birth to nine months; nine to eighteen months; eighteen months to three years; and three to five years. To accompany the above, there is a Parenthood course which covers the period beginning at pregnancy right through to the birth of the child.

The five fundamental elements of an Altram course are:

- Targeted parent-and-child-centered Gaelic language (parentese).
- Course themes built around daily experiences that one finds in the home dealing with a baby, and out and about in the community.
- Unique hands-on learning, functional language acquisition carried out in the most accessible, user-friendly way possible, by way of Total Immersion Plus strategies.
- Centering on baby care and its related language. This is then underpinned by appropriate items, utensils, products, articles, etc., all of which are used in helping a parent/student identify, name, imprint, and eventually use Gaelic with ease and confidence when speaking to a baby or very young child.
- Categorization of topics into three overlapping groups regarding the relationship between parent and baby: emotion, intellect, and nurturing.

In order to make an Altram course workable and accessible to students, the course has been formatted into themes that are all relevant to the baby and its welfare.

Emotional Interaction between Parent and Child
This area deals primarily with the language of affection, building intimate connections between the parent and child, talking, caressing, rubbing, touching, whispering, singing softly, and so on. Themes include such situations as

* Playing with the baby
* Baby is woken up by parent
* Feeding/bottle feeds
* Baby has an afternoon nap
* Visiting grandparents and friends

Intellectual Interaction between Parent and Child
The intellectual area concentrates on talking, reading/singing, introducing new experiences, touch, smells, sounds, showing picture books to the baby.

* Going to the parent-and-child group
* Going to the swimming pool
* Going to the park
* Visiting shops
* Visiting grandparents and friends

Parent and Child Nurturing
The nurturing element focuses on washing, feeding, nappy changing, safety, health checks, dressing/undressing, hygiene, clothes, and such like:

* Nappy changes through the day
* Nursing the baby
* Washing hands and face
* Clothing the baby
* Getting ready to go out
* Health, hygiene, and safety routines

The aims of the Altram course are:

- To endow parents with a comprehensive Gaelic vocabulary that allows them to speak to a baby or very young child.
- To provide parents who do not speak Gaelic with the where-withal for their child to become a fluent Gaelic speaker by the time it reaches three years.
- To help create a conducive environment outside the home, in the company of others, at varying stages of parenthood.
- To help strengthen the parent-and-child bonding, and at the same time enhance the interaction within the whole family.
- To offer, as an ongoing objective, courses that make use of the most useful and up-to-date strategies for bringing babies or very young children to a Gaelic fluency as early as possible.
- To bring together parents, irrespective of where they are placed on the parenthood spectrum, for the acquisition of Gaelic. Not only does this give them Gaelic as a lifelong skill, it will also do much to alleviate the feelings of isolation felt by all too many minority-language parents.
- To make parents aware that the knowledge they bring to their child in the home environment, prior to the child's embarking on formal school-based education, is precious and the natural pre-cursor to this next stage of their child's education.

The most important point we hope to convey to the parents is that they do indeed bring an enormous amount of knowledge to their children and at a most crucial stage in their development. Parents, in considering this, should bear in mind the large amount of time they spend with their offspring before they take up any kind of formal education. It may come as quite a surprise to find out just how much time there is between birth and three years. This is the period when parents and children are together the greatest amount of time, as well as the time when children go a long way toward acquiring their first language. If the parents want their children to be Gaelic speakers, these are the years to start making it happen.

Final Remarks

The Glasgow-based Altram/Bumps & Babies Centre will provide training and development for the acquisition of conversational Gaelic for anyone on the parenthood spectrum. We will also offer Gaelic in the Home courses and even more new courses using the Total Immersion Plus (TIP) methodologies.

We have in the pipeline plans for running TIP training courses for prospective Altram and Gaelic in the Home tutors that will last for some thirty days throughout the year and cover theory, hands-on, and practical tasks.

As always, publicity is paramount in bringing home the message and then the people onto our courses and into our centres. Posters, news releases, letters, and the media have all been used in raising awareness with regard to Gaelic acquisition for adults/parents, children, and potential staff. It is said that in Scotland it takes about seven years for a new idea to be taken up on any practical level.

Another lesson learned from our latest undertakings is that we need to attract not just learners, but also fluent speakers as well. There are many good reasons why, but perhaps the following two are the most important.

- Good examples abound, indicating clearly that fluent Gaelic speakers/helpers among the learners speed up their progress immeasurably.
- For a host of reasons, many very competent Gaelic speakers do not actually use their Gaelic. Habit, lack of confidence, no one to speak Gaelic with, and upbringing are just a few of the reasons; an Altram and Gaelic in the Home course can easily and quickly activate their motivation and speaking skills.

In conclusion, between the various programs—the Family Language Plan, the Gaelic in the Home course, and the Altram course—we believe that the Gaelic language in Scotland has much improved prospects for the future.

Postscript

Everything in life has an "expiry date" which one, if wise, accepts gracefully and then moves on. Though the demise of the Taic organisation was sad, I believe I have accepted it and moved on to greater things with the creation of the Moray Language Centre.

This being my latest and most exciting venture, it has the sum total of all my experience of what and what not to do with regard to teaching Gaelic to adults; how to make the process of Gaelic conversational language acquisition ever more accessible and user-friendly; and the quickest ways for learners to reach their desired levels of fluency. Of course my overarching objective is to make the whole learning experience both satisfying and enjoyable.

Above all this, the Moray Language Centre allows me the freedom to explore innovative ideas that would not have been practical within the long-standing structures of the Taic organisation.

And so I enthusiastically look forward with a renewed commitment to an even brighter and more dynamic future for Gaelic language learning.

Manuals and Courses by F. M. Macleoid and D. Farber
(finlay@fmdf.org.uk; www.ti-plus.co.uk or www.gaelicworld.co.uk; telephone (0044) 1542-836322)

Family Language Plan Resources
*   1(G) Family Language Plan Meetings: The Officer's Handbook
*   2(G) Family Language Action Plan: The Parent's Handbook
*   4(G) Family Language Plan: Book One: Neither Parent Gaelic Speaking
*   5(G) Family Language Plan: Omnibus Edition
*   37(G) The Gaelic Language Tracker

TIP and Gaelic in the Home Resources
*   6(G) Gaelic in the Home Group: The Committee Handbook
*   7(G) Total Immersion Plus for Adults: The Student's Handbook
*   8(G) Total Immersion Plus for Adults: The Course Handbook
*   9(G) Total Immersion Plus for Adults: The Tutor's Handbook
*   100(G) TIP Conversation Strategies
*   16(G) Gaelic in the Home Course: Theme Packs
*   120(G) 6 Week Gaelic in the Home TIP Course Framework Book One

- 121(G) 6 Week Gaelic in the Home TIP Course Framework Book Two
- 122(G) 3 Week Gaelic in the Home TIP Course Framework Book Three
- 141(G) Gaelic in the Home TIP Sessional Framework
- 153(G) 6 Week TIP Social Situations Course Framework (Book One)
- 154(G) 6 Week TIP Social Situations Course Framework (Book Two)

Staff, Parents, and Pre-School Children Ages 2 to 5
- 17(G) Total Immersion Plus: The Parents' Manual
- 18(G) Creating a Total Gaelic Environment
- 19(G) Total Immersion Plus for Pre-School Children
- 20(G) Circle Time for Two-Year-Olds

Pre-birth Altram/Bumps & Babies, to 3 years old
- 170(G) The Parenthood Course
- 27(G) Altram/Bumps & Babies Gaelic Course: Theme Pack
- 181(G) 6 Week TIP Bumps & Babies Course Framework
- 186(G) The Bumps & Babies TIP Sessional Framework
- 95(G) Bumps & Babies Language of Endearment

Pre-School Staff Gaelic Courses
- 33(G) Pre-School Staff Gaelic Course: Theme Pack

Parent and Child Gaelic Courses
- 220(G) The Pre-School Gaelic Course 6 Week TIP Framework (Book One)
- 221(G) The Pre-School Gaelic Course 6 Week TIP Framework (Book Two)
- 222(G) The Pre-School Gaelic Course 6 Week TIP Framework (Book Three)

CONCLUSION:
BRINGING YOUR LANGUAGE INTO YOUR OWN HOME

BRINGING YOUR LANGUAGE INTO YOUR OWN HOME

Leanne Hinton

The families who wrote most of the chapters of this book are language pioneers in a broad, non-centralized social movement of language reclamation. To them, language is one of the most important aspects of maintaining an indigenous identity in the face of the juggernaut of social and political forces that threaten to erase that identity. And yet the parents' decision to bring their family's heritage language into their home was beyond political. The decision was a very personal one—based on the desire to give an important gift to their children. The heritage language is a most precious gift of connection to family, community, history, and identity.

There are many who would like to give this gift to their own children but may not know where to start or how to proceed. This chapter, then, is for those readers who would like to do what the parents in this book are doing—to bring your heritage language into your home to use with your family. Or perhaps you are already doing this, and could just use some ideas, or some encouragement that you are doing it "right." The preceding chapters have in them many lessons for the rest of us, which we will utilize here as a guide.

Becoming Bilingual

My grandnephew Walter is five years old, and at this point in his life he is completely bilingual in English and Dutch. I expect he will remain so all his life, because he has strong input from both languages and strong motivation for using both. Unlike all the other stories in this book, it is actually English in this case that is the "minority" language. Walter's parents are from America but are now naturalized citizens of Holland. They still have strong ties to relatives in the United States (me, for example!) and visiting occurs in both directions every couple of years. They were not fluent in Dutch when he was born, and they still use English at home all the time, except when Dutch friends and playmates come over. When Walter was three he knew English better than Dutch, but now, at age seven and going to school, he speaks Dutch flawlessly. Walter did tell his mother once that he "likes Dutch better than English." It is common to prefer the language that one's friends, schoolmates, and teachers speak. This might have been interpreted as a danger sign for his English, were it not that English is well respected in Holland and always taught in the later grades in school, and will continue as the main language of home. Many Dutch people are conversant in English, and every library and bookstore has a section filled with English-language books. And visits from relatives or to the "homeland" always give a new shot of energy to English. Furthermore, since English is one of the dominant languages of the world, opportunities to use it will always be there for him.

The choice made by Walter's parents to speak English at home was what gave him the opportunity to be bilingual. Had they decided to speak Dutch at home to give him a "head start" for his schooling, he would probably be heavily dominant in Dutch now. It is the language least used in the surrounding society that must be emphasized at home in order to help a child become bilingual.

For children learning an endangered language, the path to bilingualism will not be as easy as it has been for young Walter. The endangered language is not waiting everywhere for a child. No bookstores or libraries are likely to have books in the endangered language. There is no country to go to where the language fills the environment. In most cases, there is no support for the language in the schools. For a child to learn an endangered language, the parents have to find ways to make sure there is a sufficient amount of input for the child to learn, and to make the language beloved of the child. Margaret Noori puts it well:

> Sometimes it is like waging war on English and you must have
> strong defenses, offensive strategies and an endless supply of

Margaret Noori with her daughter Fionna and a friend, Marlie Libbs. Photograph courtesy of Margaret Noori

patience and assistance. At other times it is the most natural and easy form of play, a blanket of comfort that shelters a small community from the larger, sometimes harsher, landscape. I will be honest, we don't yet have days where everyone speaks Anishinaabemowin all the time, and perhaps we never will. But we do try and I think that is what matters. We make space and give children a foundation for bilingual learning in the place where it matters the most, the home.[1]

Family Language Planning

Let us suppose that you are a parent or future parent interested in raising your children to know and use your endangered heritage language. It is very useful to start with creating a language plan (see Chapters 12 and 13).

As Finlay Macleoid describes for Scottish Gaelic in Chapter 13, your language plan should itemize the resources available to you, both human—relatives and friends who speak the language—and material—books, schools, language lessons, cultural programs in your community, etc. Your plan might also involve seeking out resources you do not know about yet, or working to create your own. There will be ups and downs during the journey toward family bilingualism, and it is helpful to refer back to your plan (and perhaps modify it) when problems arise.

The Kawaiisu family plan described in Chapter 12 included setting milestones and monthly goals for family language learning. Both Kawaiisu and Gaelic involved community-level programs to assist families, but a language plan can also be made without any outside agency.

Full Immersion, OPOL, or Starting to Learn Together

An important step in language planning is to take stock of what linguistic situation you are in. Are you a speaker of this language? Is your spouse also a speaker? Or are neither of you fluent in the language? We will approach these alternatives one at a time.

Both parents fluent in the language. If you are both fluent in the language, congratulations! All you need to do is start talking to each other and to your children in your language. Later in this chapter, you'll find some pointers to help in getting started. But it is never too early to start—today would be a good time.

You may well be thinking that this is easier said than done, and you are right. Some of the issues that make this difficult are discussed later in this chapter.

One parent fluent in the language. The "One-parent, one-language" (OPOL) approach is often used when only one parent is fluent in the desired language. It is a well-studied approach to developing bilingual children, and there are a number of guidebooks that can help parents understand and succeed in this approach. For example, see Suzanne Barron-Hauwaert's *Language Strategies for Bilingual Families,* which has a great deal of important advice for successful use of the OPOL approach.[2]

Another example is in Chapter 11. Ezra Hale's father, the celebrated linguist Ken Hale, spoke only Warlpiri to him, and Ezra's mother spoke English. Similarly, Margaret Peters's daughter speaks Mohawk to her little son, but his father speaks mainly English to him. And Hana O'Regan (Chapter 6) writes:

> The children's father only spoke English, so we adopted the OPOL (one-parent, one-language) practice of bilingualism, although in fairness there weren't many other options available to us. Despite the challenges, we have managed to raise our two children as fluent speakers of both Māori and English.

I have a friend who is from Iceland and speaks only Icelandic to his children. His wife, who is American, speaks only English. Their children switch flawlessly and automatically from one language to the other depending on who they are talking to. I know other couples in the United States who leave aside English altogether when speaking to their children. In one case, one parent uses Swedish while the other uses Arabic. The parents use English with each other, and also in their three- and four-way conversations within the family, and trust this exposure, along with school and the general English-speaking environment, to bring the children along in that language. A four-year-old child I met in Finland was already speaking four languages with ease—Finnish, Russian, and two Saami languages. Cedric Sunray and his wife, Randi, speak Kiowa, Choctaw, and English in the home, and for some time, while they were working in a Cherokee community, their oldest child attended a Cherokee immersion school. Cedric writes:

We speak Choctaw, Kiowa, and English in our home. We call
it "Kiotaw" jokingly. My wife's mom lives with us about four
days/evenings a week and is wonderful in contributing to the
usage of the Kiowa language....We both speak both languages
to the kids more and more. So the language people hear our
kids speaking a mix of Kiowa, Choctaw, and English. And it
varies as well. Sometimes my kids may define the same thing
or the same question depending on the day, their mood, or the
location they are in. I hear more Kiowa at Kiowa activities,
more Choctaw at Choctaw activities, and more English around
monolingual English-speaking people.[3]

Children are perfectly capable of growing up bilingual, trilingual, or even quadrilingual. But the parents must create an environment where both (or all) of the languages can thrive. Barron-Hauwaert
points out that a child must hear the minority language 40 to 60 percent of the time in order to become a balanced bilingual. Some of the
important factors that lead to success in the OPOL approach include
(1) consistency in the use of the minority language with the children;
(2) both parents being supportive of the approach (e.g., if one parent feels resentful because he doesn't know the language being used by
the other, he or she could undercut the efforts of the other); (3) having
some encouragement from outside the household, such as contact with
relatives or friends who also use the language, or a school program, to
help the children to realize that the language is useful beyond the walls
of their household.[4]

In order to support the second language being used in their household, many spouses make strong efforts to learn as much as they can of
that language, even if English will remain their main language of communication. The Baldwin family (Chapter 1) is one example: Karen
Baldwin does not know Miami as well as her husband but supports the
language in many ways and continually strives to learn more and use
it when she can. Similarly, Brian Bielenberg (Chapter 10), the English
speaker in an OPOL household, is still learning Kypriaka and uses it
increasingly over time.

Always, though, the endangered language is the one that needs the
most care and support, for English is all around and can easily crowd
your language out if you don't find plenty of time and ways to bring it
to your children.

Neither parent fluent in the language. If neither of you knows the language fluently, you must of course learn it in order for it to become a language of home. In this situation, the family will learn the language together. Everything the parent learns should be shared with the children, either simultaneously or later the same day. This family learning project can be fun and fulfilling for all members.

Some of the parents in this book learned their language as a first language from their own parents. Margaret and Theodore Peters (Chapter 5) were such parents. But other parents who wanted to use their language at home with their children had to learn in other ways, and in most cases are still learning. Determination is the main factor in the language learning of the parents in this book. They learned in any and every way available to them. Hana O'Regan (Chapter 6) developed her love of *Te Reo* through an elder and honed her skills in a boarding school and college. Kauanoe Kamanā and William Wilson (Chapter 7) learned most of their Hawaiian at the university. Phil and Ellie Albers (Chapter 3) learned and are still learning Karuk from elder speakers, simply by listening, asking questions, and practicing with them—using an adult learning model, the Master-Apprentice Language Learning Program.[5] Similarly, Richard Grounds (Chapter 4) took his children to work with elders and learned along with them. Daryl Baldwin (Chapter 1) and Jessie Little Doe Baird (Chapter 2) both learned their heritage tongues entirely from documentation, getting master's degrees in linguistics in order to handle the difficult tasks of understanding the sounds and grammar described in the written documents available to them. Many Native parents in California are learning from documentation on their own, without degrees, but getting some mentoring through the Breath of Life Language Restoration Workshops held biennially at the University of California.[6] Parents in Scotland who want to use their language with their children can learn Scottish Gaelic through the Family Language Plan program, where language learning is geared toward home language.

Richard Grounds (Chapter 4) points out a key strategy for parents who are learning their language along with their kids:

> Once I learned to ask *sOdEt@ha wahAha?* (Your shoes—where are they?), then I never said it in English again. As a parent my use of the language focused on parent survival language. I

became very quick with *n@ KAê thla* (Don't do that!), or *s'@hA wE* (Get down!). Of course, there were other parenting essentials, such as *n@zAKw@ˆthl@ˆ* (Don't hang on me!).

There are two important points in this statement: (1) If you are just learning the language, focus on "parent survival language"—language you will use with your children daily; and (2) Once you know something in your heritage language, never say it in English again.

If you are a parent or future parent who needs to learn your language in order to use it at home, you need to find your way to whatever means might be available to you. Here are some possible resources, some of which might be available for your language.

Learning from speakers. If you have relatives or friends who are speakers, it is not only possible to learn from them, but the very best way to learn. You can ask the speakers in your circle to teach you words and phrases, and even to simply speak the language to you at every opportunity. The Master-Apprentice Language Learning Program mentioned in Chapter 3 is an intensive program designed for one-on-one learning from a speaker. The published manual for the master-apprentice method can guide you in learning from a speaker.[7] Another excellent book on how to learn a language from speakers is *Language Acquisition Made Practical: Field Methods for Language Learners,* which gives step-by-step guidance on language learning from speakers.[8]

Community support programs. If you are lucky, your community has language programs that can directly or indirectly support your language learning. Some communities run immersion schools, and these often have adult learning classes for parents. Some communities run summer camps. Some have developed documentation programs where community members document the elders. Any kind of language program, large or small, can provide support and encouragement to adults trying to learn and use their language. If you are not already involved in these programs, just becoming associated with them can benefit your language learning. While reading this book, it may have become obvious to you that many of the people using their language at home are leaders and even founders of community language programs. If there is nothing going on yet in your community, your own zeal for your language may well put you on a path toward leadership in a language program.

College programs and courses for your language. Universities, tribal colleges, and community colleges may have classes to help you learn your language. Some schools are developing distance-learning options that you may want to look into if you do not live nearby.

Books and recordings geared toward language learning. You might be able to find materials to help with learning your language: pedagogical grammars, recorded language lessons, and dictionaries are available for some endangered languages. Such materials are less available for endangered languages than for world languages, but you never know if there is something out there until you look.

Linguistic materials and old documents. For many endangered languages, there may be old documents available from a period of literacy. Hawaiian and Māori, for example, have many books, newspapers, Bible translations, and other materials written in those languages. Linguists may have developed grammars and dictionaries and collected traditional tales. For languages with no speakers, these materials provide the only path to language revitalization. While these documents are not geared toward language learning, they can be used to learn. You may have to search in archives at universities and museums to find them. The Internet can be an important guide in this search. You may find that you need to take courses in linguistics in order to learn how to use these materials. Some universities have institutes to facilitate finding and using linguistic materials—such as the aforementioned Breath of Life workshops in Berkeley. Oklahoma began holding a regular Breath of Life Institute in 2010, and a similar institute was held in Washington, DC, in 2011 at the National Anthropological Archives, Library of Congress, and National Museum of the American Indian.

Working with linguists. Some languages do not have very much documentation, but if there are no speakers, you have to find a way to work with this limited material. Linguists can be helpful in reconstructing a language, by utilizing the structures that are found in the documentation to develop new words, for example, or comparing related languages that have speakers or better documentation and figuring out how words from those languages would sound in your own. In the Miami chapter of this book (Chapter 1), Daryl Baldwin writes of David Costa, whose dissertation on Miami syntax galvanized the Miami language revitalization movement and who is now employed as the tribal linguist. Another example of a linguist working together with people seeking to regain their languages is David Shaul, who has developed a great deal of the grammar and vocabulary of Esselen (a California language) from a small amount of documentation.[9] In Australia, too, linguists and aboriginal people have worked together to reconstruct languages and revitalize their use.[10]

Linguists can also be very helpful in assisting you to understand and make use of linguistic documents in your language. If there is a university or college near you with a linguistics department, go visit, and see if you can find someone who might help you out. And like Daryl Baldwin and Jessie Little Doe Baird, consider taking courses to develop your own expertise in linguistics.

The Breath of Life workshops and institutes generally give participants a linguist to work one-on-one with for the duration of the event. This helps the participants learn a good deal about linguistics and may even result in a longer-term relationship of value to your language revitalization goals.

Practice and use. No matter the quality of any method you use to learn your language, learning will not take place without regular intensive practice and use of the language. Keep notes in your pocket. Put labels around the house naming objects and reminding you to use those names. Play CDs in your language in the car or on your home stereo. Whatever you have learned, use it wherever you can. Speak your language to your friends, to your dog, to yourself. Your own children will be your best group to practice with. And be warned: they will learn faster than you!

More Issues about Fluency

Parents are often afraid to speak to their children in the endangered language for fear of making mistakes, having a bad accent, etc. Here's what the parents in this book have to say about that. Jessie Little Doe Baird (Chapter 2) writes:

> Maybe we do not want to talk about it because we feel that we may not be good enough speakers to try to pass on what we do know. i have thought about all of these things and felt the emotion from these thoughts too. i also know that if i put out the language i do have, then i have given my child everything i have. i have given her a chance and can feel satisfied with my efforts to pass on my culture.

Richard Grounds writes in Chapter 4:

A surprising realization that has become clearer to me over the last few years concerns the benefit of exposing *dEzA'y@nE,* my daughter, and *dEzAs'@nE,* my son, to the language at an early age even though, at the time, I was quite aware of my own limitations in the language. (For an embarrassingly long time I was forced to read off a card on the refrigerator door just to call the kids to eat, *k'agOthl@nE hElA sh@ˆsh@ˆ, a @gû k'a@thl@nô.*) My concern was that I was not better able to give them exposure to more advanced forms of the language and therefore the advantages growing from our efforts would have a minimum long-term effect. Yet to my surprise *dEzEOtOtOhAnû,* my children, did develop the ability to hear and understand the language in an immediate, direct way in spite of my limitations. I think this is promising for those who are forced to launch into a family learning program for all the family members at the same time. Due to the urgency and paucity of access to our original languages most of us cannot now afford the luxury of a two-stage learning process wherein the care-givers develop fluency in the language first and then begin to teach their children. Our approach was to make sure that what was being said—even though given in limited quantities—was said with the correct rhythm and with precise pronunciation. Being assured of a high quality of exchange in the language, the children were indeed enabled to develop a natural "ear" for the language as they continued with their learning.

Daryl Baldwin (Chapter 1) writes:

My first two children were still very young and so they naturally became part of the learning process, as rudimentary as our effort was....Household items, birds, animals, and other familiar items common to everyday activities served as our starting point. Word lists taped to walls, counters, and cabinets served as the learning mechanism, along with folded notes in my pockets as I went about my day.

We see Hana O'Regan (Chapter 6) on a website in support of the Kotahi Mano Kāika "1000 Homes" program for Māori. Short videos encourage parents to use Māori at home, whether or not they are fluent:[11]

- Start with what you know and use it as much as you can.
- Start with little things like teatime, and some rituals around that.
- You don't have to be fluent at all. Everyone's got to start somewhere.
- You've got to maintain the consistency and speak Māori even if your Māori's no good! It's better than nothing. They get used to hearing the sounds, they get used to hearing the way things flow...
- Even if you don't necessarily have *Te Reo* speakers around the place, you've still got the opportunity to go online and get books and support resources, things like word lists...

So the lesson here is that you must not let the imperfections of your own knowledge of the language keep you from speaking it. And if there are other speakers around, fluent or not, who can also speak the language to your children, the kids will pick it all up, sort it out, and learn more than they could ever learn from you alone.

What If You Can't Become Fluent?
Sometimes parents just don't have the opportunity to become very fluent, or maybe they don't have time to take full advantage of the opportunities that are out there. Some languages have no speakers and there isn't enough documentation for anyone to learn to use them as full-fledged languages of communication. I mentioned above that some groups are trying to reconstruct their languages out of small amounts of data, but this is a process that may take a generation or more; even the most dedicated parent might not be able to learn enough to make such a language primary in the home.

All that aside, you can use what you have available to you at home. Use words and phrases from your language that you know, even if the rest of the time you have to use English. Think up games and activities that you can do in your heritage language. Even if you can never make the language your main language of communication, you and your children can still give this beloved language of yours a place in your home and hearts.

How to Get Started Using Your Language at Home

It's never too soon to start using your language at home. It's also never too late. Whether you have children yet or not, and however old they are, the best time to start is right now.

Before children. Often parents start thinking seriously about language in the home when they find out they are pregnant. But there is plenty of reason not to wait even that long. The most difficult part of using the language at home with your family is to begin doing it. Part of the problem of getting started is the awkwardness of using a different language. This is true even if both parents know the language. Recall Wilson and Kamanā's struggle (Chapter 7) during the first week of using their language with each other. If all your communication with your family has been in English, it may seem strange, even artificial, a block to real communication, to switch to this other language. It might even feel like you are losing intimacy with your family members by speaking in this different—yes, within the family—language. But you can take heart from Wilson and Kamanā, who found that it only took a week for it to feel natural to use Hawaiian with each other.

Pregnancy. Your baby hears even while in the womb. Speak your language to each other and to your baby before it is born. The Albers family (Chapter 3) writes that they thought about the Karuk language constantly during pregnancy, asking their relatives for vocabulary they knew they would need for babies, learning as much and using as much as possible. Ellie played tapes of the Karuk language to their baby before his birth, holding the player against her belly when she would go to bed at night.

Birth and beyond. Parents who start out their linguistic family adventure by speaking to each other in the language will have a head start when the babies come along. But even then, as O'Regan noted for Māori (Chapter 6) and the Alberses noted for Karuk (Chapter 3), many things come up with your baby that you never once thought about saying before, and may not know how to say. The Alberses were constantly calling up or visiting their great-aunt to get words and phrases they needed for interaction with their young sons. Hana O'Regan also felt at a loss when her first child was born:

> Yet when the time arrived, I learnt very quickly that I didn't
> have at my disposal the language I needed, and it wasn't just
> the vocabulary: it was the idiom, the turn of phrase, the terms

of endearment. I didn't know the term for winding or burping a child, or how to say, "Let's put your legs up so I can clean you up"; these weren't structures or sentences I had ever had to use in the lecture room or with my peers!

These are the kinds of linguistic challenges that all parents trying to bring their endangered language home will come up against, but everyone finds solutions. Working with an elder will bring the missing vocabulary and has many benefits beyond that, in the way of connecting generations and bringing more exposure to the language for you and your family. Or perhaps it will be through a program like the Kawaiisu Language at Home program (Chapter 12), or Gaelic in the Home courses (Chapter 13), or simply more research on the documentation of your language. You may even decide to make up your own words sometimes, as some of the authors in this volume have (more on that below).

Starting out with older children. It might seem a daunting task to start using your language at home if you are switching languages on older children who already know English and don't know your heritage language. For one thing, speaking to someone who doesn't understand you is a very difficult task; and it's frustrating for the addressee as well. Also, communication may be stilted—if your children and perhaps you are dominant in English, it may not be possible to communicate everything you might wish to in your heritage language. Your children might resist the step of changing languages in the home. To minimize the potential of this, start by having fun. Work with the kids to make recordings of the words for household objects around the house. Play games in the language. Play traditional games or board games: games like Guess Who and UNO, Chutes and Ladders, and Bingo can all provide structured practice in the heritage language while people are having fun. Make up little games like the Baldwins' penny jar: if someone says something in English when they know the word in the heritage tongue, the person who catches it takes a penny from the guilty one's jar and puts it in his or her own. (Catching the parents is the most fun of all.) Focus on bringing common words and phrases into the household, such as greetings, phrases like "I love you" and "Come and eat!", kinship terms, and other frequently uttered phrases. Set certain times and situations where you will use the language together, such as dinnertime or bedtime story time.

Margaret Noori writes:

> The first step is to begin transferring as much of the day as pos-
> sible into Anishinaabe. "*Wenesh waa biiskaman?* / What are you
> going to put on?" is common in the morning. We can say "*miig-*
> *wetch*" for our meals or "*gaye nishisnoo* / it's not fair" when
> we have to eat our broccoli. One wall has been made into a
> chalkboard and each week below the Anishinaabe name of the
> month the seven days of the week appear in Anishinaabe as
> well. The "*ezhichige* / to do" list is written below that. These
> may seem like mundane and obvious habits, but this is where
> the learning begins. To say "*jiimshin* / give me a kiss" each
> night before bedtime, or "*booniikwishin* / leave me alone" when
> you need some space. These instinctive utterances need to grad-
> ually be transferred from one language to another.[12]

In other words, all these everyday intimate family communications
are what now need to take place in the heritage language.

One key decision as you develop usage of the heritage language will
be whether family members will start using kinship address terms in
the language. That is, will you stop calling your daughters by name and
use the kinship term from your heritage language instead? Will your
children stop calling you "Dad" and replace it with a word from your
language? The names you use when addressing kin carry a deep emotional connection. Changing the terms you address your relatives by has
emotional consequences and is a particularly important symbolic way
of connecting to the other language. Renée Grounds (Chapter 4) writes
about it well:

> When I was little, there was a transitional period in which
> *dEzAt'ê* demanded I stop calling him "Dad" in English and
> instead refer to him only as *dEzAt'ê*. It was difficult for me to
> break my English habit of saying "Dad" but I have come to
> appreciate the significance of using Yuchi family terms to iden-
> tify each other. Yuchi family names continually reinforce our
> connection as a Yuchi family, in the midst of an English-
> speaking culture.

Increasing the Presence of Your Language in Your Family Members' Lives

Margaret Peters (Chapter 5) writes:

> There was no magic formula that we had for passing the language on to our children. We just spoke it to them, and not at them or around them, but directly to them. We spoke it to them in the house, in the car, at the restaurant, at the lacrosse games, at the movie theatre, at the laundromat, in the shopping malls, at the park, and the occasional times we attended church services, such as funerals and weddings, and just everywhere we went we spoke it to them. We didn't break it down or use baby talk. We just spoke it to them naturally and that was how they responded.

That is a great goal for family language revitalization—just use it everywhere and everywhen. Not all families can do this, however, especially not at first, and especially in languages that have not been used for a long time. It is often difficult to talk about topics in modern culture; there are great gaps in vocabulary in a language like Miami, where there have been no speakers for a long time, or like Karuk or Yuchi, where even people who remember their heritage language have been talking in English for many years and the language has not "kept up with the times." You may find it more comfortable to talk in your heritage language in situations where the language has been used a lot in the past—where the language feels comfortable. This is the "one-language, one-context" method, as Brian Bielenberg calls it.[13] The Baldwins, who are not rigid about using Miami all the time at home, nevertheless have a number of activities where Miami is always used. On their farm, for example, all the work with their crops and animals takes place in Miami. You might find that various outdoor activities are comfortable for your language, such as hunting or boating, or perhaps working with certain arts, crafts, and skills, or cooking traditional foods, or telling old tales. In that case, it is good to make these activities a big part of your life. The heritage language is not separate from your heritage culture and heritage values, as you have seen in this book. Keep your heritage culture strong in your lives, and language follows.

But modern living brings other things to talk about as well, and one of the features of human language is that it can even talk about things it has never talked about before. If you use the language only in traditional situations, there is a potential danger that your children will come to think of it as old-fashioned and irrelevant, especially when they enter the teen years. Bringing the language to the activities and interests of young people is an important part of language revitalization. Describing new things and developing new vocabulary can itself be an activity full of fun and learning. Noori (Chapter 8) writes about one example:

> One recent example in our home was a shape game created by my daughters because I had simply never taken time to teach them geometric words. We cooked, we cleaned, we got ready for school, we came home and stayed quite busy, much of which we could, if pressed, describe in Anishinaabemowin, but we had never taken time to learn one of the concepts that belonged only to the realm of school. The outcome was a wonderful lesson in etymology and description as we worked with Howard Kimewon and Francis Fox, realizing that, of course, the words "*giiwaajiwaayaa*" (oval) and "*giiwaajikaakadeyaa*" (rectangle) are literally composed of a morpheme for "elongated" added to the words for "circle" and "square."

Here is a list of a few of the many activities, old and new, that you can do in your language to help your children learn it. Some of these you may do already in English, in which case you should work to start using your heritage language instead. Some might be things you haven't done in the past but could bring into your home life as tools for language learning.

Games
- Board games
- Card games
- Dominos
- Jigsaw puzzles
- Traditional games
- Making plays and skits

Books
- Books written in your language
- Picture books without words
- Picture books with the English blocked out with tape

Arts, Crafts, and Skills
- Drawing and painting
- Making things
- Finger puppets, pottery, clay figurines, origami figures, model kits, carpentry
- Traditional skills: basket making, working hides, leather-work, beading, making traditional clothing and regalia

Music
- Traditional singing
- Making new songs

Cooking and Eating
- Making meals together
- Eating together
- Cleaning up together

Chores
- Washing clothes
- Washing dishes
- Making beds, cleaning rooms
- Feeding pets or stock
- Fix-it projects around the house

Sports and Other Outdoor Activities
- Playing softball, kickball, and other sports for families
- Traditional sports and outdoor activities
- Camping out, backpacking

In *7 Steps to Raising a Bilingual Child,* Naomi Steiner and her coauthors also put forward many excellent ideas for increasing the amount of input your child gets in the target language. She suggests singing nursery rhymes and songs, or making or acquiring CDs that your child can sing along with. She also suggests traveling to other communities where there are speakers of your language (if such exist). Her book has many pointers on raising bilingual children.[14]

Show your own love for and delight in the language. Because your children love you, and because you are displaying your togetherness

Howard Kimewon with canoe-making students. Photograph courtesy of Margaret Noori

with them through the fun things you are doing in the language, they will bond with the language.

But language revitalization, both at home and in the community, is best served by making sure that the language is not insulated from the outside world. Noori (Chapter 8) writes:

> When the learning is continual and includes everyone who crosses the threshold, the children can pick up the passion for the language and move from being students of something sacred to also being teachers of a practical skill. Every kid who visits needs to learn and use a little Anishinaabemowin. We don't hesitate to teach nonnative friends the language, and we don't save Anishinaabemowin for when people leave. We welcome everyone into the family. Adults are encouraged to use Anishinaabemowin if they know it, and asked to try saying a few words if they don't. This practice of counting friends as family and allowing the community to define connections can be extraordinarily empowering for kids. It is important to keep the habits of language use close to the heart, but it is also important to bring everyone who is part of the family circle into the project. Otherwise the language becomes a barrier between the home and the "real world," and using the language becomes a burden that divides relatives and friends.

Problems—and Solutions—along the Way

People often experience obstacles along the way when they are raising their children to speak their endangered heritage language. Every chapter in this book talks about the problems that come up from speaking a minority language at home, and discusses the ways the authors deal with them. Here are some of the issues.

Will my children learn English if I speak our heritage language to them? Parents' own doubts about using a minority language with their children are often the biggest problem of all in language revitalization. Parents want their children to be able to do well in the situations the majority culture throws at them—especially school and jobs. Few parents would want to raise their children unable to function in the dominant society. But it is no longer the case that children who learn endangered languages are going to be isolated from English. They may get it from one parent (OPOL) or they may have learned it before the family began to use the minority language. But even if both parents speak to their child in the minority language at all times, the child is going to have plenty of exposure to English—through friends, school, television, and so on. Do not make the mistake many parents have made, of deciding to teach English first and the heritage language later—"later" almost never comes. Don't let teachers and other naysayers stop you from using your language with your child! For a child to learn a language well at home, the child must be spoken to a significant portion of the time in that language. Parents need to establish the habit of speaking in the heritage language early on; the longer you wait, the harder it is to change to a different language within the family. Margaret Peters comments about her family's doubts and experience:

> We too were afraid that teaching our kids in an immersion setting might be a detriment to them at some point, but now that they are older and have their own children, speak their language, and are strong in their identity, they tell us that we made the right choice for them.[15]

People who know the heritage language won't speak it to you or your children. People who are out of the habit of speaking their language may resist speaking it, or they may just forget to speak it even if you have asked for their help. Theodore Peters writes of Mohawk (Chapter 5):

If you have relatives that still speak Kanien'kéha, ask them to speak to your children in the language. If they forget, remind them, train your children to remind speakers to speak to them in the language. "Use it or lose it" is the simplest way to put it. I have found that our elders have been conditioned to speak to children in English....Our elders have to be constantly reminded to speak to the children in our language, because most of them are in autopilot mode when it comes to speaking our language. It will work but you must do your part and remind them. When you hear the children speaking in your language and you are able to have a conversation with them you will become very proud and happy.

Your children might reject the language. When one talks to elders about language loss, it is not uncommon to hear the complaint "Our children didn't want to learn our language." Indeed, children frequently say that they don't want to speak the language anymore, especially when they start their studies in an English-speaking school and start befriending their English-speaking peers.

Aigli Pittaka and Brian Bielenberg (Chapter 10) had a different school-related problem—in order to help their son learn Kypriaka Greek, they moved to Cyprus, to be with family members and participate in a community where the language was spoken. They found that this was hard on their son, who at that time was dominant in English:

> Doubts concerning the wisdom of our decision rose up early on as our son experienced bumps with family and school, often misunderstanding the comments made by his grandparents or other children, which led him, initially, to withdraw. In his own words:
> "I (Aliosha) guess that you can imagine my difficulty becoming comfortable in the mostly Kypriaka environment I was coming into. I remember one night in particular, the eve of my first day in 'Greek school,' I think, when I started stomping around the room, half-shouting half-crying 'NO! NO!'"

These events might wring a parent's heart, but your constancy in the language will win out. After only a few weeks, Aliosha was excited to be going to school, and he was soon singing, writing poems, and dreaming in Kypriaka.

As Theodore Peters wrote in Chapter 5 about his own children's resistance:

> There was a minor protest from Teioswáthe when we switched from her first language, English, to Kanien'kéha. Her sister, Kawennahén:te, didn't mind, she just went with the flow. For Nihahsennà:a, our son, it was a natural way of acquiring his language. Later on they had no problems learning to speak, read, and write in Kanien'kéha and English. They just transferred the things that they learned in immersion to learning the English language.

Pila Wilson and Kauanoe Kamanā had to face stronger resistance from their children, who during their teen years had trouble adjusting to their parents' dual roles as parents and teachers in the immersion school the children attended:

> Our own family, however, was far from immune from the challenges of adolescence. When Pila volunteered to teach Keli'i's class a social studies course, she refused to respond to him as a teacher and actively promoted children speaking English in class, to force her father to abandon teaching it. Her tactics did not work. Hulilau also rebelled against the rules of the school. Pila was seriously worried that his rebelliousness would drive off the young teachers and other families. Kauanoe held the line firm and Hulilau complied after a few incidents.

Share with your children your ideas about why it is important for them to learn the language. This can help make them proud and happy with their heritage language. Jarrid Baldwin writes in Chapter 1:

> Growing up, my parents always told me that being bilingual was a very important skill. They told me it would help me when I'm older to be able to understand situations from a different point of view, so this is the outlook I've always had on learning the language.

Your children's peer group speaks English. Even if the children are not rebelling against the language overtly, there is still the problem of making sure their environment is conducive to using the language. A child with an English-speaking peer group gets less input and develops less in the way of natural habits of speaking the heritage language. Aodán Mac Póilin sees this problem cropping up in the Shaw's Road Gaeltacht:

> Twenty or so years ago a large estate of more than one hundred houses was built as an extension of the original access road. Although the estate attracted a small number of families where one or both parents spoke Irish, most of the children in this development speak only English. These children, naturally, play with the children of Pobal Feirste. As a result, whatever language or languages are used the homes of the Pobal Feirste children, their default language on the street tends to be English.

This change from the 1970s, when the neighborhood was physically isolated from English influences and children all spoke to each other in Gaelic, has created a major worry that in the long run Gaelic may not survive in Shaw's Road Gaeltacht.

On the other hand, parents in this book whose home and community environments at first offered far less of the heritage language have still been able to raise children who are fluent and committed to it. Renée Grounds and her brother (Chapter 4) are the only proficient speakers of their generation, as are Jarrid and Jessie Baldwin (Chapter 1). Ezra Hale is a fluent Warlpiri speaker despite never having been to Australia and only once meeting anyone outside the family who spoke the language. He writes in Chapter 11:

> I loved my dad very much and I wanted to be as close as possible to him. I thought that Warlpiri was the key, that it would bring us even closer together than we already were. But upon reflection I don't really think it mattered what language we spoke. It was more about spending the time together, speaking together.

Love and respect for one's parents, then, can be a strong motivation for children to learn the language their parents want them to learn.

And yet, Ezra's chapter carries a sad undertone. Since his father's death, Ezra has no one to talk to in Warlpiri. Nor will Ezra's fluency in Warlpiri have any impact on the long-term survival of the language, since he is half a world away from any communal effort at language revitalization that might exist. He may be the youngest speaker of Warlpiri, but he may also be the last speaker—and certainly is, within his own family.

Margaret and Theodore Peters point out that the prominence of English in their environment also puts obstacles in the way:

> People always say that we are the exception because we had the language and could give it to our children, but this was not the case. We were still in an all-English environment, like that of any learner. We had to make the efforts and make an attitude adjustment as parents to teach our children the language....Our newest grandchild, who is now a year old, is at a point where we will make or break his language learning. Because we all work, his mom may have to place him in a daycare setting that will be all-English, and even if they have fluent speaking people who work there,...they are conditioned to use English. So this will be another hurdle that we have to face. My niece is the supervisor for one of our daycare centers and I have been asked to help set up an immersion program, and I am very excited about doing this. I have worked long and hard to get our council to have at least one of our daycares be in the language, and it may become a reality. I just hope it will not be too late for our grandson.[16]

Cedric Sunray says this about his family's efforts to overcome the hegemony of English in their children's environment:

> Language is a constant struggle as our children go to English-only schools, so we have to find creative ways to increase the prestige of our languages, as you well know. I teach Choctaw every Wednesday at their public school as a volunteer and our kids participate in the big Native American Language Fair hosted by the University of Oklahoma each year, which brings tribal communities from across the nation to

"compete." We read in our languages, so as to not only live vocally in the language, but show that English should not be the only focus of literacy. Their language fluency or our own is not at the level we all wish it could be. We are a continual work in progress. We still go community to community when asked and model our home language nest to other tribal communities. This past month we went to Euchee and then to Creek communities and worked with their language families on effective ways to continue our commitments to living in our language. My kids go with me to all of these and try their best as nine-, five-, and two-year-olds to be solid examples. I always feel a small bit uncomfortable, as I never want my kids to be seen as "dancing bears." Fortunately, my nine- and five-year-old like to take the lead as facilitators and teachers in the situations about 50 percent of the time.[17]

Criticism or lack of support from within or outside the community. People may tell you that your decision to use your heritage language at home will keep your child from learning English and give him problems in school. Community members, speaking from bitterness, may say that trying to teach your child the language is useless, and that the language has no use in the world anymore. Teachers in an English medium school may counsel you to use English with your child. This very situation is what caused many families to abandon their languages, and what brought your language to the endangered state it is in today. Your willingness to persevere despite these criticisms is what will bring your language back into use again. As the quest for language revitalization gains a foothold in the community, many critical voices are silenced or change to praise. Criticism from within the community usually ends when people hear the miracle of a child speaking to them in a language that no child has spoken since the critics themselves were young.

Each family, each community will have its own particular problems. Some families have no support outside the home for their language, and others have some but wish for more. Internal politics sometimes mars community programs and creates obstacles. As Theodore Peters shows (Chapter 5), a long-term commitment can see its way through all these problems:

Problems along the way: not enough support for the immersion program from those that could have provided these things, not enough teachers for all of the things that we wanted to do. I think every community that wants to revitalize their language encounters the same obstacles but we are slowly turning things around. The young people that have gone through the immersion programs are now returning to become the leaders, teachers, and decision makers. There is a changing of the guard and this is a good thing because these are now the parents and they want their children to have a better experience than they did.

Who is there to talk to? If the community of people their age who speak the language is very small, parents and the younger generation alike will feel it. Finding or developing a community of speakers is a major issue for families. If the family cannot be part of a larger community effort in which other children are also learning to speak the language, then there is still little hope for its long-term survival. At a recent gathering, Dustin Rivers (a very talented young man in British Columbia who is an advanced learner of Skwxwú7mesh, or Squamish), described his fantasy of finding four or five friends who would room together and learn and use the language with each other. "Who will I have to talk to, otherwise?" he complains.

So we see that community is essential for families trying to use their language at home. Margaret Noori discusses this in Chapter 8:

> How can a language that takes hold in the safety of a home, much like the children themselves, venture out into the wider world and be welcomed and find support and acceptance? There is a need for both orality and literacy beyond the walls of comfort and shelter. Parents and children working hard to save endangered languages need to hear the words of their people in culturally supportive classrooms, at friendly local businesses, around the drum, and in the digital space created by computers and cell phones.

Will the language change? You bet! Even if the parents are native speakers, there are many reasons why their children will probably speak differently.

1. Languages always change! Sometimes the change between generations is minor enough that it is not noticed consciously, but
whether it is just a little or a lot, it will definitely be different.
In the situation of language decline and revitalization, languages
change more quickly, and the change is more noticeable by older
generations.

2. In many cases, language decline has caused the loss of some of
the richness of traditional speech. Oratorical styles, metaphor,
and poetic ways of speaking may already have been lost to the
last generation of otherwise fluent speakers. Maybe they can be
regained through the study of documentation, or maybe not.
Maybe new rich forms of speaking will develop. In any case, this
represents language change.

3. Even in situations where two languages get equal exposure, there
is usually some influence of one on the other, which can result
in a special "accent" or the use of "calques" and other linguistic
contact phenomena.

4. Peer groups have at least as much influence on speech development as parents do. Any family with teenagers knows that they
use special pronunciations, style, and slang terminology. Even in
situations where immersion schools are present so that a child
gets full exposure to the endangered language outside the home,
a "peer group variety" of the language will develop.

5. Again almost by definition, if it has been some time since the
language was in common use, there will be everyday topics that
native speakers have never discussed. As people have been drawn
into new ways of life, they have been using English instead of
their heritage tongue, and so vocabulary in the heritage language
has not kept up with the times. In any language revitalization situation, new vocabulary has to be developed for aspects of modern daily life. New topics will be talked about, and new words
will come about. This vocabulary development will be one of the
major aspects of language change under revitalization. Sometimes your own children will be the ones taking the lead in this.

What Are the Rewards?

The primary parental motives that have been demonstrated in this book
are love of the language itself (e.g., Ezra Hale's father's love of Warlpiri,

Chapter 11) and a sense of membership within the heritage community (e.g., Māori, Chapter 6).

Theodore Peters writes in Chapter 5 about a spiritual motivation for raising children in Mohawk:

> In our language we will remember who we are, where we came from, and where we are going. Our Creator told us, "When you come back to the Skyworld, make sure you speak the language I gave you, have your Onkwehón:we name, have your personal song, have your clothing, and know your ceremonies. If you don't have these things then you will really have "problems along the way."

Research shows that bilingual children have cognitive advantages over people that know only one language;[18] and there are also the social and experiential advantages of being part of diverse cultures—especially your heritage culture. As Renée Grounds writes in Chapter 4:

> These face-to-face language sessions with Mose Cahwee, William Cahwee, Jim Brown, Maggie Marsey, Dimmy Washburn, and later Addie George gave me insight into a completely different world—the Yuchi world.

Parents may get their greatest rewards from watching their children grow up and become language activists themselves. The joy of helping Mohawk be passed on to yet another generation is clear in Margaret Peters's writing (Chapter 5):

> As [my grandson] grew we continued speaking to him in Mohawk and he would amaze us with the vocabulary and phrases he began using. His mother, who had been most resistant to speaking Mohawk [as a child], was now using only the language with her son. His aunt Kawennahén:te and his uncle Nihahsennà:a spoke only Mohawk to him.

The rewards are there too for the children. As they grow up, they find benefits both large and small for being bilingual and knowing their language of heritage. Jarrid Baldwin writes in Chapter 1:

Children of the Shaw's Road community in Belfast, Ireland. Photograph by Fiontánn Ó Mealláin, courtesy of Aodán Mac Póilin

As for my thoughts on how I feel about the language, I am really glad I grew up learning to speak it at home. It is something different and very unique about me that I can put on resumés, scholarship applications, etc., and I feel good knowing a language and culture other than English. I have grown up learning the language and culture of an oppressed people, so that has really helped me relate to other groups of people who are going through things similar to what my ancestors went through.

Best of all is when the generation who grew up with their heritage language at home understand the value of spreading it further and see it as a pleasurable activity. You can see from the Yuchi chapter (Chapter 4), for example, that Renée has developed a passion for the language as strong as her father's. She has not only become a speaker but also a linguist, motivated by her fascination with the structure of the language to elicit complex paradigms from the elders in order to master them, but clearly also just for the love of it. She writes:

In the same way that a fire can be relit even if there are only
a few coals left, we are reviving our language even with only
a few speakers left. I believe that if my generation continues to revive the use of Yuchi language—even if only by a few
families now—we will one day again have strong medicine at
s'@ˆs@ˆhA, like our ancestors.

Jarrid Baldwin's older sister, Jessie, puts it like this (Chapter 1):

There are many benefits I have realized to knowing my own
language. Most important is just being able to pass it on and
teach my younger siblings and other tribal members. In order to
keep our language alive we have to spread it around and share
it with others. If we just kept the language to ourselves where
would it be today? I help pass it on to my younger siblings and
will pass it on to our future children.

In the video mentioned above about the Māori 1000 Homes program,
Hana O'Regan talks with pride about her five-year-old son's fierce adop-
tion of language values:

Last night, I was speaking to my niece Reremoana from Ngati
Porous, who was staying at our house. I was speaking to her
in English, when I heard a voice call from the other end of the
house. It was my son, who said, "Mum, you must stop speaking to Rere in English. Mum, you will be the death of our language. You are contributing to the extinction of our language,
Mum." I continue speaking English to Rere, then my five-year-
old child comes and hands me a letter. He had written a letter which said, "Do not forget, Mum, you must speak Māori to
Rere. Leave it in your room, so you remember."[19]

Keli'i Wilson's conclusion in her contribution to her family's chapter
on Hawaiian (Chapter 7) shows the hope for the future that has been
engendered in the younger generation by all the brave families who
have written chapters for this book:

When Hawaiian is the language of the home, our mother
tongue lives on. As we know, when it exists in the family, the

very core unit from the time of our ancestors, it lives and is carried through the generations. This is how we will assure that our language lives on, and Hulilau and I plan to contribute to this as we have our own families in the future and raise our children in the same way.

This book can end on Jessie Little Doe's short and powerful statement in Chapter 2: "Children have a birthright to their language."

Notes

1. Margaret Noori, "Wenesh Waa Oshkii-Bmaadizijig Noondamowaad? What Will The Young Children Hear?" in *Indigenous Language Revitalization*, ed. Jon Reyhner and Louise Lockard (Flagstaff, AZ: Northern Arizona Univ., 2009), available at http://jan. ucc.nau.edu/~jar/ILR/.
2. Suzanne Barron-Hauwaert, *Language Strategies for Bilingual Families: The One-Parent-One-Language Approach* (Clevedon, UK and Buffalo, NY: Multilingual Matters, 2004).
3. Cedric Sunray, personal communication, December 14, 2010.
4. Susanne Döpke, *One Parent—One Language: An Interactional Approach* (Amsterdam, NL, and Philadelphia: John Benjamins Publishing, 1992).
5. Leanne Hinton, *How to Keep Your Language Alive* (Berkeley: Heyday, 2002).
6. Leanne Hinton, "Breath of Life—Silent No More: The Native California Language Restoration Workshop" in *News from Native California* 10, no. 1 (1996), pp. 13–16.
7. Hinton, *How to Keep Your Language Alive.*
8. E. Thomas Brewster and Elizabeth S. Brewster, *Language Acquisition Made Practical* (Colorado Springs, CO: Lingua House, 1976).
9. Louise J. Miranda Ramirez, "Breathing Language" in *News from Native California* 22, no. 2 (2009), pp. 8–12.
10. Rob Amery, *Warrabarna Kaurna! Reclaiming an Australian Language* (Oxford and New York: Taylor & Francis, 2000); Nicholas Thieberger, *Paper and Talk: A Manual for Reconstituting Materials in Australian Aboriginal Languages* (Canberra: Aboriginal Studies Press, 1995).
11. Kotahi Mano Kāika, http://www.kmk.maori.nz/gallery (accessed August 2012).
12. Noori, "Wenesh Waa Oshkii-Bmaadizijig Noondamowaad?"
13. Brian Bielenberg, personal communication, February 16, 2011.
14. Naomi Steiner, M.D., Susan L. Hayes, and Steven Parker, M.D., *7 Steps to Raising a Bilingual Child* (New York: AMACOM, 2008).
15. Margaret Peters, personal communication, January 26, 2011.
16. Ibid.
17. Cedric Sunray, personal communication, December 14, 2010.
18. See, for example, E. Peal and W. E. Lambert, "The Relation of Bilingualism to Intelligence" in *Psychological Monographs* 76, no. 546 (1962), pp. 1–23; Kenji Hakuta and Rafael M. Diaz, "The Relationship between Degree of Bilingualism and Cognitive Ability" in *Children's Language*, Vol. 5, ed. K. E. Nelson (Hillsdale, NJ: L. Erlbaum, 1985); and Vivian Cook, "The Consequences of Bilingualism for Cognitive Processing" in *Tutorials in Bilingualism*, ed. A. de Groot and J. F. Kroll (Mahwah, NJ: L. Erlbaum, 1997).
19. "Ngāi Tahu Māori Language Revitalisation Strategy" video, part 1 of 3, 15 August 2010, http://www.youtube.com/watch?v=HU52Flbfnbg.

CONTRIBUTOR BIOGRAPHIES

Daryl Baldwin has an M.A. with emphasis on Native American linguistics from the University of Montana, and **Karen Baldwin** has a B.S. in education from Bowling Green State University. Daryl and Karen began homeschooling their children in 1991. Their main objective for this effort was to have more control over curricular content and to infuse Myaamia (Miami) language and culture into their children's educational experience. Their homeschooling efforts continue with their youngest children, Awansaapia (12) and Amehkoonsa (14).

Darryl's tribe has been developing a relationship with Miami University since the early 1970s, and in 2001 Daryl was asked to become the founding director of the Myaamia Project there. The Myaamia Project's mission is to advance the language and cultural educational needs of the Miami Tribe community. This opportunity allowed Daryl to utilize his training in linguistics and his experience in home education to begin developing programs for the benefit of his tribal community. Miami reclamation efforts and the work of the Myaamia Project have received national attention. With the commitments of both Miami University and the Miami Tribe, the project continues to grow and impacts a new generation of tribal youth.

The Baldwins' eldest daughter, **Jessie Baldwin,** is currently graduating from Miami University with a B.S. in early childhood education. For her senior project she designed a language curriculum, which she plans to implement, for the Miami Tribe's daycare in Oklahoma. **Jarrid Baldwin** plans to pursue a degree in anthropology.

jessie little doe baird is a citizen of the Mashpee Wampanoag Tribe and Wampanoag Women's Medicine Society. She lives in Mashpee and in Aquinnah, MA, with her husband, Jason Baird, of the Aquinnah Wampanoag Tribe.

jessie is the cofounder of the Wôpanâak Language Reclamation Project, which began in 1993-94. This is an intertribal effort between the Mashpee, Herring Pond, Aquinnah, and Assonet Wampanoag communities. The aim of the project is to reclaim Wôpanâôt8âôk as a spoken language. There were no speakers of the language for six generations.

little doe also teaches Wôpanâôt8âôk in Aquinnah and Mashpee. She received her M.S. in linguistics from MIT in 2000. She has written an introduction to the grammar of the language, has created the first curriculum for teaching the language, and is currently working with Professor Norvin Richards toward the completion of a dictionary that holds eleven thousand words.

jessie is the current director for 'Nuwôpanâôt8âm', a master-apprentice fluency project funded by the Administration for Native Americans. She is a current National Science Foundation Documenting Endangered Languages Fellow and a 2010 MacArthur "Genius Award" Fellow.

little doe served one term on the Mashpee Housing Authority as a commissioner and two terms on the Mashpee Wampanoag Indian Tribal Council Board of Directors. She has also served in an advisory capacity for past and current Wampanoag cultural projects for various organizations and film productions. She lectures for colleges and universities and advises tribal communities and governments in the area of language project policy and curriculum development. little doe recently completed a contact timeline history regarding contact between the Mashpee Wampanoag Tribe and non-native settlers to the area. The timeline is used on the Mashpee Wampanoag Tribe's website. Other of her passions include Wampanoag history and cooking.

Elaina Supahan Albers and **Phil Albers Jr.** have been working on the Karuk language together since they met in September of 2000. Since birth, Elaina had grown up hearing the beautiful speech patterns and rhythm of the Karuk language. Phil had experience with words and phrases throughout childhood, yet he had minimal exposure to fluent speech until meeting Elaina and spending time with her great-aunt Violet Super. Both Elaina and Phil have successfully utilized the

Master-Apprentice Language Learning Program (MALLP) sponsored by Advocates for Indigenous California Language Survival and co-instructed MALLP workshops for other tribal languages.

Phil has taught language for the past ten years, at Yreka Karuk Head Start, Discovery High School, Hoopa Valley High School, Orleans Elementary School, Southern Oregon University, and many community language classes. He has worked with the Karuk Language Program in developing curriculum, organizing language events, writing and facilitating small grants for language awareness and immersion, and much more.

Elaina has worked to incorporate her Karuk language into her education, occupation, and family life. She co-taught community classes at Southern Oregon University with Phil and her twin sister, Nisha Supahan, presented Karuk language and culture at elementary schools across Southern Oregon and Northern California, and was even chosen, along with Nisha, to give the student commencement speech for graduation at Southern Oregon University; they gave their speech in Karuk and English in 2005.

Together, Elaina and Phil have devoted their lives to Karuk language revitalization through their dedication to raising their children as first-language speakers. They have used many language resources, the Master-Apprentice Language Learning Program, and each other to progress from beginners to confident Karuk speakers. They are constantly working to stay one step ahead of their children.

Richard A. Grounds is of Yuchi and Seminole heritage. He is project director of the Euchee (Yuchi) Language Project based in Sapulpa, Oklahoma, working with the five remaining fluent Yuchi speakers. After completing his Ph.D. in the history of religions at the Princeton Theological Seminary, he taught at St. Olaf College and at the University of Tulsa. He has been faculty with the Pew Foundation Program in Religion and American History, and co-chair of the Native Traditions in the Americas Group at the American Academy of Religion. He served for seven years on the Central Committee of the World Council of Churches. He was co-convener of the hemispheric Indigenous conference "Our Living Languages, Our Living Cultures," Oklahoma City (2002). He is currently co-chair of the Program Council for Cultural Survival and continues to call for an "International Year of Indigenous

Languages" at the Permanent Forum on Indigenous Issues at the United Nations in New York. Dr. Grounds has published on Native language issues in the *Encyclopedia of Religion and Nature* (2005) as well as *Cultural Survival Quarterly* (1996, 2007, 2011) and coedited, along with George Tinker (Osage) and David Wilkins (Lumbee), *Native Voices: American Indian Identity and Resistance* (University of Kansas Press, 2003).

Renée h@IA Grounds is Richard Grounds's daughter. After receiving her B.A. in linguistics from Dartmouth College, she went home to Oklahoma to devote herself to revitalizing the Yuchi language in her community. She is the lead instructor for the children's immersion program at the Euchee-Yuchi Language Project. Through her work with elders since childhood, she has become a highly proficient speaker of Yuchi and has often given talks in the Yuchi language. She has traveled to twenty-four countries and five continents as an advocate for Indigenous Peoples and languages. She has also been a delegate to the United Nations Permanent Forum on Indigenous Issues and to the World Council of Churches. She has written articles for *Cultural Survival Quarterly* (2005, 2011). She and Richard Grounds both appear on the *Our Mother Tongues* website (OurMotherTongues.org). Visit YuchiLanguage.org for more information about the Euchee-Yuchi Language Project.

Margaret and Theodore Peters, of the Ahkwesáhsne Mohawk Nation, are both advocates for language survival on a personal and professional level. Both work for the Ahkwesáhsne Mohawk Board of Education. Margaret's position is Kanien'kéha (Mohawk language) specialist, developing curriculum and resources and networking with other First Nations and Tribes. Theodore has been a teacher for thirteen years.

Both are members of the Sweetgrass First Nations Language Council. Theodore is a committee member and Margaret is the First Speaker for the council. Both have traveled extensively to share their experiences in language survival and in the process have learned from others on their own successes towards language survival.

Three of the Peters's youngest children are fluent in the Mohawk language, and they all work as teachers at the Ahkwesáhsne Freedom School. Four grandchildren are fluent in the language, something the family has worked hard to accomplish. Margaret explains, "Language is not a pastime for us but a common mission to ensure its survival, and a passion because we love what we do. And our successes are reflected in our children and our grandchildren."

Hana O'Regan is the youngest of five children of Sir Tipene and Lady Sandra O'Regan. Raised in Wellington, New Zealand, she spent her secondary schooling years at Queen Victoria Māori Girls Boarding School before spending a year in Thailand as an exchange student. She returned to New Zealand to pursue a B.A. degree, majoring in political science and Māori language. At twenty-one she was lecturing in Māori language and creative writing in Māori at the University of Otago, where she went on to get her M.A. Her thesis became the basis of her first book on tribal identity development. Since that time Hana has spent her professional career in tertiary education and tribal language development. She was a member of the Māori Language Commission for six years and has been on a number of government review panels on issues of Māori language. She was one of the founding members of the Kotahi Mano Kāika working group, who developed and led the Kāi Tahu language strategy. She has remained an active member and driver of her tribal language strategy and works closely in the community as a teacher and language advocate. Hana currently holds the positions of *kaiarahi*/director of Māori and Pasifika and director of student support at Christchurch Institute of Technology. She is the proud mother of two children, Manuhaea Rena and Te Rautawhiri Mahaki, who have been raised as first-language speakers of Māori language. They are her world.

Kauanoe Kamanā is the daughter of Paul Kia'ipō Kamanā and Ella Kauanoe Ka'ai Kamanā of Moloka'i, Hawai'i. Along with her husband, William H. Wilson, she is a faculty member of Ka Haka 'Ula O Ke'elikōlani College of Hawaiian Language at the University of Hawai'i at Hilo. She developed and directs the college's preschool-to-grade-12 Hawaiian medium laboratory school, Nāwahīokalani'ōpu'u. She is also the president of the 'Aha Pūnana Leo, the nonprofit that is credited with beginning the Hawaiian language revitalization movement.

William H. Wilson, also known as Pila, is originally from Honolulu but lives with his wife, Kauanoe Kamanā, in Hilo on the island of Hawai'i. They moved to Hilo to establish a Hawaiian studies degree taught through the Hawaiian language at the University of Hawai'i at Hilo. Over the past thirty years Pila has been the primary planner for the expansion of that program into a Hawaiian language medium college with programs through to the doctorate.

Margaret Noori / Giiwedinoodin (Anishinaabe heritage, waabzheshi-inh doodem) received an M.F.A. in creative writing and a Ph.D. in English and linguistics from the University of Minnesota. She is director of the Comprehensive Studies Program and teaches American Indian literature at the University of Michigan. Her work focuses on the recovery and maintenance of Anishinaabe language and literature. Current research includes language proficiency and assessment, and the study of indigenous literary aesthetics. To see and hear current projects visit www.ojibwe.net, where she and her colleague Howard Kimewon, along with friends and family, have created a space for language shared by academics and the native community.

Aodán Mac Póilin is an Irish language activist from Northern Ireland and lives in an Irish-speaking community in his native city of Belfast. He has written and lectured on cultural and linguistic politics, language planning, education, broadcasting, literature, and the arts, and has published translations of poetry and prose from Irish.

He has been active in a number of organisations, including the European Bureau for Lesser-Used Languages; the Northern Ireland Community Relations Council; Colmcille, which aims to strengthen cultural links between Gaelic Scotland and Ireland; An Foras Teanga (the Cross-Border Language Body set up under the peace process); the Seamus Heaney Centre for Poetry; and the Broadcasting Council for Northern Ireland. He was chairperson of the first Irish medium school in Northern Ireland and is a current board member and former chair of Comhairle na Gaelscolaíochta (Council for Irish-Medium Education) as well as a member of Northern Ireland Screen. He was Irish-language editor of the literary magazine *Krino* and is coeditor of Padraic Fiacc's *Ruined Pages: Selected Poems*. Since 1990 Aodán has been director of the ULTACH Trust, a cross-community Irish-language organisation based in Belfast. He is interested in history, cultural politics, literature (particularly Anglo-Irish, Irish language, and Scottish Gaelic), and traditional singing in Irish, English, and Scottish Gaelic.

Brian Bielenberg was born in the United States and raised speaking English. He has been involved with language revitalization projects in the US and Cyprus. **Aigli Pittaka** was born in Cyprus and raised speaking Kypriaka. She is an anthropologist who studies cultures of peace. Their son, Aliosha, has been socialized into both languages and both cultures from birth. He is an avid learner and a comfortable citizen of the world.

Born in Nuevo León, Mexico, in 1960, **Laura Grant** learned to appreciate diverse cultures as she followed her parents to several countries through their work in the US diplomatic service. She dedicated herself to developing indigenous language revitalization programs beginning in 1996 when she met Norma Nelson, Paiute elder and teacher, who became her friend and mentor. "Since then," Grant says, "I have been privileged to work beside and learn from many fine people in California and from around the world in their selfless work to restore indigenous languages and cultures back to their communities. They have brought beauty and meaning to the lives of so many." Grant continues to be nomadic but as of fall 2011 lives in Tehachapi, California, and can be found most reliably at bigheadlg@earthlink.net.

Julie Turner is a Kawaiisu tribal member, born and raised in the Central Valley of California. Language revitalization work and production of language learning materials and archives are her biggest interests. She works very closely with her father, Luther Girado, and his two sisters, Betty Hernandez and Lucille Hicks, to preserve their language and heritage for future generations. As tribal secretary, she works with the Kern Valley Indian Communities towards tribal restoration from the federal government. Turner says, "It's very important to me to share the knowledge that I've gained with all Native American communities. There is little being done in many very remote areas to preserve and document endangered languages and to improve the skills of California's indigenous people so that they can preserve their heritage and languages. For many, these are on the verge of extinction."

Finlay M. Macleoid was born in the Western Isles of Scotland in December 1954 and at the appropriate time entered and completed the journey through the Scottish education system. In 1982, in partnership with a small group of like-minded people, he created Comhairle nan Sgoiltean Araich (CNSA), an organisation with the remit of reviving the Gaelic language and culture, by way of a range of imaginative Gaelic medium preschool groups. By 2011 there were some 150 preschool groups and 90 parent-and-child groups which had served some ten thousand children and their parents over approximately thirty years.

Macleoid has also been instrumental to a significant degree in the furtherance of the Gaelic language and culture in Nova Scotia, an effort and result he is most proud of. His latest and most exciting venture is the Moray Language Centre, a place of innovation, stimulation, and learning of the highest calibre.

Leanne Hinton is professor emerita at the University of California, Berkeley, and a founding member of the board of the Advocates for Indigenous California Language Survival (AICLS). She began her career as an ethnomusicologist and linguist working with the music of the Havasupai tribe of Grand Canyon (culminating in her dissertation and subsequent book *Havasupai Songs: A Linguistic Perspective*). Invited to work with the Havasupais on bilingual education and literacy development, she found herself turning more and more to issues relating to language maintenance and revitalization. She has authored many articles and several books on language revitalization, including *Flutes of Fire: Essays on California Indian Languages, The Green Book of Language Revitalization in Practice* (edited with Ken Hale), and *How to Keep Your Language Alive* (with Matt Vera and Nancy Steele). She has worked with AICLS to develop and implement the Master-Apprentice Language Learning Program and the Breath of Life Language Workshops, both of which have expanded throughout the US and internationally. In 2005 she received the Cultural Freedom Award from the Lannan Foundation for her work on the revitalization of endangered languages. Leanne lives in Berkeley, California, with her husband, Gary Scott, and delights in family time with their four children and eight grandchildren.

HEYDAY
into California

About Heyday

Heyday is an independent, nonprofit publisher and unique cultural institution. We promote widespread awareness and celebration of California's many cultures, landscapes, and boundary-breaking ideas. Through our well-crafted books, public events, and innovative outreach programs we are building a vibrant community of readers, writers, and thinkers.

Thank You

It takes the collective effort of many to create a thriving literary culture. We are thankful to all the thoughtful people we have the privilege to engage with. Cheers to our writers, artists, editors, storytellers, designers, printers, bookstores, critics, cultural organizations, readers, and book lovers everywhere!

We are especially grateful for the generous funding we've received for our publications and programs during the past year from foundations and hundreds of individual donors. Major supporters include:

Anonymous (2); Acorn Naturalists; Alliance for California Traditional Arts; Judy Avery; James J. Baechle; BayTree Fund; S. D. Bechtel, Jr. Foundation; Barbara Jean and Fred Berensmeier; Berkeley Civic Arts Program and Civic Arts Commission; Joan Berman; Buena Vista Rancheria/ Jesse Flyingcloud Pope Foundation; Lewis and Sheana Butler; California Civil Liberties Public Education Program; Cal Humanities; California Indian Heritage Center Foundation; California State Library; California State Parks Foundation; Keith Campbell Foundation; Candelaria Fund; John and Nancy Cassidy Family Foundation, through Silicon Valley Community Foundation; The Center for California Studies; Graham Chisholm; The Christensen Fund; Jon Christensen; Community Futures Collective; Compton Foundation; Creative Work Fund; Lawrence Crooks; Nik Dehejia; Frances Dinkelspiel and Gary Wayne; Durfee Foundation; Troy Duster; Earth Island Institute; Eaton Kenyon Fund of the Sacramento

Region Community Foundation; Exhibit Envoy; Euclid Fund at the East Bay Community Foundation; Furthur Foundation; The Fred Gellert Family Foundation; Wallace Alexander Gerbode Foundation; Nicola W. Gordon; Wanda Lee Graves and Stephen Duscha; The Walter and Elise Haas Fund; Coke and James Hallowell; G. Scott Hong Charitable Trust; Donna Ewald Huggins; Humboldt Area Foundation; James Irvine Foundation; Claudia Jurmain; Kendeda Fund; Marty and Pamela Krasney; Guy Lampard and Suzanne Badenhoop; Christine Leefeldt, in celebration of Ernest Callenbach and Malcolm Margolin's friendship; LEF Foundation; Thomas Lockard; Thomas J. Long Foundation; Judith and Brad Lowry-Croul; Kermit Lynch Wine Merchant; Michael McCone; Nion McEvoy and Leslie Berriman; Michael Mitrani; Moore Family Foundation; Michael J. Moratto, in memory of Ernest L. Cassel; Richard Nagler; National Endowment for the Arts; National Wildlife Federation; Native Cultures Fund; The Nature Conservancy; Nightingale Family Foundation; Steven Nightingale; Northern California Water Association; Pacific Legacy, Inc.; The David and Lucile Packard Foundation; Patagonia, Inc.; PhotoWings; Robin Ridder; Alan Rosenus; The San Francisco Foundation; San Manuel Band of Mission Indians; Greg Sarris; Savory Thymes; Sonoma Land Trust; Stanley Smith Horticultural Trust; Stone Soup Fresno; Roselyne Chroman Swig; Swinerton Family Fund; Thendara Foundation; Sedge Thomson and Sylvia Brownrigg; TomKat Charitable Trust; Lisa Van Cleef and Mark Gunson; Patricia Wakida; Whole Systems Foundation; John Wiley & Sons, Inc.; Peter Booth Wiley and Valerie Barth; Bobby Winston; Dean Witter Foundation; The Work-in-Progress Fund of Tides Foundation; and Yocha Dehe Community Fund.

Getting Involved
To learn more about our publications, events, membership club, and other ways you can participate, please visit www.heydaybooks.com.

ECO-FRIENDLY BOOKS
Made in the USA